What Is a Heavenly Tribal Messiah?

Heavenly Tribal Messiah Collection 1

|PHILOSOPHY|

What Is a Heavenly Tribal Messiah?

Heavenly Tribal Messiah Academy

PREFACE

What is a heavenly tribal messiah? Heavenly tribal messiahs are people entrusted with the providence of finding and establishing the ideal family, which should have been realized by the original family, Adam's family, in the garden of Eden. What kind of a place was the original garden of Eden? It was the cradle of the new civilization centered on Heavenly Parent. It was also the homeland of Adam and Eve. However, Adam and Eve fell and were driven out of the garden of Eden. They lost their original homeland. What would have happened if Adam and Eve had not fallen? They would have become the ancestors of humanity and the true parents of their own clan. After becoming the true parents, Adam and Eve would have become one with Cain and Abel, with Heavenly Parent at the center of their family, realized the three great kingships and the four great realms of heart, and perfected the model of the ideal family. Then at that very place, the lineage of goodness based on Heavenly Parent and the world of the culture of heart, which never could be invaded by Satan, would have been established.

Therefore, heavenly tribal messiahs have the mission of appeasing the bitter sorrow of Adam and Eve, who were unable to realize the dream that should have come true in the original garden of Eden, and also resolving the bitter sorrow of Jesus, who was manifested as the second Adam to finish what the first Adam was unable to achieve but who also failed to achieve that Will himself. They also have the mission of resolving the bitter sorrow of True Parents, who came as the third Adam to finish what the second Adam was unable to fulfill. True Parents' words tell us that the bitter sorrow of the first Adam and Eve is that they failed to form an ideal family; that the bitter sorrow of Jesus, the second Adam, is that he failed to build the ideal nation; and that the bitter sorrow of the third Adam, True Parents, is that they failed to realize the ideal world. Therefore, it is the mission of heavenly tribal messiahs to realize the ideal family in the original garden of Eden and, going further, to realize the ideal tribe, ideal nation and ideal world.

The most fundamental mission in attaining Heavenly Parent's dream is to perfect the ideal family, which He desired to realize in the garden of Eden through Adam and Eve before the Fall. That ideal family must be realized in its original form, and humanity that has expanded through the Fall must be brought together on the tribal level and be restored. Then the families of that tribe should be blessed to convert their lineage and be guided to form ideal families, so that together they can build a community of tribes. To fulfill this mission, heavenly tribal messiahs first need to resolve the problem caused by the fact that the children of Adam in the first family, Cain and Abel, became divided and then expanded to become today's humanity. Secondly, they need to follow the path by which Adam and Eve can personally attend Heavenly Parent, restore the Abel and Cain realms, and ultimately restore their position as parents. Thirdly, they need to walk the path of perfecting the realm of the royal family, in which they can become Heavenly Parent's own children.

This book explains heavenly tribal messiah activities from a theoretical point of view. We have explained the value and definition of the heavenly tribal messiahs and methods of achieving their mission with quotes from True Parents' words, and we did our best not to miss any of the core contents.

Chapter 1 is "Heavenly Parent's Dream and the Heavenly Tribal Messiah." It explains the original dream that Heavenly Parent wished to realize and the path of humankind who should return to the original homeland.

Chapter 2 is "What Is a Heavenly Tribal Messiah?" It elucidates the tasks and mission that heavenly tribal messiahs must fulfill and gives an easily understandable explanation of the process by which the movement was developed in accordance with the progress of the providence.

Chapter 3 addresses the question "Why Should We Fulfill the Heavenly Tribal Messiah Mission?" It explains that the perfection of one's family is achieved while enabling one's tribe to become perfect. It also sheds light on what the world will be like when human beings, who should walk the path of Heavenly Parent's object partner of love, realize the original tribe, nation and world.

Chapter 4 is on "How to Fulfill the Heavenly Tribal Messiah Mission." It introduces True Parents' words on the attitude and methods of carrying out the activities of heavenly tribal messiahs, as well as the cooperation of the spirit world and the creation of the environment.

Chapter 5 is titled "What Happens When You Fulfill the Heavenly Tribal Messiah Mission?" It explains that, when heavenly tribal messiahs accomplish their mission, they perfect Heavenly Parent's creativity and subjectivity, they earn the authority to have dominion over the angelic world, they come to experience heaven's wisdom, and they receive the blessing of entering the realm of the royal family.

Chapter 6 is "Life Principles for Those Who Fulfill the Heavenly Tribal Messiah Mission." It elucidates what comes after the heavenly tribal messiah mission is fulfilled, including the perfection of parentism and the life principles thereof, the fact that the spirit self must be perfected on earth, principles and realities of life in the spirit and physical worlds, and the nature of a life in which Heavenly Parent comes down to earth to experience human character and the people on earth experience Heavenly Parent's divine character.

The overall contents of this book explain the continuous flow of the providence by which the heavenly tribal messiah providence came to be, starting with the home church age—the providence of restoring the authority of the eldest son; then the tribal messiah age—the providence of restoring the authority of parents; the hoondok family church age—the providence of restoring the kingship; and the heavenly tribal messiah age—the providence of restoring the realm of the royal family.

We also tried to compile the contents in such a way that our readers could gain a deep understanding of the Cheon Il Guk heavenly tribal messiah providence, through which all parts of the providence that have been carried out in stages until now are brought together and fulfilled at the same time. We hope that heavenly fortune will be with the blessed central families who read the volumes of this heavenly tribal messiah series, so that they all can become victors who can accomplish their tribal responsibility and, by doing so, perfect their family.

February 1, 2018
Family Federation for World Peace and Unification
International Headquarters

CONTENTS

PREFACE 4

Introduction 11

Chapter 1   Heavenly Parent's Dream and the Heavenly Tribal Messiah

Section 1   Heavenly Parent's Dream 19
Section 2   The Path Returning to the Original Hometown 29
Section 3   Heavenly Tribal Messiahs Who Attend Heavenly Parent   40
Section 4   The Dream in Which I Can Become Perfect by Enabling My Partner to Become Perfect 47
Section 5   The Perfection of Love and the Spirit World 52

Chapter 2   What Is a Heavenly Tribal Messiah?

Section 1   The World Based on the Culture of Heart and Hyojeong   71
Section 2   What Is a Heavenly Tribal Messiah? — What Kind of Path Does a Heavenly Tribal Messiah Follow? 98
Section 3   The Historic Era and the Meaning of the Heavenly Tribal Messiahs 108
Section 4   A New Age for Heavenly Tribal Messiahs Who Attend Heavenly Parent 133

Chapter 3	**Why Should We Fulfill the Heavenly Tribal Messiah Mission?**	
Section 1	The Blessing of Perfecting My Family	143
Section 2	Completing and Blessing My Tribe	161
Section 3	For the Sake of Building and Expanding My Nation of Cheon Il Guk	186

Chapter 4	**How to Fulfill the Heavenly Tribal Messiah Mission**	
Section 1	Heavenly Tribal Messiah Code of Conduct	205
Section 2	Visiting Spirits in the Area	226
Section 3	Visits of True Love in the Heavenly Tribe	245

Chapter 5	**What Happens When You Fulfill the Heavenly Tribal Messiah Mission?**	
Section 1	You Inherit Heaven's Creativity and Subjectivity	265
Section 2	Receive the Wisdom of Heaven, by Which Creativity Is Manifested	279
Section 3	You Enter Heaven's Realm of the Royal Family	293

Chapter 6 Life Principles for Those Who Fulfill the Heavenly Tribal Messiah Mission

Section 1   The Perfection of Parentism by the
             Heavenly Tribal Messiah 311
Section 2   Spirit World Citizens Who Have Reached Perfection
             on Earth 332
Section 3   Human Beings on Earth Who Resemble Divine Character
             345
Section 4   Free People Living in Accordance with the Voice of the
             Conscience 354

Endnotes and Bibliography

Endnotes 367
Bibliography 385

A GLOSSARY OF KEY TERMS 390

Introduction

On April 17, 1935, True Father received the command from God, "Save and bring with you all of humankind who have been living a wandering life for thousands of years as orphans, born of the fallen lineage!" [1] No one could disobey such a command, which was a heavenly calling. This heavenly calling was not decided based on an agreement between Heavenly Parent and True Father. The command was proposed and passed down unilaterally. When one receives a heavenly calling, it is a mission that one cannot add to or decrease. True Father humbly accepted this heavenly calling. And he determined to take on this heavenly calling and live his life for the sake of the liberation of Heavenly Parent, the salvation of humankind and the eternal realization of a world of peace.

True Mother clearly knew what her mission was before she married True Father in 1960. Through spiritual discourse with God, True Mother resolved: "I will complete the course of restoration through indemnity during my lifetime. I will absolutely liberate

Heavenly Parent." [2] This resolution by True Mother became a reality when she began walking this path together with True Father after the Holy Wedding. With the principle that a true subject creates a true object, and a true object completes a true subject, True Parents have been victorious as partners of the providence.

Ever since True Father accepted his heavenly calling, he has lived a life of carrying the "cross of suffering and persecution" to fulfill the mission. True Mother has been carrying the "cross of sacrifice and mercy" to fulfill the resolution to realize Heavenly Parent's Will. Even now, True Father in the spirit world and True Mother on earth are walking the path of the "cross of true love" to bring fallen humankind to become Heavenly Parent's children. [3]

The result of True Parents' course of the cross of true love is that, through the grace of True Parents, all blessed families worldwide were registered as citizens of Cheon Il Guk on the Foundation Day of Cheon Il Guk in 2013. Now, if all the blessed families who participated in the Cheon Il Guk Foundation Day Registration Blessing Ceremony can fulfill their portion of responsibility, they can be restored as perfected human beings who have no trace of the Fall.

Therefore, we have returned to the realm of the garden of Eden which was the original ideal of creation. [4] True Parents have pioneered the way with blood, sweat and tears and shown us the model of the Principle. They have opened the path for humankind to follow that model and accomplish the three great blessings. Satan's power of opposition has been abolished, and the foundation has been laid for Cheon Il Guk citizens who attend Heavenly Parent to create at will.

True Parents also have bestowed on blessed central families the privilege of guiding their family and tribe to the same realm of merit. Therefore, all blessed families have been granted the title of heavenly tribal messiah and given the blessing, "Like me, you too must walk the path of a messiah for your tribe in your hometown and mobilization area." Therefore, True Parents have said that blessed families must inherit the standard of True Parents who have been victorious in heaven and earth, restore their family and nation, and connect them to True Parents' realm of fortune. We should establish Cheon Il Guk substantially in one nation as a model and then further expand that to the world.

> Today, as I have returned the conclusion of the final perfection to You, Father, I know that up to this moment I have offered my whole life to You. I am spending this time now to bring my life to its conclusion, to bring it to a close with utmost jeongseong, in accordance with Your Will. In order that we may return to the original garden of Eden, the garden with no trace of the Fall, and surmount everything that came to be connected to Adam's portion of responsibility following the error committed by his betrothed, I, who have the authority to grant liberation and complete freedom to everything, declare that anyone who follows True Parents, be it someone in the fourth dimension or be it someone who otherwise would go even to the fourteenth dimension of hell, will be adopted into the kingdom of heaven and

registered in the fourth dimension. I declare that if, centering on the fourteen sons and daughters, the tribal messiahs can fulfill the calling of national representatives and restore the 387 nations [194 nations of the Abel UN + 193 nations of the Cain UN = 387 nations mentioned by True Father a few times, without a full explanation], everything will be brought to a conclusion. I have accomplished everything for this. I have completed everything. Aju! [5]

In this book, *What Is a Heavenly Tribal Messiah?* it is revealed that the heavenly tribal messiah mission that True Parents have bestowed on the blessed families after the Foundation Day of Cheon Il Guk is the greatest of all blessings. All blessed families will come to experience Heavenly Parent and True Parents' blessing and gift through doing heavenly tribal messiah activities with a heart of gratitude.

True Parents, who have granted us the title of heavenly tribal messiah, have blessed us, saying, "Do not worry about whether or not it will work. True Parents have established the realm of fortune in heaven and on earth, so you will see miracles wherever you pursue your mission and wherever you proclaim True Parents." [6]

Chapter 1

Heavenly Parent's Dream and the Heavenly Tribal Messiah

Section 1 Heavenly Parent's Dream

Heavenly Parent had a great dream before the Creation. This dream was to become one with human beings and live with them. [1] His hope was for the very first human beings that he created, Adam and Eve, to become husband and wife and become the true parents of humankind. [2] The kingdom of heaven on earth is a world where the dream of Heavenly Parent and human beings are one and the same and this dream has been realized. The kingdom of heaven in heaven is the world where human beings live when they go to the spirit world after having lived in the kingdom of heaven on earth. [3] The model of heaven where this ideal has been realized completely is a world where we are one human family under Heavenly Parent.

1. Heavenly Parent's hope, heart and situation

Before creating human beings, Heavenly Parent created the most favorable environment for human beings to live in. He first created water, earth, air, sunlight and all the environment that human beings would need while living on the earth after being born. Only after that, He created male and female human beings, with elements to resemble His internal nature and external form.

Heavenly Parent's great dream began when He created human beings. He hoped for the first human beings He created, Adam and Eve, to follow His Will and grow well. He hoped that a mature Adam and Eve would marry with His approval, become an ideal couple, give birth to children and realize an ideal family. When Adam and Eve realize an ideal family centering on Heaven's Will, then Heavenly Parent's dream becomes a reality.

> God originally created true human beings to live in joy. Our minds and bodies were meant to be united with God's love and be intoxicated by it. God created human beings so that He could experience infinite joy by participating in true families' lives of happiness. Then, by establishing oneness and harmony with human beings, He desired to appear in the human world through the oneness thus created between the substantial world and the insubstantial world. [4]

If Adam and Eve had given birth to children and realized an ideal family, Heavenly Parent would have lived together with them and presided over them directly. The tribe, people, nation and world would have been realized through the multiplication of that family. Through their children, an ideal world and ideal heaven would have been realized. [5] That would have meant the substantiation in the world of the dream that Heavenly Parent had: to become True Parents through the first human beings. [6] Through this, He hoped to share the joys and sorrows of life with human beings and live eternally feeling great joy through His children who resemble Him in mind and body.

Heavenly Parent on His own cannot realize His dream of becoming one with human beings and living with them. If Heavenly Parent were able to realize that dream on His own, the creation would not have been necessary, but a choice. Heavenly Parent has the ability to achieve all things, and nothing is impossible for Him. However, there is one thing that even such a Heavenly Parent cannot achieve alone. What is that? It is love.

> Even though God is a Supreme Being, He cannot be happy alone. The phrases "It is good" and "I am happy" cannot exist on their own. They can be used only where there is a relationship with a partner. If someone who has been a singer all his life sings at the top of his lungs on a deserted island all alone, can he be happy? In the same way, in order to be happy the self-existent Heavenly Parent absolutely needs an object partner of love with whom He can have a give-and-take relationship. [7]

Heavenly Parent is love. [8] However, even Heavenly Parent, who is the essence of love itself, cannot realize love on His own. Love can happen only when there is an object partner and there is give-and-take action. Then love is created as that action grows. Before the Creation, Heavenly Parent, who was all alone, was very lonely. Even if He is the essence of love, if there is no object partner of love, then He cannot feel, touch or taste that love. That is why He created human beings as His children who can have the same dream as He does. He created human beings and designed them to complete His world. Therefore, He created Adam and then created Eve for Adam, who looked as lonely as He was. That is because, for human beings as well, it is only when they have a give-and-take relationship with an object partner that they can perfect love. If we look at the blueprint of creation, Adam and Eve were supposed to have had absolute faith, absolute love and absolute obedience to Heavenly Parent's word while they were not yet in the completion stage. They needed to go through the growth period in which they would learn the basic order and rules of the created world and master the operating principles of creation. They should have waited and learned the Will of Heavenly Parent who created them, the significance of the parent–child relationship and what kind of world they would have to expand while moving forward. They should have gone through that process and followed the path to become people who resemble Heavenly Parent, embrace His ideal and become inheritors who can have dominion over the creation.

2. The path of the father–son relationship (face to face)

Heavenly Parent and human beings were meant to be in a relationship of parent and child. In the parent–child relationship Heavenly Parent is the parent of human beings and human beings are the children of Heavenly Parent. [9] The parent–child relationship is the best and greatest relationship among all relationships.

When Adam and Eve were born as babies, what was Heavenly Parent's heart at the time? Adam and Eve, who were created according to plan on the foundation of thousands of years of sincere jeongseong, were His blood, His flesh and His everything. Most probably Heavenly Parent looked at His substantial partners who resembled Him "face to face" and expressed how moved He was. "It is good. I cannot be any happier than this!" As He gazed at His newborn children, it brought Him more happiness than anything else in the world. Human beings are His children born with a connection of love, life and lineage and are the result of total investment. When Adam and Eve had gone through the growth period, become an ideal couple and realized an ideal family, Heavenly Parent hoped to bequeath to them the creation and have them become His representatives. The joy that Heavenly Parent felt while looking at Adam and Eve at that time would have been even greater than at the time of Creation.

In this place with the beautiful fragrance of Heaven, how do you think Heavenly Parent educated Adam and Eve? He looked at Adam and Eve face to face, gazed into their eyes and taught them by answering their questions one by one. If Adam and Eve had a question, they could go to ask Him anytime. If they had something to report to Heavenly Parent, they could do so directly anytime. And Heavenly Parent and Adam and Eve would have shared their hearts freely and had a spiritual exchange.

What name did Adam and Eve call Heavenly Parent during the growth period? They must have used some name indicating that Heavenly Parent was their parent. Before the Fall, Adam and Eve called Him "Father." If Adam and Eve had formed an ideal couple and given birth to children, those children would have followed Adam and Eve and called Heavenly Parent "Father" as well. This is because Heavenly Parent has the dual characteristics of masculinity and femininity but exists as one entity with both characteristics combined. [10]

However, Adam and Eve gave in to temptation during the growth period, could not control themselves and fell. They came to stand in a position with no connection to Heavenly Parent and became tied to a fallen lineage and fate. The result of Adam and Eve's Fall is that the connection of lineage between human beings and Heavenly Parent was rendered irrelevant. Furthermore, the parent–child relationship was also severed. Heavenly Parent could no longer have a direct relationship with human beings. Heavenly Parent can have a direct relationship with children of His lineage, but He cannot do so with human beings whose connection of lineage has been severed. This is because they can receive Satan's attacks. That is how crucial lineage is. Lineage follows the owner. Heavenly Parent could not relate directly with fallen human beings whose lineage was severed, so from then on, our pitiful Heavenly Parent had to relate with human beings through the remaining angels who had not fallen. He passed on his commands to human beings as revelations through the angels and held onto the rope of the providence of salvation by trying to develop what was left of people's original minds. Noah, Abraham, Isaac, Jacob, Moses and other central figures in the Bible also received Heavenly Parent's commands through the angels and reported back to Him through the angels.

We can get a better understanding if we look at Moses, who liberated the Israelites who suffered 430 years of slavery in Egypt. When Moses was in the Midian wilderness, he met Heavenly Parent face to face on Mount Horeb. Moses received the mission to liberate the Israelites, and he was granted the ability to carry out that mission. However, it was not Heavenly Parent who gave Moses that mission and ability on Mount Horeb. It was one sent by God; in other words, it was an angel. [Exodus 3:1–2] In Chapter 7 of the Acts of the Apostles, it is revealed that the one who appeared to Moses was an angel.

> When Moses saw it, he wondered at the sight; and as he drew near to look, the voice of the Lord came, "I am the God of your fathers, the God of Abraham and of Isaac and of Jacob." And Moses trembled and did not dare to look. And the Lord said to him, "Take off the shoes from your feet, for the place where you are standing is holy ground. I have surely seen the ill-treatment of

> my people that are in Egypt and heard their groaning, and I have come down to deliver them. And now come; I will send you to Egypt." This Moses whom they refused, saying, "Who made you a ruler and a judge?" God sent as both ruler and deliverer by the hand of the angel that appeared to him in the bush. [Acts 7:31-35]

What name do the angels have for Heavenly Parent? Heavenly Parent and the angels do not have a parent-child relationship. They are in a relationship of master and servants; therefore, the angels call Heavenly Parent "Lord." The central figures who received God's command through the angels could not call Heavenly Parent "Father" either. Just like the angels, they called Heavenly Parent either "Lord" or "Adoni." According to the Book of John 8:54 Jesus called Heavenly Parent "Father." He was the first person to call Heavenly Parent "Father." According to Jesus' words, the Jewish leaders at the time called Heavenly Parent "Adoni." This was a great source of sorrow to Heavenly Parent. After the Fall of humankind, the fact that nobody could call Him "Father" and that He had to be called "Adoni" was a very sorrowful thing.

> In history, a source of great sorrow for Heavenly Parent was that He was supposed to have been called "Father," standing in the position of a parent, father and mother, but instead He was called "God." Jesus also said in God's name, "Repent! The kingdom of heaven is at hand!" Repentance means reversing what went wrong, taking the opposite and making it go the right way. When

fallen human beings repent and return to a position that is 180 degrees different from where they were, in which they can refer to God as a parent, then they will come to feel all the tears that Heavenly Parent shed. When that happens, they will let out a heart-wrenching cry of pain that will last many days.

Saint Paul, who was a great missionary and theologian in the New Testament Age, explained about love in 1 Corinthians 13. He said that we only know and prophesize in part but when completion comes, prophesying in part will disappear. Right now, when you look in the mirror, you see a vague reflection of yourself, but when the time comes, you will see face to face.

Love never ends; as for prophecies, they will pass away; as for tongues, they will cease; as for knowledge, it will pass away. For our knowledge is imperfect and our prophecy is imperfect; but when the perfect comes, the imperfect will pass away. When I was a child, I spoke like a child, I thought like a child, I reasoned like a child; when I became a man, I gave up childish ways. For now we see in a mirror dimly, but then face to face. Now I know in part; then I shall understand fully, even as I have been fully understood. [1 Cor 13:8–12]

True Parents were born as the original human beings. They were born as direct children that Heavenly Parent can call "My son! My daughter!" Just like Adam and Eve in the early days before the Fall,

True Parents grew up face to face with Heavenly Parent and were taught by Heavenly Parent. They lived while experiencing the reality of the spirit world. From very young, they lived a life of confirming and practicing the truths about heaven and the spirit world that they experienced. They put into practice in the two-dimensional earthly world what they experienced in the three-dimensional spirit world and explained it to us in plain language understandable to human beings.

Heavenly Parent and True Parents live face to face. This face to face is not just superficial and physical. We look at the mirror every morning. At first, we see the surface, but by looking at our facial expression, we can perceive the state of our heart. In other words, we can see our heart. To be face to face with an incorporeal Heavenly Parent means to resemble His heart such that created human beings can communicate and talk heart to heart. Heavenly Parent is not a concept but is always present in our day-to-day lives. True Parents' life with Heavenly Parent did not end with the truth and communication. They live together with Heavenly Parent, experiencing Him directly.

> God is not an abstract God. He is alive in each of our lives, and we can feel His touch. I am constantly hearing the beat of God's pulse. I breathe as He breathes. I can feel the warmth of His body against my own. I have come to know the heart of God and have shed rivers of tears from the knowledge that His heart is bursting with the sorrow of having lost humankind through the Fall. [11]

Section 2 The Path Returning to the Original Hometown

Adam and Eve developed self-centered desires during the growth period when it was not the right time. They fell into temptation under the influence of evil, without knowing the ideal world that had been prepared for them and without knowing what their roles were. What was the result of that? They were kicked out of the garden of Eden. They married and multiplied outside the garden of Eden, centering on the archangel Lucifer who was degraded to Satan.

Just as the value of Heavenly Parent's existence is absolute, unique, unchanging and eternal, the value of His Will is also absolute, unique, unchanging and eternal. His plan at the start was clear and His goal was also clear. The beginning and end are always the same, and He cannot change the Principle of Creation that He established. Even though humankind fell and stained the lineage, because the motivation for creation came from Heavenly Parent, He absolutely must save fallen humankind and restore them to their original state. Heavenly Parent is filled with sorrow and grief, and He shed many tears after losing the children that He created to be His absolute object partners. However, even today He goes in search of human beings with the heart of a parent.

1. The path of searching and returning

How does Heavenly Parent lead the providence of salvation of fallen human beings? He has to lead the providence of salvation by working in the opposite order from the course that human beings took when they fell. Then what was the order of the course of the human Fall, and what was lost through it and how?

First, humankind was severed from Heavenly Parent, who is the original parent. The relationship in which they could ask and receive answers one on one was severed, and they left the garden of Eden, which was the home where they had lived together with Heavenly Parent. What is the reverse order required to return? For fallen humankind to return to Heavenly Parent, the original parent, they must meet the True Parents, the Messiah and Lord of the Second Advent, who can guide them to that path. Therefore, they must meet the son (Messiah) who has not fallen and was sent by Heavenly Parent, establish him as a treasure and be born again. And they must reverse and overcome the situation in which they became severed from Heavenly Parent.

Second, the first son, Adam was taken away by Satan. Originally, Heavenly Parent wanted to raise Adam up and give him the right of inheritance and the authority to rule this world. However, because Adam fell, the authority of the eldest son, of standing in the position to receive that right of inheritance, was taken away from him. Therefore, Heavenly Parent had to find and establish an object partner in Cain or Abel, Adam and Eve's children, who would put Heavenly Parent at the center. However, the first child, Cain, became the object of evil and worshipped the world. Therefore, Heavenly Parent established the second son, Abel, as the model of good. Abel became the one who would have to realize the dream that Adam could not realize. He had to restore the position of the elder son and do his best to fulfill the responsibility to realize Heavenly Parent's dream. And he also had to inherit the work left unfinished by Heavenly Parent.

Unfortunately, until today human history has been progressing as the history of the Abel realm centered on Heavenly Parent that tries to restore the world to its origin and the history of the Cain realm that tries to maintain the evil, fallen world. Our world of today is a world that has been divided by these two brothers who are the result of the Fall of Adam's family.

The division of this first family has expanded to the world. This is manifested in the Abel-type view of life and Cain-type view of life. In politics, economics, religion, culture and every field it has become a siblings' struggle between the value of good centered on the conscience and that which is self-centered and concerned only with its own interests. The world has gone from being a whirlpool of conflict and war to a world that moans and groans.

Third, the providence to bring back unity to the world divided by the brothers must be carried out. Only the parents can stop the fighting between siblings. The persons who have appeared as the parents of humankind are the True Parents who came as the Messiah and Lord of the Second Advent. Divided humankind must be engrafted onto their good lineage, love and world of heart. Those who receive the Blessing from them become the Abel tribe centering on Heavenly Parent. In other words, they are starting off as the descendants of good who found the lost existence of Heavenly Parent. To realize one human family, they must carry out activities for the Cain realm of the world, introduce Heavenly Parent and True Parents, and bring about the restoration of the realm of siblings (restoration of the authority of the eldest son). Through this, they must bring an end to the path of chaos of the orphans of humankind and help them find Heavenly Parent, who is the original parent of humankind.

When this happens and the Cain realm is restored, the division of the two brothers from Adam and Eve's family who were the first human ancestors can be restored. There no longer will be struggle or conflict between the siblings. There will be no clash between Heavenly Parent-centered goodness and self-centered evil. The place will be recovered where the two lost brothers become one and reconcile centering on the one Heavenly Parent.

In this way, Heavenly Parent looks for us in order to restore the ideal world that was lost. From the moment that human beings fell until now, Heavenly Parent has been lonely and full of sorrow and grief. Heavenly Parent's sorrow is so great that it cannot be described in words. There was no one in history who could understand this deep sorrow of Heavenly Parent

However, because Heavenly Parent had the dream of living together as one with human beings, He led the providence of restoration by choosing central figures from the Abel realm who can attend Heavenly Parent at the level of the individual, family, tribe, race and nation. He has been carrying out the history of the providence of salvation by having them pay indemnity.

A fallen human being cannot save fallen human beings, so Heavenly Parent went through 4,000 years of preparation and sent Jesus Christ, His only begotten son, 2,000 years ago. Jesus cannot realize the Will of Heavenly Parent on his own either. The cooperation of the surrounding environment prepared by Heaven is necessary. However, all those in the prepared environment surrounding Jesus turned to faithlessness. Even John the Baptist, who received a direct revelation and vision from Heavenly Parent and received the teaching "This is my Son, whom I love; with him I am well pleased" [Matt. 3:17], ended up faithless.

> If John the Baptist had clearly understood and fulfilled his responsibility in the position of Cain, how could Jesus have died on the cross? Yet, despite receiving direct revelations and visions from Heaven, and despite hearing Jesus' guidance that Jesus was

himself the Lord and Abel, in the end John the Baptist could not meet the challenge of living by absolute faith, absolute love and absolute obedience. [12]

Jesus died on the cross saying, "I will come again!" He will come again and perform the Marriage Supper of the Lamb. [John 19:20] Jesus came as the lamb of Heavenly Parent. He was supposed to find a bride and hold the marriage feast. Heavenly Parent's ideal of creation was to realize the ideal family and ideal world by creating Adam and Eve as his object partners. Therefore, for Heavenly Parent's dream to be realized, Jesus must carry out the marriage feast and absolutely needs to find a bride. The 2,000 years of Christian history were to prepare the bride, who was to meet Jesus, and hold the marriage feast. However, Christianity was not aware of this Will and could not prepare at all.

Jesus could not hold the marriage feast and died on the cross without realizing the Will. Then, 2,000 years later, Heavenly Parent sent the True Parents to earth. After the Fall of Adam and Eve, for the first time in 6,000 years Heavenly Parent sent to earth his one son and one daughter—True Father (Sun Myung Moon) and True Mother (Hak Ja Han)—who could realize His dream. Heavenly Parent sent His direct son and daughter, of whom he could call out, "This is my son! This is my daughter!" and had them go through a period of growth. Through the Marriage Supper of the Lamb in 1960, they became the True Parents. Before True Parents could appear, 6,000 long years passed. It was 6,000 years, according to the record in the Bible; however, the history of humankind lasted for much longer than 6,000 years.

The time has come when the dream that Heavenly Parent has hoped for since the beginning of time can be realized completely. Centering on the hope, situation and heart of Heavenly Parent, True Parents overcame all their trials and were victorious in the restoration through indemnity. Through the victory of the providence of establishing the condition on earth, they realized total oneness between husband and wife and became the True Parents of Heaven, Earth and Humankind. Through achieving oneness with Heavenly Parent, True Parents realized the hope of Heavenly Parent. And they understood Heavenly Parent's situation and were able to experience joy together in heart. [13] Oneness of Heavenly Parent and True Parents' hope, situation and heart was achieved, and the four-position foundation could be accomplished. True Parents' family achieved the four-position foundation, so Heavenly Parent could come and reside in their family and feel infinite joy. Heavenly Parent and True Parents always live together with the standard of having achieved total oneness. Even today, they look at each other face to face and discuss how to carry out the providence of Heaven.

True Father directly experienced the spirit world with Heavenly Parent. He is putting into practice on the earth all the things that he experienced and has proclaimed the systematic truth. We absolutely must believe in the words that True Parents have proclaimed. If we just put them into practice, we can go to the same world of experience as True Parents. True Parents have said that the era is now open for all blessed families to live while feeling the presence of Heavenly Parent. In other words, the era has been opened in which we can converse harmoniously with Heavenly Parent face to face, if we fulfill our responsibility during this time and environment and achieve individual perfection. True Parents have opened the era in which we can perceive Heavenly Parent with our original mind. [14]

True Parents, who have achieved oneness centering on Heavenly Parent's hope, situation and heart, have asked all blessed families around the world to achieve oneness with Heavenly Parent and True Parents centering on the hope, situation and heart of Heaven. This means that we blessed families must return to the position of the original family of Adam and Eve and realize the ideal of the perfected couple and family.

The idea of the original family of Adam and Eve means a family that has the same lineage as Heavenly Parent, in which the couple is centered on Heavenly Parent and the family is united. With a different lineage, they cannot call Him "Heavenly Parent" or meet Him as a parent. This is because the realm of dominion is different.

Therefore, we must change our lineage through the True Parents and find Heavenly Parent. This means meeting True Parents, receiving the Blessing, going through the path of rebirth and establishing as a couple a relationship of parent and child with True Parents. Then we must stand in the position in which we can be recognized as the direct children of Heavenly Parent. This is the path that the blessed families must take.

The condition for a couple to become one centering on Heavenly

Parent and realize the ideal family is to find and raise up the lost children of the Abel realm (biological children) and Cain realm (spiritual children) centering on Heavenly Parent. The two realms of children must become one, centering on one set of parents, attend the parents and restore the family model. If the two children had not fallen, they would have stood in equal positions as siblings. Therefore, just as the blessed families found the position of the direct children through the True Parents, they must restore the Cain realm tribe, have them meet the True Parents, be reborn and go the path of the Blessing. They must make sure that their lineage is changed. The realm of dominion must be reversed, and they must return to the realm of dominion of Heavenly Parent and True Parents before the Fall. In other words, the Cain realm tribe and Abel realm tribe should meet and become one. In Adam's family, Cain and Abel were divided, and this was expanded to humankind. Therefore, this is the providence to find and raise up again the Cain realm tribe as a condition centering on your own tribe. When you are establishing that standard, through blessed central families finding and raising up the realm of children that were lost and are in confusion, you can gain strength in their contribution and become the parent of the tribe as the heavenly tribal messiah. Therefore, it is through finding and establishing the standard of True Parents' victorious restoration of the authority of the eldest son that we also can become messiahs of our tribe and parents of our tribe. Then we will be able to build the original ideal of the family, tribe, village and nation centering on Heavenly Parent. Based on that foundation, if we can connect with the victorious world and cosmic foundation of True Parents, that can become the condition to restore this cosmos into the world that Heavenly Parent lost.

Heavenly Parent's dream is to become one with human beings and to live together with them. Heavenly Parent's hope was the providence to reverse the world that was expanded from the Fall of the first family of Adam and restore it to its original state. It is the providence to find and establish one family, tribe, nation and world centering on Heavenly Parent to the original state of one human family. Heavenly tribal messiahs are the heroes who have received this mission in this important era. [15]

We are living in an era when our dream and Heavenly Parent's dream can become one and the same. [16] We are living in a deeply moving era when we can meet Heavenly Parent and have a conversation with him face to face while living day-to-day life. First we must unite the children of the Abel realm tribe and Cain realm tribe, which expanded into two worlds because of the Fall of Adam and Eve. Only then can we live a substantial life. The heavenly tribal messiah, who is in the position of the parent, should bring the children of the two tribes together. Then the two siblings must become one and build the ideal family and ideal village. Within their area, they must find and establish again the ideal of the garden of Eden in which Heavenly Parent can come to live together with them. The hometown could not be realized in the beginning of time. The place where the ideal family and ideal village are built, centering on the two realms of children, is the tribe's hometown.

True Parents said that when heavenly tribal messiahs, in order to realize the dream of Heavenly Parent, fulfill the ideal of 12 heavenly tribes in one nation, that nation can be restored.

Section 3 Heavenly Tribal Messiahs Who Attend Heavenly Parent

True Parents have lived their lives for the sake of realizing the dream of one human family under Heavenly Parent in which all humankind will attend one Heavenly Parent and live as brothers and sisters. The dream of one human family under Heavenly Parent is a providence that starts from one and expands to all. In that course, True Parents first walked the model life course and bequeathed that victorious foundation to the blessed families. Therefore, blessed families can walk and follow in their footsteps. [17]

1. The way that all blessed families must go

True Parents conducted the Holy Wedding Ceremony in 1960 and then walked the first seven-year course until 1967. They victoriously concluded the providence of the first seven-year course to establish the family. After the second seven-year course began in 1968, True Parents used the term "tribal messiah" for the first time. The first seven-year course was a course in which the True Parents bore the family-level cross of love to establish the foundation of the true family. [18] This is the providence in which True Mother, as the restored Eve, had to find and establish, stage by stage, the foundation that was lost by fallen Eve. Through that, members had to become one with True Mother by carrying the cross of love. [19]

The second seven-year course, which began in 1968, was the course to be walked by the blessed families who inherited the victorious foundation of True Parents' first seven-year course. For blessed families, on the foundation of "family messiah," "it was a period of fulfilling the mission of tribal messiah and people's messiah that Jesus could not fulfill." [20] Through the three-year course that Jesus walked, Father talked about witnessing to 12 people and used the term "tribal messiah" for the first time. After that, at every opportunity and on countless occasions he would use the term.

True Parents have adjusted the activities for the providence of restoration for each stage of the providence as it advanced—focusing on home church in 1978, local breakthrough (*tongban gyeokpa*) in 1987, tribal messiah in 1991, and hoondok home church in 2005. After proclaiming the founding year of Cheon Il Guk in 2013, they have been leading the substantial providence by expanding Cheon Il Guk from the tribal level to the national level, then from the national level to the world level, through heavenly tribal messiah activities. The concepts or terms used in the advancement of the providence have changed along the way, but the goal and direction of the providence are ultimately the same. [21]

What was the difference between the dispatching of tribal messiahs and heavenly tribal messiahs? Let us first look at the dispatching of tribal messiahs. On August 29, 1991, True Parents appointed all blessed families as tribal messiahs and sent them out to their hometown. They told blessed families to go back to their hometown and do various activities to liberate their hometown, ancestors and Heavenly Parent. [22] At the summit with Soviet President Mikhail Gorbachev in 1990, True Parents restored the authority of the eldest son with the representative of communism on a worldwide level and communism came to an end. On December 6, 1991, they traveled to North Korea as representatives of the chosen and met Kim Il Sung of North Korea, thus realizing the substantial restoration of the authority of the eldest son. On the foundation of the "Proclamation Ceremony of God's Eternal Blessing" of July 1, 1991, Kim Il Sung, who was the object partner of the restoration of the authority of the eldest son and the restoration partner of the authority of the parents, began to implement his promise [to strive for unification] to True Parents, with the result that North Korea began to develop. During the same time, the tribal messiahs who had been send out were the starting point to connect the restoration of the authority of the eldest son to the restoration of the authority of the parents. [23]

Let us look at the background of the dispatching of heavenly tribal messiahs. First, there was the stage of proclaiming that all blessed families must do their best to fulfill their responsibility as heavenly tribal messiahs. On the 1st day of the 3rd month, 2012, by the heavenly calendar (April 21), on the way back to Korea from Las Vegas, in mid-air above Alaska, True Parents called a Korean leader and gave him directions, "We will arrive in CheongPyeong in 10 hours. Gather 30,000 members at the CheongShim Peace World Center to meet us when we arrive in Korea."

The word was spread quickly, 30,000 blessed family members gathered at CheongPyeong in time for True Parents' arrival, and the "Victorious Welcoming Rally for the True Parents of Heaven, Earth and Humankind" was held. True Parents read the speech from the Cosmic Assemblies for the Settlement of the True Parents of Heaven, Earth and Humankind Who, as God's Embodiment, Proclaim the Word and explained the content. They also explained the meaning of the subtitle of the speech, *Shin Jongjok* (Tribal) Messiah. *Shin* can mean either "new" or "heavenly." They emphasized that through the Cheon Il Guk Foundation Day Registration Blessing, all blessed families who are reborn like the original Adam and Eve in the garden of Eden must become "heavenly tribal messiahs."

The second stage was the Special 30-day Heavenly Tribal Messiah Original Divine Principle Workshop for 3,600 people. On the 5th day of the 3rd month by the heavenly calendar (April 25, 2012), True Parents invited 358 Korean church leaders to participate in hoondokhae at Cheon Jeong Gung. During hoondokhae, True Parents gave the direction for this workshop to be held. They said that this 30-day special workshop would be the foundation to allow the participants the grace of being able to register in Cheon Il Guk on Foundation Day.

> When I move to a new place and enter the 4th Heaven, there is no one apart from these people (grandchildren) that I can take with me. This workshop is not like other workshops in the past. It is a special workshop. The 30 days of Original Divine Principle education must be done again. This is the final Original Divine Principle workshop for heavenly tribal messiahs to inherit the position of representatives of the Second Advent.

Participating in the Cheon Il Guk Foundation Day event was the greatest blessing among blessings. It is the greatest grace. True Parents permitted the Special 30-day Heavenly Tribal Messiah Original Divine Principle Workshop for 3,600 people because they wanted to create the condition to take us with them on Cheon Il Guk Foundation Day. The special workshop was held in Korea in 2012 from 3.27 to 4.29, by the heavenly calendar.

The third stage was when the heavenly tribal messiahs could inherit the position of representatives of True Parents. True Parents have said that Cheon Il Guk is "a nation where two become one." In the garden of Eden of the original ideal of creation, these two people are the perfected Adam and the perfected Eve. The substantial Cheon Il Guk is the nation where Heavenly Parent and human beings are one. Cheon Il Guk Foundation Day could begin because

Heavenly Parent and True Parents achieved oneness. [24]

Cheon Il Guk Foundation Day, held on February 22, 2013 (1.13 HC), was celebrated in two ceremonies, part one and two. The first part was the Cheon Il Guk Foundation Day Coronation Ceremony. This Cheon Il Guk Foundation Day Coronation Ceremony was held based on the foundation of Heavenly Parent and True Parents having achieved total oneness. [25] True Parents oversaw the Cheon Il Guk Coronation Ceremony as the Holy Wedding Ceremony and Coronation Ceremony of the True Parents of Heaven, Earth and Humankind and opened the gates to Cheon Il Guk. Then they proclaimed 1.3 (HC), 2013, as the first day of the Founding Year of Cheon Il Guk.

The second part was the Cheon Il Guk Foundation Day Registration Blessing Ceremony. With the authority of Cheon Il Guk, True Parents unconditionally embraced wide and high the blessed families as citizens of Cheon Il Guk. [26] And they blessed all the blessed families as heavenly tribal messiahs. They bequeathed to all blessed families the position of representatives of True Parents. [27]

The fourth stage was sending out the heavenly tribal messiahs. At the Victory of Vision 2020! World Joint Service for the Completion of Mission of Heavenly Tribal Messiahs, held at CheongPyeong on 9.3 in the 2nd year of Cheon Il Guk by the heavenly calendar (October 26, 2014), True Mother praised and encouraged the two families who accomplished the Blessing of 430 couples as heavenly tribal messiahs and their tribes. She told all the blessed families, "Let us remember True Father's request to us to fulfill the mission of tribal messiahs as he passed away. The Cheon Il Guk Foundation Day Registration Blessing was given through the True Parents. You must repay this by fulfilling the heavenly tribal messiah mission." [28]

True Mother said that until that time, blessed families had not been able to fulfill their mission as tribal messiahs. She said that we are not new tribal messiahs but rather heavenly tribal messiahs who should attend Heavenly Parent. Through the accord between Heavenly Parent and True Parents and through the grace of being born anew, all the blessed families could now become heavenly tribal messiahs.

> Why did True Father say that you have to be *shin jongjok* messiahs? The *shin* here does not mean to be a new tribal messiah but to be a tribal messiah who attends Heavenly Parent. This *shin* does not mean "new" (新) but "God" (神). I pray for the victory of all our members as heavenly tribal messiahs attending Heavenly Parent! [29]

Section 4 The Dream in Which I Can Become Perfect by Enabling My Partner to Become Perfect

What does it mean to be an ideal family that resembles Heavenly Parent? It refers to the tradition of living for the sake of others and enabling the object partner to reach perfection, centering on Heavenly Parent's attributes, so that I can reach perfection. In other words, the value and perfection of the husband does not lie with himself but with the wife. This is because he does not call himself "husband" but rather it is his wife who calls him that. There may be many women in the world, but the only one who calls you "husband" is your wife. Likewise, the value of the wife does not lie with herself, but is created and perfected through the husband. Therefore, there is no perfection for the person in the family who simply says "Follow me." You must move according to the object partner who enables you to reach perfection. Only then can your position be recognized and you can go the path of perfection. In conclusion, the perfection of my value does not lie with me It can be perfected only through my partner. Therefore, to become perfect, we must put effort into enabling our object partner to become perfect. Only then can your position be perfected.

This also applies to the parent–child relationship. The parent cannot fulfill the position of parents on his or her own. It is created by the child. Even if you are a married couple, if you do not give birth to children, then you have no object partners to call you "Mom" and "Dad." Then you cannot become parents. The value of mom and dad, the value of parents, does not lie with the parents but rather with the children who call them parents. That is why parents go the path of sacrifice: because it is only when the parents enable the child to become perfect that their position as parents can be fulfilled.

The same principle can be seen when the position of the master can be perfected only when the disciple acknowledges that position, and the position of the president of a country can be perfected only when the citizens acknowledge it. Therefore, we must go the path that the partner wants to go and the path of enabling our partner to become perfect in order for our position to be fulfilled. In the same way, why did Heavenly Parent create human beings? This is because He cannot become a parent without creating human beings as His children and enabling them to become perfect.

The conclusion is that our perfection does not lie with us. However, people in the world say, "If you help me and complete me, I will complete you." This is the method that Satan used when he tempted Adam and Eve, in the form of a serpent. "For God knows that when you eat the fruit of the tree of knowledge of good and evil, your eyes will be opened like Heavenly Parent. Eat it, then your eyes will be opened." Ultimately, he tempted them to put his own benefit first. He tempted human beings to preserve his own position.

The original ideal world is a world where I can become perfected by enabling my partner to become perfect. It is a world where we are acknowledged and reach perfection by living for the sake of others. If we invest and sacrifice to try to enable our partner to become perfect, our position also can be perfected as our partner becomes perfect. For example, there may be parents who only graduated elementary school, but if they invest and sacrifice to raise their child up to be the president of the country, they can be recognized as the parents of the president, having the same value as the child who has reached perfection. From this perspective, why do we do heavenly tribal messiah activities?

First: Only when our family accomplishes completes the Cain tribe, can our family be perfected as a heavenly family. If there is no Cain tribe, our family cannot become perfect. This is because the path for Satan to enter is wide open. However, if the Cain tribe is restored, Satan cannot attack. This is because the Cain realm is the symbol of the lineage of the people who followed Satan. Therefore, the Abel tribe can be protected by the defense barrier of the Cain realm. That is why the Abel tribe must love the Cain tribe until the very end, guide them to take the path to knowing Heavenly Parent, and realize the restoration of the authority of siblings (restoration of the authority of the eldest son).

Second is to perfect love. If we love many people and enable them to reach perfection, it may seem like we went the path of investing and sacrificing for our partner, but at some point, we will receive recognition from many people and stand in the position of parents and receive the right of inheritance. We will be born as a heavenly tribal messiah who resembles Heavenly Parent. Therefore, in the end, the completion of the restoration of the tribe is not a burden but a hopeful movement. It is the only path by which I perfect myself, by enabling my partner to reach perfection, and for my family to be perfected by going the path of restoration of the tribe. It is the movement in which all humankind is building one family under the original parents. It is the movement in which we ascend as the parents of the tribe. Based on that foundation, the perfection of the people, nation and cosmos can be realized.

We have come to know that the restoration of the tribe is the path for the perfection of my family. All blessed families of the Family Federation who have first received the calling of God's Will and have participated in the Blessing are blessed central families centered on Heavenly Parent. In other words, the position in which we can inherit the position of the unfallen Adam and Eve family has been secured. Therefore, we must establish the model of an unfallen family and go the path that can be a model for others. The establishment of that model family cannot be realized when we try to perfect our family alone. Only when we form tribes of large numbers and try to enable them to be perfected, can our family be protected and be perfected. That is how our family can be perfected through our partner. Blessed families should follow the attributes of Heavenly Parent and fulfill the needs of the tribe who are our spiritual children, practicing true love and work on their shortcomings so they can be more complete individuals. what is lacking in them. When that happens, the members of our tribe will acknowledge our family and say, "Our heavenly tribal messiah is a model family centered on Heavenly Parent." Then that model can be expanded and manifested as the tribal community, the masterpiece of our life. Through that, our family can find again the original model of the unfallen family of Adam and Eve, and the tribe members will come to have the name and the realm of authority of parents.

Section 5 The Perfection of Love and the Spirit World

Heavenly Parent created human beings after creating the best environment for them to live freely. True Parents also have created the best environment for blessed families to accomplish their mission of heavenly tribal messiah. The most precious thing is that they have created the environment in which the spirit world can cooperate with us. They opened the era in which the spirit world can come and cooperate if blessed families just proclaim that they will complete their mission as heavenly tribal messiahs. All the barriers that existed between the spirit world and physical world have been brought down, and a new era has been opened in which the spirit world can cooperate with us freely.

1. The three stages of life and the spirit world

All human beings are created to go through three stages during their life course: nine months in the womb, 100 years on the earth, and eternity in the spirit world. The time in the womb is a period of preparation for the time on earth. The time on earth is a period of preparation for the eternal spirit world. Human beings are born on the earth after nine months in the womb have passed. After 100 years have passed on the earth, they will be born again as a spirit in the spirit world and live there for eternity. Heavenly Parent has created human beings to live and go through three stages of creation.

We spend nine months in water in the womb, so it is called the underwater era. We breathe air for 100 years on earth, so it is called the era of air. And we breathe love in the spirit world, so it is called the era of love. For the nine months in the womb, we eat food and breathe through the umbilical cord. For the 100 years on earth, we eat with our mouth and breathe with our nose. In the eternal spirit world, we breathe through our spirit's nose and the cells on the top of our head. In the spirit world, we feel and bond through these love-breathing organs and live in a carefree environment without limits. It is important for human beings to prepare their love-breathing organs during their 100 years on earth, so that they can use them in the world of love. [30]

When a baby who was in the womb is born on the earth, its umbilical cord is cut. In the era of the womb, this is considered death, but in the era of the earth, it means the birth of new life. When the life of a human being who was living on the earth ends and he or she stops breathing, this is considered death in the era of the earth, but in the era of the spirit world, it means the birth of a new life. Therefore, when we end our time in the womb and are born again on the earth or when we end our time on the earth and are born again in the spirit world, we must go through the gateway of death. In the original world, the term "death" is not a noun of suffering but a sacred word.

> True Parents have created the term "Seonghwa" to teach the true significance of death. The moment we enter the spirit world should be a time of joy and victory, as we enter with the fruits borne of our life on earth. It is a time for those remaining on earth to send off the departed with joy. It should be a time for great celebration. We should be shedding tears of joy, not of sadness. That is the way of the sacred and noble Seonghwa Ceremony, the first step that the spirit of the departed takes toward enjoying eternal life in attendance of God, within His embrace. At the moment of death, our spirit should feel more excited and thrilled than a newlywed bride feels when she goes to her groom's home for the first time. [31]

Just as the goal of going through the time in the womb is to prepare to live well on the earth, the goal of our life on the earth is not to live well on the earth but to prepare to live well in the spirit world. Therefore, the life of a human being who must live through three stages is not to prepare for the era in which he or she currently lives but to prepare for the next era. The time in the womb is preparation for the earth. The eyes, nose, ears and mouth to be used on the earth must be well prepared. This is also the case with regard to the world of the spirit. Through the umbilical cord, the baby can understand the outside world that the parent sees, and when the parent eats normal food and takes in proper nutrients, the baby can develop into a normal baby. However, what would happen if a baby were born on the earth without developing the parts necessary in the outside world? That baby would live with deformities in the outside world. Therefore, if the baby does not receive the proper nutrients from the parent while in the womb, he or she will have a problem living on the earth. In the same way, human beings living on the earth for 100 years should not just be caught up with living on the earth. They should fill up on and complete the necessary requisites for the spirit world. They have to go through the era of water (liquid) in the womb, the era of land (solid) on earth, and prepare the elements necessary in the air of the heavenly world (gas). If we are born in the spirit world without having prepared elements necessary in the heavenly world while on the earth, we may live like a child with deformities when we are in the heavenly world.

Therefore, glory is not something to be received on the earth. Glory is to be received in the spirit world after you die. A human being on the earth should live in accordance with the standard of the spirit world. This means being in step with the spirit world while on the earth and practicing true love. We should communicate with the spirit world through jeongseong and prayer and live as a spiritual being who has achieved perfection on the earth. [32]

Human beings are in a dual structure of spirit self and physical self. It is a dual structure of spirit and physical and mind and body. We are created in a dual structure of the "spirit me" and the "physical me" or the "inside me" and "outside me." Just as a human being's physical self has five physical senses, the spirit self has five spiritual senses. Just as the physical self has a brain, the spirit self also has a brain. Human beings have cosmic value because they have a dual structure. [33]

> Human beings have both a mind and a body. Above our mind is our spirit, and above our spirit is God. This is why we can become perfect when we become completely one with God. Though a person is only one small entity, because he or she represents all of history as well as all future relationships, he or she possesses cosmic value. [34]

What does it mean for a human being to live well on the earth? This means to unite the spirit and physical and the mind and body. It means having the spirit self and physical self become one, uniting the "spirit me" and "physical me" and uniting the "inside me" and "outside me." If human beings had not fallen, the spirit self and physical self would have become one. The spirit self and physical self become one in a place of resonance. When something matches the vibration frequency of a tuning fork, when you hit it, it will resonate with sound. In the same way as the tuning fork, the spirit self and physical self become one through the realm of resonance. What happens when the spirit self and physical self become one?

> When our spiritual and physical selves harmonize and resonate with each other in God's love, the spiritual cells and physical cells interact perfectly. When we open our eyes and they are working perfectly, we can see everything throughout heaven and earth for the first time. When we use a highly efficient microphone, our voice will ring out fully everywhere. Similarly, once our physical and spiritual selves become one and attain an explosive state through the power of love, that complete union emits a light on the same wavelength as the heavenly world, the earthly world, and even God Himself. [35]

When the spirit self and physical self are in a place of resonance, the physical world and heavenly world become connected as one. A person who communicates with the spirit world while living as a spirit self who has achieved perfection on the earth can feel the reality of the spirit world while still on the earth through his or her five spiritual senses. In the original world, there is no boundary between the spirit world and the earth. In the original world, the spirit world is also one single realm of the spirit. In the original world, the physical world is one world and the spirit world is one world and the spirit world and the earth form one connected world. We live 100 years on the earth, but we live while experiencing the spirit world and then leave our physical selves behind and enter the eternal world. It is like a tree whose fruit becomes ripe and falls down in the autumn. The fruit decomposes, but the seeds inside it remain alive.

In the original plan of creation, there are no national boundaries in the earthly world. There are no boundaries in the heavenly world either. There is no boundary between the spirit world and the earth either. The physical self lives on the earth for about 100 years and then leaves, but the spirit self was created to live forever, transcending time and space. The world after life, the spirit world, exists on the grounds of the physical world, but we cannot see it with our eyes. In other words, although we have shed our physical body, it is an automatic and inevitable extension of the earthly life. Heavenly Parent created the spirit world to be the eternal hometown for human beings. People who have perfected their spirit self on the earth can live while experiencing the spirit world through their five spiritual senses, even while still living on the earth.

A person who knows the reality of the spirit world clearly and who feels the spirit world through his five spiritual senses will feel greater pain in living centering on himself rather than living for the sake of others. Such a person will feel that a selfish life is not natural, and their cells will cry out if they live a life of making others suffer or feel pain. People who know and experience the spirit world live up to the standard of the order of the spirit world as they live the moments of their earthly life. They live while prioritizing the practice of true love. The same goes for space. The reason why the planets centering on the sun do not collide with each other and maintain their constant distance while rotating and revolving is to care and live for the sake of the other. That is why there is no destruction within that order.

The original spirit world that Heavenly Parent created is called the principled realm of the spirit world. The principled spirit world, as the only spirit world, refers to heaven. It refers to the spirit world where people who have realized ideal families can enter as a family unit and live forever. The level in the spirit world is based on how much we practiced true love while on the earth. When we come to stand in the position of God's object partner of love, we can feel what Heavenly Parent does. [36] With regard to what we inherit from Heaven, the spirit world is a place where our thoughts become reality, so we can create anything we desire as much as we like.

> In the spirit world, when you think, "I want to do such and such a thing," it becomes a reality. That is why in the next world, whenever you wish for something with an earnest heart of love, it is made possible. It is a place where, if you desire to make ten million beautiful outfits and to dress your loved ones in them all at once, you can do that. If you want to dress your beloved in clothes woven of gold thread, that clothing will appear just as you imagined it. [37]

> The spirit world is a place that transcends time and space. In the spirit world you can freely eat whatever you want. There is no need to worry about food or water. There is no need to worry about what to drink or what to wear. It transcends everything— be it food, clothing or shelter. Would you need a car there? Would

> there be car factories, food factories or clothing factories? There would be no such things. In the spirit world you can go back and forth, covering billions of miles in an instant. You can do so with the power of love. If you wish to see someone you love, that person will appear immediately before you. [38]

The spirit world is a world where our intuitive senses become reality, depending on the level of our spirit. [39] In the spirit world, we can receive anything we want instantaneously. The spirit world is a place where if we say, "Appear" to someone we want, that person will appear immediately. However, there is one thing that is not possible in the spirit world. It does not work if we say "appear" for our own sake. [40]

The spirit world transcends the limits of the physical body and is an infinite world. It is an extrasensory world that transcends the senses of the physical body. Heavenly Parent created the infinite spirit world first before creating the finite earth. He prepared this infinite world for human beings, and even at this very moment He is calling out to us to become ideal couples who have realized ideal families on earth. He is calling us to come to this place, "Let's live together!"

2. The pathway to harmony and unity

In the original world without the Fall, the spirit world would exist as one entity. It would exist as spirit world with only one realm. That is the kingdom of heaven in heaven. The spirit world that Heavenly Parent originally created was not divided into different structures such as heaven, paradise, middle spirit world and hell. These structures have nothing to do with Heavenly Parent. [41] These structures of the spirit world only came into existence after the Fall of human beings. The nations and the boundaries between nations in the earthly world also came into existence after the Fall. The boundary between the spirit world and the physical world also came after the Fall. These things resulted from the Fall because human beings tried to construct their own world.

First, after the Fall the spirit world was divided into many levels, and this had nothing to do with Heavenly Parent. It was generally divided into heaven, paradise, middle spirit world and hell. Before True Parents, no one entered heaven. This is because heaven is a place that you enter after realizing an ideal family. Paradise, middle spirit world and hell are each divided into many different levels as well. The spirit world has been in a state where one could not come and go freely because of the unfathomable number of boundaries that exist.

Second, after the Fall many boundaries were created on earth as well. After the Fall extreme individualism and self-centeredness came to be. This extreme individualism and self-centeredness created many boundaries. They created a boundary between the mind and body on a smaller scale and a boundary between the spirit world and the physical world on a bigger scale. There exist an unfathomable number of boundaries on this earth, such as boundaries between nations, between people of different skin color, between different religions, different theologies and different cultures.

Third, after the Fall there came to be a boundary between the spirit world and the physical world, so it is difficult to go back and forth freely. People living on the earth do not know the spirit world well. They do not know the existence of Heavenly Parent clearly either. They do not know the reality of the spirit world and the structure of the spirit world. They also do not know about the three stages of creation that human beings must go through. They are ignorant of the spirit world or think of it very vaguely.

The characteristic of Satan after the Fall is to encourage conflict and division. Satan cannot have dominion beyond the national level. That is why he has been trying to rule the world by dividing the earth into hundreds of nations by creating boundaries. Satan also has been trying to rule the spirit world by creating many levels there. He created the boundary between the spirit world and the physical world so that people living on the earth would not be aware of the spirit world. These kinds of boundaries were not created by Heavenly Parent but by Satan. Wherever there is a boundary, evil is lurking there. [42]

The responsibility of removing those boundaries created by Satan lies with True Parents and not Heavenly Parent. Heavenly Parent cannot be present in a place with boundaries and conflict. He can be present only in a place with harmony and unity. True Parents are the ones who remove the boundaries by using a method reversing how they came to be. Heavenly Parent is present and working in the places where the boundaries have been removed. Human beings can come and go freely between the spirit world and the physical world. From this perspective, True Parents are connecting the world divided by boundaries and breaking down the walls of the world as through an international highway, and they have been leading the providence of bringing the world together as one.

Boundaries have come into existence due to the Fall caused by false love. Boundaries came to be because of false love, so they must be removed through true love. If we can practice just true love, the boundaries naturally will be abolished. [43] What is the greatest true love? It is to love our enemy. What is the greatest way to love our enemy? First, we must be able to look at our brother with a parental heart. The second way is to marry people who come from enemy nations.

We must resemble the unchanging parental heart of True Parents, who are the causal ones, transcending age, race and theology. It is only when we place the parental heart of Heavenly Parent in human beings that we can love the enemy. We should be willing to marry people from enemy countries that had problems in history. This is the cross-cultural and interracial marriage. The cross-cultural and interracial marriage is a ceremony in which a man and a woman transcend race, religion and nationality to marry centering on Heavenly Parent's Will. This cross-cultural marriage is at the individual level, and the interracial marriage involves people in a nation or religious organization having a cross-cultural marriage. The cross-cultural and interracial marriage is the best way to practice loving the enemy, and it is the shortcut to realizing world peace. If we start resolving things that were problematic in the past here on earth, those who were enemies on earth in the past can begin to make harmony when they go to the spirit world. Then they can come again to the earth and encourage the unity of the world. In places where there is cross-cultural and interracial marriage, Satan has to step aside and boundaries come down. In places where the boundaries come down, peace can prevail and Heavenly Parent can be present.

Once the actual era of Cheon Il Guk begins, the spiritual and earthly worlds will connect and come into oneness, and the Association to Connect the Earth to the Spirit World, a new entity that we will establish on earth, will govern all creation. Moreover, we will carry out the providence according to heavenly law and the heavenly way. Elections conducted in a purely secular fashion will disappear from the face of the earth. All people will become one family through cross-cultural Marriage Blessings. We will enjoy tranquility and true love in happiness amid the sacred reign of peace. Let me say it again: This day is drawing near. [44]

Before they proclaimed the heavenly tribal messiah mission, True Parents created the greatest environment where the spirit world can cooperate with us. First, on August 18, 2000, at the celebratory banquet for the International Peace Award, held at the UN headquarters in New York, they proclaimed the removal of boundaries on the earth. There are many boundaries, beginning with the boundary between our individual mind and body; there are boundaries between families, tribes, races and nations, as well as boundaries between religions and a boundary between heaven and earth. The theology to remove these boundaries is true love, and True Parents have proclaimed that the substantial way of practicing true love is to see from Heavenly Parent's point of view and to marry people from enemy homes. [45]

Second, on September 12, 2000 (8/15 by the lunar calendar), at the Total Liberation Chuseok commemorative ceremony held at East Garden, True Parents proclaimed the removal of all the boundaries in the spirit world and the liberation of all spirits. "All the people who lived on the earth, then passed away to the spirit world until now, have been caught up in their own limitations and buried as though in a tomb. However, now the cover of that tomb has been opened, and they can go back and forth as they wish. No matter where the good spirits of the spirit world go, they can drive out Satan in the satanic world." [46]

Third, on October 16 and October 20, 2002, at the Rallies for the Harmony and Unity of Heaven and Earth held at the Korean Central Training Center and Sun Moon University, True Parents proclaimed that heaven and earth had achieved harmony and unity through true love, and thus the boundaries between heaven and earth had been removed. "The condition for the two nations of the spirit world and the physical world to become one was for the ancestors of the spirit world to come to the earth, stand in the position of the younger brother and attend the blessed descendants on the earth as their older brother and become one with the earthly world." [47]

Through true love True Parents removed the boundaries on earth, in the spirit world and those that existed between heaven and earth. They said that true love has a color. The color of false love is conflict and division, but the color of true love is harmony, unity and peace. They sent out blessed families as heavenly tribal messiahs to shine forth the light of harmony, unity and peace in heaven and on earth where the boundaries have been removed.

Through the Marriage Blessing, True Parents opened wide the gate of salvation to all the spirits in the spirit world, not just to human beings on the earth. It is not possible to have complete salvation of people on the earth without first saving all the spirits in the spirit world who lived on the earth and passed away in history. Through the providence of restoration, True Parents have been leading the work of salvation of all the spirits that went to the spirit world after Adam. Through the descendants of blessed families on the earth, the ancestors who have joined the ranks of salvation can come again to the earth and cooperate with their descendants. When that happens, the spirit world and physical world can be connected as one world and can be cleansed at a much quicker pace.

The providence of restoration puts into order the spirit world through the providence of conditions on the earth and then joins forces with the organized spirit world to bring order on the earth. The spirit world is much more complicated than the earth. If the complicated spirit world cannot be put in order, then it is impossible to put the earth in order. The spirit world can be put in order when men and women receive the Blessing. Only when all the spirits in the spirit world receive the Blessing, will the spirit world be in order. The providence to put the spirit world in order is carried out through the providence of conditions, but the providence of the ordered spirit world coming down to the earth and putting the earthly world in order is referred to as the substantial providence. Through this process, the harmony and unity between the spirit world and earthly world can come about and a peaceful world can come to be. It is when the absolute good spirits who have received the Blessing in the spirit world come down to the earth and cooperate with descendants of the same lineage that the spirit world and earthly world can be connected as one world. [48]

Heavenly Parent's Will can be completed through 95 percent Heavenly Parent's portion of responsibility and five percent human beings' portion of responsibility. The human beings who have completed this five percent portion of responsibility stand in the position of Adam and Eve, in other words, the True Parents. In June 2012, True Parents proclaimed that they had accomplished all their responsibility through the Proclamation of the Entrance into the Fourth Realm. They said that we were entering the era in which blessed families can become perfected through 96 percent True Parents' portion of responsibility and four percent blessed families' portion of responsibility. In August 2017, True Mother proclaimed that from now on, we have entered a new era in which perfection can be achieved through 99.99 percent of True Parents' victorious fulfillment of responsibility and 0.01 percent blessed families' responsibility. This means that we have entered the era when Heavenly Parent's dream of one human family under Heavenly Parent can be realized by fulfilling our 0.01 percent portion of responsibility. Being a heavenly tribal messiah means fulfilling that mission completely.

> What I am saying to you today is that we absolutely must realize God's dream. This must be realized centered on True Parents. You must have a picture of heaven on earth. Through True Parents' victorious achievements, True Parents already have achieved 99.99 percent of that great dream, God's dream. All that you, who are unstained, must do, is fulfill the 0.01 percent of the responsibility. True Parents' grand design is like a puzzle. You are the ones who have the last piece, which will complete the puzzle. Therefore, the day must quickly come when you can say and offer to Heavenly Parent, "Together with True Parents, we have created the environment through which we can realize our Heavenly Parent's dream." [49]

The realization of the dream that Heavenly Parent has long awaited and hoped for can be achieved through our actions and mobilization centering on True Parents. True Parents have created the environment. Now the time has come when, together with True Parents, we can make Heavenly Parent's dream our dream and offer it to Heavenly Parent.

Chapter 2

What Is a Heavenly Tribal Messiah?

Section 1 The World Based on the Culture of Heart and Hyojeong

At a hoondokhae session in 2011, True Father declared that from then on, the term Seunghwa (昇華) should be changed to Seonghwa (聖和); *cheongi* (天紀) to *cheongi* (天基); Foundation Day (起元節) to Foundation Day (基元節); "evolve and change" (進化) to "evolve in harmony" (進和); and culture (文化) to "culture in harmony" (文和). And he spoke about how *hwa* (化) has a strong connotation of change, but *hwa* (和) has a strong connotation of balance, harmony and unification and insisted that this *hwa* (和) be used from now on. [1]

1. Definition of the culture of heart

When we speak of culture, or *munhwa* (文化), as it is based on the written word, the essence can change, yet the essence of culture itself, *munhwa* (文和), is unchanging and brings harmony. As a culture that is based on the unchanging heart of Heavenly Parent, the "culture of heart," *shimjeong munhwa* (心情文和), is a culture that wields the ideologies of "A God–human relationship—a Parent–child relationship" and "true love travels the shortest path." When Adam and Eve and all humankind build a parent–child relationship with Heavenly Parent, their Parent whose lineage they share, their love will take the shortest path. The culture of heart is a culture in which all people achieve balance, stability and unity through living for the sake of one another.

The first principle of the dwelling place of Heavenly Parent states that a single lineage must be achieved based on the Heavenly Parent. The second principle states that God dwells in a place of balance, where perfection is achieved by living for the sake of each other, and that God dwells in a vertical position in a place where harmony is reached with the horizontal. [2]

After 2011, in which a lifestyle of the Era After the Coming of Heaven prevailed, we began to use the term "culture of heart" synonymously with "let us prosper together" based on the heart of the Heavenly Parent. The culture of heart is based on the eternal, unchanging heart, in which longing naturally wells up from the very center of one's being. It is the lifestyle that all of humankind practices as brothers and sisters to perfect themselves by enabling one another to perfect themselves, while also protecting the original lineage. The culture of heart can be understood as a culture that achieves unification in a place where a balance is reached among the heart of Heavenly Parent, the heart of humans, and the ways of the world, creating a level plane. The world where people "prosper together" with hyojeong (filial devotion) based on the heart of Heavenly Parent is truly a world of peace.

The culture of heart in the Era after the Coming of Heaven is not a culture of conflict and division but rather a culture of harmony and unification. It is a culture in which Cain and Abel achieve harmony and unity. It is a culture in which the sacred and the mundane achieve harmony and unity. It is a culture in which Heavenly Parent and humans, the spirit world and the earth harmonize and are bound to one another. Also, it is a culture in which harmony and unity are achieved based on a true love that contains absolute value (Heavenly Parent) rather than relative value. When harmony and unity are achieved based on true love, then peace and happiness follow.

2. True Parents have both initiated and exemplified hyojeong culture

In 1952, in the *Wolli Wonbon,* True Parents expressed the heart of Heaven that Heavenly Parent longs for and the heart of humans that humankind longs for. True Parents have voluntarily walked a path of hardship to attain the liberation of Heavenly Parent, based on heavenly heart, and the salvation of humankind, based on the heart of humans. In understanding True Parents' lives in terms of the culture of heart, the clearing up of that which transpired in the past due to the Fall is the return to life based on the culture of heart. In other words, the newly created history is evident when a life is lived based on the culture of heart.

Prior to the Fall, human beings were in direct communication with God. The intangible Heavenly Parent and the substantial people had a relationship in which they could see, feel and empathize with one another. Heavenly Parent intended for people to inherit all creation, and for both parties to enjoy a "parent–child relationship." Heavenly Parent gave parental love to humans, and, having received that love, humans returned beauty. This meant that the human world was one where people received inspiration from Heavenly Parent while reciprocating by giving beauty to Heavenly Parent. The point where they mutually shared their feelings could be called "affection." In Unification Thought, this is known as "heart," meaning the "love welling up from the center of Parents' being." But, when looking at it from another perspective, there is the phenomenon of filial piety by which the children of humankind, who had a deep experience of God's love, seek to return the grace back to God.

This means when heart is manifested on its own by people who intend to return the love of parents in a place where the heart of the Heavenly Parent and the heart of the children of humankind become one, then filial piety is achieved. In other words, filial piety is not about parents paying the price of sacrifice for children. When children who have received unconditional love from their parents then become parents themselves, the beautiful tradition of parental love is displayed to their children. The children and grandchildren who receive love experience the beautiful tradition of parental love and the heart that manifests as a desire to attend ancestors and the causal being, the Heavenly Parent, with gratitude.

True Mother defines hyojeong (filial devotion) as the give-and-take relationship between Heavenly Parent and humankind combined with the filial piety which displays the beauty that reciprocates the affectionate heart and love. But there is further depth to the content and significance of hyojeong as defined by True Mother. On September 3, 2012, the date of the Seonghwa of Sun Myung Moon, the True Father, True Mother started a three-year condition of memorial jeongseong. This memorial jeongseong was significant because this was the final jeongseong made as Sun Myung Moon, the True Father, went to spirit world to meet Heavenly Parent. Originally, the Messiah was supposed to come to earth and go to the spirit world on the foundation of emerging victorious in the battle with Satan, restoring God's people on behalf of all humankind, and restoring at least one nation. True Father should have met Heavenly Parent after attaining such results.

Though True Father did complete some of the criteria before passing to the heavenly realm, such as emerging victorious in the battle with Satan and fulfilling the history of restoration through indemnity, he did not accomplish the condition of creating a restored foundation on the national level. That condition must be fulfilled by all of humankind, who are in the position of children. That is why all of humankind and the children of blessed families should have made a three-year condition of atonement, with the determination to restore the nation of the land of Heavenly Parent through memorial jeongseong, starting from the date of True Father's Seonghwa. But, on behalf of the children, True Mother performed the jeongseong that should have been performed by all of humankind and expressed sorrow before Heaven. This became the "starting point for the concept of hyojeong."

This means the background for the manifestation of hyojeong is the inclusion of filial piety that is returned to the Heavenly Parent from an unfallen, original person (True Mother). Though humankind is fallen, included in the heart of a restored child is the internal goal of intending to return filial piety to the Creator, the Heavenly Parent. And the filial piety found in this hyojeong originated not from his physical parents but from the fundamental creator of humans, Heavenly Parent. Also, when we embrace the hope for the salvation of humankind, which is the original dream and ideal of Heavenly Parent, our absolute faith in Heavenly Parent will expand that form to the nation and cosmos. In that regard, blessed families are in the position of a child who must repent before Heavenly Parent and True Father for not performing filial piety to the best of their abilities. They should have the mindset of hyojeong that determines to live with a filial heart to turn the foundation of restoration to victory on the national and cosmic levels. Therefore, the definition of hyojeong is "a general term when Heavenly Parent and humankind create a parent–child relationship with an underlying motivation of heart, and love is transmitted from the parents to the children, and filial piety from the children to the parents. [3]

3. Hyojeong culture for the liberation of Heavenly Parent

After the Fall of Adam and Eve, Heavenly Parent was rendered unable to settle anywhere in the spirit world or physical world. Because there was no connection to His children by means of lineage, the spirit world and the physical world resembled a prison. Heavenly Parent, in the position of parents, could do nothing until the right time arrived, except to look on [4] in silence as humankind suffered in this prison created by Satan. [5] True Parents' realm of heart was filled with longing for the heart of heaven (天情), while physically entrapped in a bodily prison. They are filled with hyojeong to liberate Heavenly Parent and once again regain the original kingship of the Heavenly Parent.

With God's Coronation Ceremony held in 2001, True Parents completely liberated and released God's body and mind. [6] True Parents were so fully committed to dedicating God's Coronation Ceremony that they were willing to risk their lives with no concept of rest, working night and day and overcoming limitations. They alone bore the cross [7] of love and the cross [8] of heart for the liberation of Heavenly Parent, and always stuck to the standard tactic of the providence of restoration through indemnity in dealing with

Satan. This resulted in the archangel Lucifer surrendering, enabling Heavenly Parent to be completely liberated and released. [9] Within True Parents' realm of heart which liberated and released Heavenly Parent, Heavenly Parent is not limited to emotional impulse but is enabled to meet His object partners and directly feel and experience their hearts. By becoming one in body, True Father and True Mother became the absolute partner to Heavenly Parent and were the ones who enabled Heavenly Parent to experience generosity on a grand scale. Heavenly Parent was able to experience "first love" and "first heart" through the True Parents. This scene is further elaborated in the statement from the Divine Principle below.

> The place where Adam and Eve become perfectly one in heart and body as husband and wife is also the place where God, the subject partner giving love, and human beings, the object partners returning beauty, become united. This is the center of goodness where the purpose of creation is fulfilled. Here God, our Parent, draws near and abides within His perfected children and rests peacefully for eternity. This center of goodness is the object partner to God's eternal love, where God can be stimulated with joy for eternity. This is the place where the Word of God is incarnated and brought to fulfillment. It is the center of truth and the center of the original mind, which guides us to pursue the purpose of creation. [10]

First, the purpose of creation is attaining the central position of a perfected cosmos where goodness is at the center. Second, it is attaining an eternal resting place for Heavenly Parent. Third, it is attaining a place where Heavenly Parent can experience riveting joy. Fourth, it is attaining a place where the embodiment of the Word by True Parents can be achieved. Fifth, it is attaining the central position of the truth. And sixth, it is attaining the central position of original mind.

> The Heavenly Parent has eagerly awaited the day when a person could emerge to clear away all these tragedies, but the right partner and nation are yet to emerge upon the earth. If a person could appear in a nation to take the position of True Parents, the Heavenly Parent would want to create "lightning of happiness" out of thin air and make "thunder of delight," even if they would have to move the sun with a helicopter and relocate the moon. [11]

Once the heart of Heavenly Parent, which is filled through and through with longing, and the hyojeong of the True Parents of Heaven meet at the cosmic central position, an explosion of heart will transpire. Once that happens, our being will tremble with true love. Amid such trembling, the joy and delight of creation will stimulate our five spiritual and physical senses. However, fallen people have experienced a paralysis of heart and have been rendered unable to experience the explosion of heart. To be released from the paralysis of heart, an antidote is required. The antidote is holy wine. Anyone will be able to experience the explosion of heart after becoming a citizen of Cheon Il Guk and receiving the Blessing.

What will happen when human beings experience the explosion of heart? Of their own volition, they will seek the path to connect to Heavenly Parent and experience Heavenly Parent's love firsthand. What is the taste of such love? It can be described in the following metaphor. A honeybee that has known only sugar water throughout the winter then has a chance to try the nectar from blooming flowers in the spring. Such a taste is indescribable. Such a honeybee that has tasted genuine nectar would not notice if you removed its stinger using tweezers. The taste of the love of Heavenly Parent is beyond comparison with such nectar. The taste of such love cannot be compared with anything else in the world. If there is a person who truly tasted the love of Heavenly Parent, that person would never be overcome by any hardship or by any sorrow. [12]

4. Culture of heart for the salvation of humankind

True Parents' world of heart is filled with a longing to be with and a compassion for fallen humankind. True Parents gave the following diagnosis: "Due to the Fall of the ancestors of humankind, human beings descended from a false lineage. Because of this, none of them could be free from their ties with Satan and they are still wandering aimlessly in the darkness." [13] True Parents are the ones who could completely save fallen humankind, reconnecting humankind with the Heavenly Parent in a parent–child relationship. True Parents' hearts are filled with the longing of parents for humanity and the desire to create a world where we "live together."

Blessed families that have had their original sin removed by receiving the Blessing from True Parents should be born again in the garden of Eden, the original creation. The original creation of the garden of Eden is the position before Heavenly Parent gave the commandment not to eat of the fruit of the Tree of the Knowledge of Good and Evil. [14] The position prior to the commandment given by Heavenly Parent is the original creation of the garden of Eden, free from original sin and free from fallen nature. [15] Fallen people must pass through the threshold of True Parents' Blessing to be reborn in the original creation of the garden of Eden. Five stages of Blessing were implemented for the complete salvation of fallen humankind: Church Blessing, National Blessing, World Blessing, Cosmic Blessing, and Cheon Il Guk Foundation Day Registration Blessing. [16]

The holy wine ceremony is a central part of the Blessing. Through the Blessing, humankind undergoes a change of lineage from Satan's lineage to the lineage of Heavenly Parent. Through the holy wine ceremony, the original sin of fallen people can be removed and they can be reborn at a position prior to the point where God gave the commandment. This is because the holy wine is a contractual condition concluded between Heavenly Parent, Satan and True Father.

> Do you know what holy wine is? It contains intimidating ingredients. You will be changed once you drink it. It is a contractual

condition between Satan, Heavenly Parent and myself. Once you drink this, the gates to hell and the gates to heaven should be opened. Not even Satan cannot oppose, so once the Blessing crosses over into the global level, the gates of hell automatically are opened. [17]

The holy wine used at Blessing ceremonies is suffused with an adequate amount of indemnity that can satisfy both Satan and Heavenly Parent, which is why it could be offered. The amount of indemnity for saving fallen humankind cannot be completed by fallen people on their own. If they could complete that indemnity, there would be no need for a Messiah to come. The amount of indemnity to completely save fallen humans can be accomplished only by True Parents. True Parents have suffered six physical hardships, including imprisonment and a helicopter accident, [18] to set conditions for the complete salvation of fallen humankind. And they suffered the pain of witnessing five of their children pass on to spirit world.

True Parents' world of heart is a journey of blood, sweat and tears. The world of heart is one in which the unforgivable are forgiven and the unlovable are given love without end. It is a world that transcends what fallen humankind can fathom. True Parents were the ones who prayed for each member while offering jeongseong, even for those who left the church, and in this way continued the connection of heart. True Father prayed for the members three times a day while serving close to three years in the Heungnam Labor Camp. [19]

After being discharged from Seodaemun Prison, for the three years between 1957 and 1960, when the Marriage Supper of the Lamb was held, True Father called out the names of about 400 members, one by one, in prayer that was brimming with the heart of heaven and the heart of humanity. [20]

5. The flagbearer of hyojeong culture, the heavenly tribal messiah

The heavenly tribal messiah who is serving Heavenly Parent comes into existence when he becomes a love partner as well as heart partner of Heavenly Parent, so that they experience an explosion of heart. When the heart of Heavenly Parent meets the hyojeong (filial devotion) of the heavenly tribal messiah to experience an explosion of heart, Heaven will dance. When Heaven dances, the world and humanity also will dance. The heavenly tribal messiah, dancing to the beat of Heaven, will become the flag-bearer of the heartistic cultural revolution that is Heavenly Parent's wish. Let's now look at the lifestyle that such a flag-bearer must have, dividing this lifestyle into three parts for further consideration.

1) Lifestyle associated with the original lineage

The first prerequisite needed for the heavenly tribal messiah to establish a culture of heart is the lifestyle associated with the original lineage. In *Pyeong Hwa Shin Gyeong*, when human beings are connected to their original lineage, they will feel heavenly affection (receiving the love of Heavenly Parent), human affection (being loved by human beings), and material affection (being loved by all things). They also may fulfill the three great blessings given by the Heavenly Parent.

> In the veins of Heavenly Parent, there is the seed of true love, and the body of true life is alive. Therefore, when humans are connected to this line, Heavenly Parent can make the ideal human beings, that is, the perfection of the personality, and the ideal family. Furthermore, the fatherland of Heavenly Parent and the ideal nation also appear. In this way, the world of peace and the ideal is created. [21]

For a fallen person to be connected to Heavenly Parent by blood, he or she must pass through the door of the Blessing, which comes from True Parents. We have heard that if we do not pass through the door of the Blessing of True Parents who come to us as true mediators of Heaven, we cannot be connected to the heart and mind of Heavenly Parent. [22] True Father stressed that we should live with True Parents according to absolute standards. [23]

When we are connected to the lineage of Heavenly Parent, we will feel His love and heart. Heavenly Parent, who is love itself, is not able to control His love because He wants to give it to someone and is waiting for a partner who can receive it. If the blessed family is connected to the lineage of Heavenly Parent, the possibility of experiencing that love is always open. However, the precondition is that in any case, pure love and fidelity centering on "absolute sex" should be kept more precious than life. The human being connected to the original lineage is to hear Heavenly Parent through his or her conscience. Heavenly Parent meets only those related to Him through the foundation of pure lineage. This is because Heavenly Parent, who created only goodness, cannot tolerate evil. The standard of good is the true lineage, which is connected to the conscience, and through it people can meet Heavenly Parent. That is why we must defend our original lineage. The only way to make a vertical bond with Heaven is lineage.

In the Divine Principle, the motive of the Fall of the archangel is called the "feeling of loss of love." From the standpoint of the archangel, it is correct to say there was a feeling of loss of love. However, when I asked Heavenly Parent about the motive of the Fall of the archangel, He said that the archangel had a self-centered greed regarding Heavenly Parent. [24] In other words, the archangel thought that Heavenly Parent created a partner for Adam, but none for him. Therefore, he became relatively greedy. As a result, human corruption was inherited from the corruption and egoism of the archangel. Therefore, it became such that people cannot keep pure love and fidelity based on absolute sex and cannot control their greed.

Living in connection with the original lineage means living in the authority of the dominion of Heavenly Parent. It means living a new life in a state of being disconnected from Satan. As seen in the

Fall of Adam and Eve, Satan dominates humankind through the lineage. [25] It is crucial to adhere to absolute sex in order to keep and protect the purity of lineage. Absolute sex refers to the act of love only between the blessed couple serving Heavenly Parent after the Blessing. [26]

2) A lifestyle of practicing true love

The second prerequisite for a heavenly tribal messiah to found the culture of heart is the lifestyle that realizes true love at home. True love is said to be an intangible principle that is necessary for the good of the public. [27] The spirit world is the place where we breathe the air of true love and where we act by the order of true love. The minimum unit in which true love is practiced is the family. If we perfect our family through a life based on true love for each family member, each family member comes to feel the heart of Heavenly Parent.

> The relationship between God, who has a heart of true love, and humankind is a vertical relationship of parent and child. Adam and Eve, who were created as God's son and daughter, were the first to receive God's parental love and experience the heart of children as they grew up. During their growth, they also could feel the heart of brother and sister for each other. Next, after being blessed in marriage by God, they were to become a couple, and by loving each other they were to experience the heart of a husband

and wife. Finally, after having children and loving them as true parents, they were to feel the heart of parents, thereby experiencing the heart with which God loved them as children. [28]

In the culture of heart, in which we care about each other with true love, we share and experience heart together in the Unification realm of the ideal family that has achieved the four great realms of heart, namely the realms of children's love, siblings' love, conjugal love and parental love. On the basis of our perfected ideal family, we will be able to fully experience not only the heart of Heavenly Parent, who is the Parent of humanity, but also the fact that we are the children of Heavenly Parent.

Once the ideal family based on true love is perfected, we live a life caring for each other by the principle that our own viewpoint is determined in relation to the position of others. In the parent–child relationship, the parent completes the child and the child completes the parent. Therefore, the child makes the parent a parent, and the parent makes the child a child. The same is true for siblings and for marital relationships. It also should be true for the relationship between Heavenly Parent and humans. Perfection of the relationship centered on love always should be in consideration of the relationship from the other's perspective first.

In the lifestyle of caring for each other with true love, the subject is not me but always the partner. In my relationship with Heavenly Parent, I look at myself from the perspective of Heavenly Parent. For example, what if we look at the world from the perspective of

Heavenly Parent? We will feel the heart of Heavenly Parent, who wants to save humanity. In our relationship with our parents, we should think in terms of our parents. In sibling relations, for example, an older brother should think from the standpoint of the younger brother and vice versa. In a marital relationship, a husband should think from the perspective of his wife and vice versa. Even in the heavenly tribe, tribe members form a community that helps and completes each other's viewpoint. The heavenly tribal messiah treats the members of the tribe in the position of parents and views them from the perspective of the heavenly tribal messiah. When we try to fill each other's lack, harmony, love and unification can transpire. And in such a place, we feel gratitude to the partners about the fact that our growth has been achieved and completed through them. There are happy songs on the spot. These things are expanding into the dream of one family of human beings under Heavenly Parent.

3) Lifestyle that extends the practice of true love

The third prerequisite for a heavenly tribal messiah to establish a culture of heart is a lifestyle that extends the practice of true love to society, nation and the world. A person who has been grafted into the heart of Heavenly Parent as an individual through a life connected to the original lineage can be grafted to the heart of Heavenly Parent by family through the perfection of an ideal family. Anyone who has experienced the heart of Heavenly Parent in the family also can bring the surrounding relatives to be likewise grafted. He also can extend it to the tribe, people, nation and the world. [29]

These above-mentioned things may be possible if we live with the conviction that "I" am not just an individual but the center of the world that represents a whole world. Working to expand the practice of true love is to contribute to my creation and fulfillment. [30]

When I am convinced that I am a representative of the world, I can live with the awareness that my calling is to maximize my personal expertise, which is my creativity given to me by Heaven. Through hyojeong, we may experience the heart of Heavenly Parent and live with various people to create and complete a culture of heart in which all things live together. Therefore, True Parents told us to "live for the sake of others." We cannot experience living for others in a place that is centered on me. When we live giving and loving the partner's world with my individual truth incarnation, we discover that we are already in the world of heart of Heavenly Parent. In other words, we are going to experience becoming a human being of completed substance resembling Him. Therefore, just like Heavenly Parent said after creating human beings, we also can say, "It's good, I'm glad." after creating the partner's world.

4) Lifestyle as a master of re-creation

Heavenly Parent wanted Adam and Eve to grow up to marry and grow to perfection and to be love partners and heart partners of Heavenly Parent. Adam and Eve, after marrying and reaching perfection together, should have opened the era of heavenly civilization centered on Heavenly Parent. The heavenly civilization centered on Heavenly Parent is a new civilization that has never appeared on earth. Heavenly civilization is not a disappearing or circulating civilization once created. It resembles the inner main attributes of Heavenly Parent and therefore, is the only permanently existing civilization.

The civilization of humanity after the Fall of Adam and Eve is a civilization centering on the archangel. Since it was not a civilization made in cooperation between Heavenly Parent and human beings, Heavenly Parent could not visit to become a master of civilization. True Parents observed the human civilization in depth that had begun after the Fall and said that we surely might feel the Will and the breath of Heavenly Parent working behind history. [31]

If you look at the history of human civilization, its first steps formed around the world's four great rivers—the Nile, the Indus, the Tigris and the Yellow River. This parallel may make it clear that civilization has been spiraling toward one destination. destination. What is the destination? True Parents say that human civilization has moved repeatedly in a spiraling movement in search of the heavenly civilization centered on the Heavenly Parent.

> Four civilizations developed around the four rivers of the world, namely the Egyptian civilization centered on the River Nile, the Mesopotamian civilization centered on the Tigris-Euphrates Rivers, the Indus Valley civilization centered on the Indus River, and the Chinese civilization centered on the Yellow River. Then

civilization landed in the Mediterranean region, namely on the Greek peninsula and the Roman peninsula to blossom as the Mediterranean civilization.

As history continued to evolve, the Mediterranean civilization also fueled the Island civilization in Britain and so on across the Atlantic. The British Empire, which conquered the Dead Sea and proudly proclaimed "the empire on which the sun never sets," handed over the baton to the American continent. The Atlantic civilization era, centered on England and the United States, was rooted in Christianity, embracing democracy, promoting religious freedom, human rights and equality. And it brought communism, which was synonymous with atheistic evil sovereignty, to its knees.

Human civilization, which has made a full circle, has now reached the point where it is necessary to look at its completion centered on the Pacific realm. After the American continent, the Japanese archipelago, which is like the British archipelago in geological terms, is in bloom, and according to the providence of Heaven, human civilization is facing a fateful moment to bear fruit on the Korean peninsula, the fatherland of Heavenly Parent. It is the providence of Heaven that human culture should bear its fruit in the Pacific region centered on the Korean peninsula. The Korean peninsula will be the home country that combines and protects all the countries in the Pacific region by bringing them together along with the American continent. The future of humanity now depends on the preservation of the Pacific, centering on the Republic of Korea, Japan, and the United States. [32]

Heavenly Parent failed to plant the seeds of heavenly civilization in the garden of Eden due to the Fall of Adam and Eve. The Pacific civilization era means the civilization era that newly creates the heavenly civilization on earth based on Heavenly Parent. [33] It is a new civilization era centered on Heavenly Parent, which has never been experienced by humanity. In the original garden of Eden, Heavenly Parent, Adam and Eve cooperate with each other to create this civilization by sowing seeds, growing fruits and so on.

The civilization of the garden of Eden cannot be created by the efforts of Heavenly Parent alone or by the efforts of humans alone. The civilization of the garden of Eden is a new civilization that is created by Heavenly Parent and human beings together. It is a civilization in which spirit and the earth are united. Heavenly Parent is looking for the heavenly tribal messiah and the heavenly tribal community to sow the new seeds of a new civilization, expand it by building up 12 tribes, and connect it to the cosmos. Therefore, the heavenly tribal messiah is the starting point of a new Pacific civilization centering on Heavenly Parent.

5) Construction and culture style of Cheon Il Guk

Heavenly Parent wanted to feel joy by meeting object partners of love and sharing love with them. If you meet your object partner of love and share love, you naturally will feel affection. This affection, which is accumulated by exchanging love with your love partner, is called "heart."

Until you meet your object partner of love, the heart exists as a concept but not as a reality. The inexperienced heart brings forth an impulse. An impulse is "a stimulus in the mind that makes you feel like performing some action instantly." The heart of Heavenly Parent remained as an impulse because Heavenly Parent could not meet His object partner of love. He really wanted to experience and feel that impulse. [34] When the absolute partner of love appears and shares love with the partner, the impulse of affection latent in the mind of Heavenly Parent is realized and experienced. The heart will appear and explode in love. When Heavenly Parent's heart explodes, a human being, the absolute partner of Heavenly Parent, actually experiences the heart. Then, the heart of Heavenly Parent begins to appear in the human world as a specific life culture.

Heavenly Parent created Adam and Eve as partners for affectionate love. When Adam and Eve have grown up to perfect their personality and are perfected as an ideal couple, they become the partners of Heavenly Parent's love. Heavenly Parent wanted to experience an affectionate impulse by sharing love with them. [35] True Parents became the partner for the affectionate love of Heavenly Parent throughout their lives, and they showed humanity the way to be the partners for the affectionate love of Heavenly Parent. In addition, they opened a way for Heavenly Parent, human beings and all things to live together centered on affectionate true love.

Hyojeong culture is the lifestyle that specifically shows how True Parents, as humans, lived with Heavenly Parent based on their affectionate love. Hyojeong culture is a culture of peace, and it is also the culture of Cheon Il Guk. [36] The heavenly tribal messiah, who is the master of the new cultural revolution, wants to bring a settlement of hyojeong culture in which Heavenly Parent's heart and human filial piety meet. It is necessary to understand the meaning of Cheon Il Guk for a life that suits the lifestyle of hyojeong culture.

Cheon Il Guk has the form of a nation where Heavenly Parent's ideal of creation is realized. The term refers to the place where two people become one. [37] Foundation Day of Cheon Il Guk is the day when Cheon Il Guk began. [38] Cheon Il Guk is born in the central point of the cosmos, where Heavenly Parent and humans combine to form a unified body. It undergoes the process of expanding from family to society, nation, world, and the kingdom. [39] Cheon Il Guk is a new form of nation that has never existed on the earth. Cheon Il Guk is the inner heavenly kingdom, which means the kingdom of heaven in a religious concept. [40]

a. The inner Cheon Il Guk and the outer Cheon Il Guk

Cheon Il Guk has an inner Cheon Il Guk and an outer Cheon Il Guk. First, Heavenly Parent existed as the One who perfected the inner Cheon Il Guk even before the creation. From the pre-creation period, He possessed the dual characteristics of internal character and external form as well as the dual characteristics of masculine and feminine. Therefore, He has existed as the One who perfected the inner Cheon Il Guk. Heavenly Parent, who is the master of the inner Cheon Il Guk, exists alone and cannot feel emotions because He has no partners. [41] Because He had no substantial body, He could not reproduce on the earth and could not have dominion over the creation. To satisfy desire, he created human beings, dividing them into male and female. [42]

Secondly, Heavenly Parent created Adam and Eve separately, as his embodiments, and wanted to fulfill the outer Cheon Il Guk through enabling them to become perfect. After the birth of Adam and Eve, their growth to maturity, and the accomplishment of marriage, the Heavenly Parent hoped they would be an ideal couple. When Adam and Eve became the ideal married couple as well as ideal human beings, they would become the persons who completed the outer Cheon Il Guk. And they would become the partners for the absolute love of Heavenly Parent. Adam and Eve who have completed the outer Cheon Il Guk are the only ones who can satisfy all the substantial parts of Heavenly Parent that exist intangibly.

The substantial Cheon Il Guk is a combination of the inner and outer Cheon Il Guk through the motto of "Let's fulfill the ideal of the inner and outer Cheon Il Guk!" True Parents said in 2005 that the inner Cheon Il Guk refers to the Cheon Il Guk centered on Heavenly Parent and the outer Cheon Il Guk refers to the Cheon Il Guk centered on True Parents. They called the inner and outer Cheon Il Guk the substantial Cheon Il Guk. [43] The substantial Cheon Il Guk is a nation that is born when Heavenly Parent and the perfected

Adam and Eve form a united body. When the substantial Cheon Il Guk is launched, Heavenly Parent will appear as an embodiment in the spirit world and on earth by wearing the bodies of perfected Adam and Eve.

> You may not know the meaning of "inner and outer" used in the slogan here. They refer to the inner heavenly kingdom and the outer heavenly kingdom. Cheon Il Guk is the kingdom where two different beings become one. For example, the mind and the body become one, a man and a woman become one, parents and children become one, and the earth and God become one. The "inner" means Heavenly Parent, and the "outer" means the True Parents. [44]

b. The lifestyle of the substantial Cheon Il Guk

Cheon Il Guk is realized through the process of foundation and completion. The foundation and completion of the substantial Cheon Il Guk are first realized between Heavenly Parent and Adam and Eve in the original garden of Eden. If the founding is like the groundbreaking ceremony, the completion is like the dedication ceremony. The substantial Cheon Il Guk was built on June 13, 2006, through the Cheon Jeong Gung Palace Entrance Ceremony and completed on January 13, 2013, through Cheon Il Guk Foundation Day.

The substantial Cheon Il Guk is realized as a lifestyle through the process of settlement and establishment. If "settlement" refers to arriving at a certain destination, "establishment" refers to unpacking the household items and starting a concrete life. Establishment refers to experiencing "coming and going, sleeping, what's good or bad, and so on," while living together with and serving Heavenly Parent.

When we think about the settlement and establishment at the family level, settlement is the stage in which family members become Cheon Il Guk citizens, while establishment is when the family members, after settlement, live day by day starting each new day with hoondokhae (scripture study) and feeling and experiencing Heavenly Parent. [45] At the national level, settlement is the public settlement centered on the Constitution, while establishment is the stage in which the citizens living in Cheon Il Guk adhere to the Constitution and the laws in detail.

The substantial Cheon Il Guk is the country where the spirit realm and the earth are connected. The beings in the spiritual realm can freely travel on the earth, while the beings on the earth can freely experience the spiritual realm. [46] In the central point of the cosmos, a person who has combined with Heavenly Parent to form a unified body is living on earth while being aware of the spirit world. Children born to the people of Cheon Il Guk also can grow in awareness of the spirit world. Human beings born in the center of the cosmos can live as beings with five spiritual senses united with their five physical senses. A heavenly tribal messiah, who is living in the age of the substantial Cheon Il Guk, can fulfill his mission while experiencing the spiritual realm if he makes a little effort. [47]

Section 2 What Is a Heavenly Tribal Messiah? — What Kind of Path Does a Heavenly Tribal Messiah Follow?

1. Completion of Adam's family in the garden of Eden

What is a heavenly tribal messiah? A heavenly tribal messiah is the leader of the providence of finding and founding the ideal family that the original Adam's family was meant to accomplish in the garden of Eden. What was the original garden of Eden like? It was the birthplace of a new civilization focusing on Heavenly Parent. It was the home of Adam and Eve. But Adam and Eve were driven out of the garden of Eden. They lost their hometown. What if the original Adam and Eve had not fallen? Adam and Eve could have been the ancestors of humanity and become the true parents with their clan. If Adam and Eve had become the true parents, they would have served Heavenly Parent at the center of their family, and Cain and Abel would have become one, forming the three great kingships and the four great realms of heart, to complete the model of the ideal family. There could have been a pure lineage belonging to Heavenly Parent, which Satan could not enter, and a world of the culture of heart.

Originally Adam and Eve wished to grow up, be blessed in marriage, and form a beautiful family; then they would have expanded their model family to humanity. Heavenly Parent, as the invisible and intangible being, wished to be the substantial Creator by entering and wearing the bodies of Adam and Eve when they received the blessing of marriage and became one. That is why Heavenly Parent created Adam and Eve, who were the ancestors of humanity, so that they would have their children, raise them, and prosper in loving dominion over all things. In other words, it was the purpose of creation, centering on Heavenly Parent as the first generation, that Adam and Eve as the second generation, and grandchildren as the third generation, live together in harmony so that the kingship of the Heavenly Parent would be formed on the earth, and that the tradition would go on eternally.

However, Adam and Eve, the ancestors of humanity, fell. After being driven out of the original garden of Eden, they became wanderers. They lost their parents and lived as orphans. Then how can a fallen human return to the original purpose of creation and live a restored human life? The answer is, through reversing the process, finding what was lost, indemnifying the mistakes, and restoring the original humankind.

First, humanity lost Heavenly Parent, who was their original Parent. Therefore, it became the fate of humanity to meet the Messiah, True Parents, who can guide them back to Heavenly Parent.

Second, Satan took away Adam, the first son of Heavenly Parent. Originally, Heavenly Parent wanted to give Adam the power and inheritance to rule the world. However, due to the Fall of Adam, he was removed from the position of firstborn with the right of inheritance. Therefore, Heavenly Parent had to choose a partner among those who were centered on themselves, between Cain and Abel, the children of Adam and Eve. Their first son, Cain, became a partner of evil and a servant of the gods of the world. Therefore, Heavenly Parent set up Abel as the symbol of goodness, and Abel proceeded to come to Heavenly Parent through religion. The separation of these two brothers became the world of humanity. This first division of the family expanded to the world level and formed the Abel-type and Cain-type realms in human society. This has resulted in the struggle between the good value of conscience and self-centered egotism in all areas: politics, economy, religion, and culture. And the human world has been groaning in the vortex of conflict and war.

Therefore, humanity needs True Parents, who appeared as the Savior, Messiah, and ancestors of goodness. Humanity must be grafted on to their good lineage as well as love and culture of heart. Those who are blessed by them are the Abel tribe centered on Heavenly Parent. In other words, humanity starts off as the descendants of goodness, who have found the existence of the lost Heavenly

Parent. Therefore, the blessed families should first target the Cain realm in the world by introducing them to Heavenly Parent and True Parents, so that they could be blessed in order to realize the hope of Heavenly Parent and humanity, that is, one family of humanity. By doing so, they must end their wandering path as the orphans of humanity and find Heavenly Parent as their original Parents of humanity.

When the tribe of the realm of Cain is restored in that way, it is possible to restore the division of two brothers in the family of the first human ancestors, Adam and Eve. There no longer will be fighting or conflict among siblings. There will be no conflict between the worship of Heavenly Parent centered on good and the value of evil centered on selfishness. Centered on Heavenly Parent, the two lost brothers become one and harmonious. In other words, it is the community movement of the heavenly tribal messiah to create an ideal family of the brothers centered on Heavenly Parent. It is the providence to integrate the world, which had been divided into Abel's realm and Cain's realm by the first family's Fall, by restoring it to the original family community before the Fall.

What is the mission of a heavenly tribal messiah? It is to restore and re-establish the kind of family community under Heavenly Parent that was meant to be established in the original family of Adam and Eve. That is, it is the providence to restore the family of Adam and Eve, which fell and became divided into Abel's realm and Cain's realm, and to unify the brothers by making Abel, the first son on the side of Heaven, as the center, and then having Abel bring

Cain to surrender naturally by loving him.

When the ideal of unifying the brothers is fulfilled, it means that a family blessed by the Messiah, True Parents, has united his Cain-realm children, established through heavenly tribal messiah activities, and brought them together with his second-generation children, who are his Abel-realm children. At this time, the two sons, Cain and Abel, finally will live together, united in one extended tribal family with Heavenly Parent at the center. The tribal messiah couple, the parents of the tribe, who have restored these two sons, divided since the time of Adam and Eve, stand in the position of restored parents. This place is where the ideal of creation, which Heavenly Parent has been seeking to establish since the beginning, with good true parents giving birth to good children through the family of Adam and Eve in the beginning, is finally to be realized. A blessed family that has restored the positions of the two children, Abel and Cain, through the heavenly tribal messiah mission will recover their parental authority. In other words, we are in the position of true parents who serve Heavenly Parent and inherit the heart of Heavenly Parent through our Abel and Cain children.

When this parental realm has been restored, Heavenly Parent will recover the kingship, so He can enter and live by manifesting through the body of the heavenly tribal messiah, who has been set up in the place of the parents. It is then that the intangible Heavenly Parent becomes the Heavenly Parent wearing the embodiment, and the world of tangible and intangible embodiment is completed. In that place, three major kingships are being achieved, namely, the kingship of Heavenly Parent who is the king of this world, the kingship of the parents who restored the two sons, Abel and Cain, and the kingship of the children who inherit the kingship of the future world. Through the completion of these three kingships, it is possible to live eternally as citizens of the heavenly kingdom.

In conclusion, the task of heavenly tribal messiah is to find the position in which they receive the right for Heavenly Parent to reside within their body and their spouse's and to restore the position of Adam and Eve before the Fall.

2. Blessings at the place where four great realms of heart are completed

In the family where three great kingships (the kingship of Heavenly Parent, the kingship of parents, and the kingship of future children) were created, parental love, conjugal love, siblings' love and children's love will harmonize to create a model of the heavenly kingdom. The heavenly tribal messiah has a mission to form a model that accomplishes the four great realms of heart and to pass down the model to the Abel and Cain tribes. Then what are the four great realms of heart?

First, it is the love of a married couple.

In the beginning, Heavenly Parent wanted Adam and Eve to grow up and achieve the ideal of unity with Heavenly Parent. Therefore, it is recorded in the scriptures that He created Adam, but Adam looked lonely in his solitude, so Heavenly Parent used Adam's rib to create Eve. This part should not be interpreted as the matter of who was created first, Adam or Eve. The fact that Eve was created from Adam's rib is to emphasize that they were created as one body, two parts of an inseparable pair. Therefore, the love of a couple is the order of creation in which the absolute subject partner must create the absolute object partner while the absolute object partner also must create and complete the absolute subject partner. In other words, the only person among all the numerous women in the world who calls a man "husband" and confirms his status as a husband is his wife. Upon her recognition of that man as her husband, his place as a husband is perfected. Likewise, the place of a wife is perfected by her husband's recognition. Therefore, the love of a couple is the life that adjusts itself to their partners so that their places can be perfected because the partners complete each other and have authority. This is because a partner cannot complete me if I put myself at the center. And the only thing I can do is to fill my partner's needs and help my partner grow, so that my position can be as high as that of my partner. The perfection of the wife's position does not depend on herself alone, but on how much her husband has helped her grow. The perfection of the husband's position also depends on how much the wife has helped him grow. For example, when a husband becomes an attorney with the indispensable help of his wife, the position of the wife also is upgraded, equal to the position of the husband. In other words, she will be qualified as a lawyer's wife. Therefore, when both parties complete each other and focus on fulfilling each other's needs, they become an ideal married couple whom their Heavenly Parent dreamed of.

Second it is the heart of the parents.

As mentioned above, the place of the parent is not determined by the parents themselves. When their children call them parents, the position and value of the parent are determined. In the end, the value of the parents will be determined by how much they have enabled the perfection of their children. Therefore, the parents of the world are slaves to their children. Why? It is because the parents will maintain the title of parents only if they enable the perfection of their children. Parents will be assessed by how well their children have matured. Therefore, the reason why Heavenly Parent proceeded with the history of human salvation is because His children, humankind, should call him "Parent" in order to complete His place as a parent. Therefore, Heavenly Parent has been pursuing the providence of salvation, without giving up, for more than 6,000 years, because His perfection depends on His children, humankind.

Third is the heart of the child.

Our children are in a position where they soon will be parents. A child who has been loved devotedly by his parents will be recognized by his parents as the person who responds to their love. Therefore, they will take over the position of parents in the future, and as adult children, they will attain the right of lineage, inheritance rights, right of equal status and right of participation as equals, coming to a place in the world where they can act together with their parents on an equal footing. Therefore, the perfection of a child is not in asserting himself but in the parents' recognition of the child, so the position and value of the child will be established.

Fourth is the heart of siblings.

The Fall of humanity has been aggravated by the division into Abel and Cain realms that grew out from the family of Adam and Eve. Heavenly Parent, who is the original Parents, wants the brothers to be one and return to their Parents. Therefore, we must bring not only our own children but also the lost Cain brothers to unify as children and brothers. In other words, the siblings must live for the sake of each other. My position as a brother or sister is not made by myself but is perfected when it is acknowledged by my siblings. Our worth is determined when we are acknowledged by our relatives, who say, "That brother is a true man." We do not determine our own value. This is because the perfection of an individual depends on the partner, not on the individual alone.

If these four great realms of heart are broken, what will follow are incompleteness in the marriage realm, incompleteness in the parental realm, incompleteness in the children's realm, and incompleteness in the siblings' realm. It is in one's own family that these four great realms of heart can be realized. This practice one should then expand to the tribe, the society, and the nation with the love of the four great realms of heart that people learned in their own homes. In other words, the three great kingships and the four great realms of heart refer to the completion of Adam and Eve and the family before the Fall. Before the Fall, Adam and Eve should have been the royal family as the immediate family of Heavenly Parent through the three great kingships and four great realms of heart. The ultimate goal of the providence is to restore fallen humanity and form a royal family. Blessed families must fulfill this mission. We are trying to build an absolute standard centering on the families created by Heavenly Parent, so we should have a grandparent model, a parent model, a couple model, and a child model. The people of Korea, a chosen people, are the people of Heaven who have pursued an extended family. The heavenly tribal messiah pursues a traditional situation in which seven generations of Abel tribes and Cain tribes can live together in one community.

Section 3 The Historic Era and the Meaning of the Heavenly Tribal Messiahs

A heavenly tribal messiah must melt the bitter grief of Adam and Eve, who could not realize the dream that was supposed to be realized in the original garden of Eden, and melt the bitter grief of Jesus, who came as the Second Adam to realize what the first Adam could not achieve but had to leave without achieving it. We also can say that a heavenly tribal messiah has the mission to melt the bitter grief of the third Adam, True Parents, who came to realize what the second Adam could not realize.

The bitter grief of the first Adam and Eve was that they could not have an ideal family. The bitter grief of the second Adam, Jesus, was that he could not have the ideal nation, and the bitter grief of the third Adam, True Parents, is that they could not have an ideal world. Therefore, the mission of the heavenly tribal messiah is to find the ideal family in the original garden of Eden and find the ideal tribe, nation and world.

The most basic mission to fulfill Heavenly Parent's dream is to realize the ideal family that Heavenly Parent wanted to achieve through Adam and Eve in the garden of Eden before the Fall. To realize an ideal family, heavenly tribal messiahs first must resolve the issue of Adam's children who were divided into Cain and Abel and whose division was expanded to all humankind. Second, Adam himself must attend Heavenly Parent, restore the Abel and Cain realms and recover the position of parents. Third, they must complete the realm of the royal family who are the direct children of Heavenly Parent.

Let us first get to know the tribal messiah providence that has unfolded in history up until today. Heavenly tribal messiahs, first of all, must restore the Cain realm through a home group and become the messiahs of the tribe. Second, they must bring together the Cain tribe and Abel tribe and become the tribal messiah. Third, based on the foundation of having brought the Cain tribe and Abel tribe together, they must join their family to those tribes and go through the era of expanding the hoondok family church. Fourth, centering on the hoondok family church, they must directly attend Heavenly Parent at the tribal level and go through the four stages to become a heavenly tribal messiah. In this way, True Parents advanced the providence through home church, tribal messiah, hoondok family church and heavenly tribal messiah activities based on the spirit of the times.

However, the conclusion is that all of this is to find the position of completing the ideal family that Adam's family should have realized originally. Through the Fall of the first ancestors, Adam and Eve, their children were divided into the Cain tribe and Abel tribe and this was expanded to humankind. Heavenly tribal messiahs must bring those two divided tribes together and restore the authority of the eldest son. Then on the foundation of success of the restoration of the authority of the eldest son, the authority of the parents must be recognized. Next, they must realize the restoration of the authority of the king centering on Heavenly Parent. Then they must go up to the position of the realm of the royal family and become the direct children of Heavenly Parent. In this way, they realize the restoration of the authority of the eldest son (restoration of the realm of siblings), restoration of the authority of the parents, and restoration of the right of kingship (restoration of the realm of the royal family), and pass on to the heavenly nation to live in the eternal world after having lived on the earth. This is the path of a heavenly tribal messiah.

Before the title "heavenly tribal messiah" came to be, as mentioned above, there are four stages based on the advancement of the providence. Let us look at each stage in turn, which will bring us to the definition of a heavenly tribal messiah.

1. The era of the Cain tribe messiah through home church (the gateway and key to opening heaven)

Home church, which began in the United States in 1978, refers to the family-type church in which Adam's family lives completely united through love centering on Heavenly Parent in the garden of Eden. True Parents have explained that when the home church expands into the home tribe church, home people church, home nation church and home world church, then one ideal world can come to be centered on the ideal of the family. [48]

The home church movement seeks to create a sanctuary in which each of the 360 families living in the area where the blessed family resides can attend Heavenly Parent. The home church movement is not a movement in which the home where the blessed family lives becomes a home church that witnesses to 360 families. Rather it is a movement in which 360 families are guided to live with and attend Heavenly Parent in their family and live a life of home church. [49]

Jesus left the key to the gate of Heaven to his best disciple, Peter, and went the way of the cross. True Parents have given the key to the gate of Heaven to the blessed families on the earth. The key to the gate of Heaven is the home church movement. This means that the gate to Heaven can be opened freely through the home church movement. Just as Jesus said, "Verily I say unto you, whatsoever ye shall bind on earth shall be bound in heaven: and whatsoever ye shall loose on earth shall be loosed in heaven" [Matt. 18:18], if blessed families can realize the home church movement on the earth, the gate to Heaven will be opened. This also means that if we cannot create home church on the earth, we cannot enter Heaven.

> I give the key to Heaven to the members of the Unification Church. When I go to the spirit world, I can come down anytime and I can go back and forth whenever I want. When I come back, I will not be looking for a church, but I will look for a home church. The home church is the place where God can reside, where True Parents can reside, where sons and daughters can live and a place where the family can live. [50]

True Parents did not give us the key to Heaven for our individual selves, but they gave us the key that can save the tribe. Blessed families who have received the key to Heaven must become home church messiahs who can save the Cain tribe.

> Until now, the goal of religion was individual salvation, but our goal is salvation of the tribe. We are saying that the tribe can be saved all at once. It is the movement that says, "Let us get the ticket of universally shared values where we can live and our tribe can enter Heaven!" Not "Let me go to Heaven when I die." [51]

A home church sign should be put up in each home, and education to attend Heavenly Parent must be carried out. If we can attend Heavenly Parent in each family, True Parents can establish the Family Federation and can immediately carry out the national movement.

Based on that foundation and through the home church, a genealogy for the new heavenly nation can be made. [52]

The principle is for blessed families to be recognized and approved by the Cain tribe, "That person is a good person. They are truly a person of Heavenly Parent," receive the certificate and then receive the Blessing. It is only when we can get the recognition and victorious condition at the home church that we can go easily through the gate of Heaven and go before Heavenly Parent. The home church is the base of Heaven, so at the home church we can meet Heavenly Parent, the Messiah, True Parents. Cain and Abel can become one and meet, and all the lost enemies, tribes and humankind can be found. [53]

How will we create the kingdom of heaven on earth? It will be done when 360 families themselves can unify, find the realm of the indemnity condition for the home church, and enter heaven. The family purification that is to be carried out going forward will be realized through the home church organization. At the home church where bonds have been created through the relationship of love, Satan's shadow cannot appear even for a moment. When the home church expands to the tribe church, people's church, nation's church and world church, and the entire nation believes in True Parents, then it will become the national church. [54]

The 360-home church movement in the United States took place when the members who lived at church centers received the Blessing and went to their assigned area and began to create ideal societies.

This kind of home church centered on 360 families was the movement to become Cain-level tribal messiahs. The reason they were Cain-level tribal messiahs is because rather than relationships with their own relatives tied by lineage, the blessed families lived a life of serving and devoting themselves to the people in the neighborhoods where they were living.

When the home church movement would conclude successfully, blessed families would return to their hometown. Through serving and devoting themselves for the sake of their tribe, they would be sent out to carry out the Abel tribal messiah movement that shares the heart of Heavenly Parent. [55]

When the 360-home church movement first began in 1978, the Unification community welcomed this movement and participated with a joyful heart. "When I heard that the substantial conclusion of all the faith and sincere jeongseong until now would be realized in the 360 families, I felt that the concepts contained in the Divine Principle were being established clearly." [56]

There was much focus on the home church movement, so much so that the Unification community's yearly motto for five years, beginning in 1979, had to do with home church: "Home church and the completion of the kingdom of heaven" (1979), "Home church is the base of heaven" (1980), "Home church is my kingdom of heaven" (1981), "Victory of home church" (1982), "Home church is our land of settlement" (1983).

Following that, the annual mottos had to do with the homeland's independence: "Creating and building the fatherland" (1984), "Creating and building the kingdom of heaven" (1985), "Unification of the kingdom of heaven" (1986), "Unification of the fatherland" (1987), "Unification of my country" (1988), "Unification of the new nation" (1989).

1) Restoration of the family church and the authority of the eldest son

The home church movement, which began in February 1978, was not just a movement to save the Cain tribe. It was directly connected to the providence of finding the authority of the eldest son that Heavenly Parent lost through the Fall of Adam and Eve. In Kodiak, Alaska, on August 31, 1989, during the time when the home church movement was being carried out in the United States, Korea, Japan and worldwide, True Parents proclaimed the *Pal Jeong Sik* Ceremony for the Settlement of Eight Stages. This was a ceremony in which True Parents proclaimed beforehand that they would restore from Satan the realm of the authority of the eldest son.

Satan divided the spirit world and physical world into eight vertical stages (servant of servant, servant, adopted son, stepson, son, mother, father, God) and eight horizontal stages (individual, family, tribe, people, nation, world, cosmos, God) to make a total of 64 stages and ruled over each of them separately. True Parents paid the indemnity conditions and banished Satan from the 64 stages, removed the boundaries between them, and traveled the path to restore the authority of the eldest son. As a substantial condition, in April 1990 they embraced with true love President Mikhail Gorbachev of the

Soviet Union, who stood in the position of the world-level eldest son and in the position of Satan on the earth, and thus restored substantially the authority of the eldest son. Based on that foundation, on July 1, 1991, True Parents held the ceremony for the Proclamation of God's Eternal Blessing (*Chil Il Jeol*). [57]

To connect the restoration of the authority of the eldest son to the restoration of the authority of the parents, True Parents proclaimed the providence of returning to the hometown, and on September 1, 1991, the blessed families who were dedicated to the home church movement were appointed as tribal messiahs and sent to their hometowns. [58]

In this way, based on the foundation of the home church movement, True Parents finalized and proclaimed the restoration of the authority of the eldest son, which is important in Heaven's providence. It was very weak but, based on the foundation of the activities of blessed families, Heaven's providence to restore the authority of the eldest son could be advanced. The result is that, based on the foundation of the Cain tribe home church, blessed families also could restore the Abel tribe, embrace the Cain tribe and Abel tribe, and go the path of a tribal messiah that restores the authority of the parents.

2. The Cain realm and Abel realm tribal messiah era (The providence to find the original hometown)

The original hometown refers to the garden of Eden. It is the place where Heavenly Parent and human beings breathed, conversed and lived together. The original hometown is the place where Heavenly Parent gave birth to Adam and Eve. It is also the place where He gave birth to Jesus and True Parents. Therefore, the hometown is the place where we can attend Heavenly Parent from a place unaffected by the Fall.

However, human beings started out as false ancestors who were kicked out of the hometown. They could not begin with the original heart. Therefore, blessed families must return to the hometown where they were born and, based on the foundation of having restored the Cain tribe, find the authority of the parent. And when they become tribal messiahs, they become the restored Adam. The place where Adam lives is the original hometown. [59] In other words, the original hometown does not refer simply to the place where we were born physically. It refers to the area where we complete our mission as a tribal messiah. It is the symbolical restoration of the place where Heavenly Parent and Adam and Eve lived together in the original garden of Eden.

The original hometown is the place where blessed families who are born again and pass on to the spirit world must live in while going back and forth constantly. Blessed families who have inherited true love and heart return to their hometown to plant the tradition of the true parent again. [60] When tribal messiahs go back to their hometown, they are going back to their original home. The original home is the hometown of the perfected Adam and Eve and the place where Heavenly Parent resides. [61]

It is important for tribal messiahs to attain the restored standard and stand in the position of the unfallen Adam before they return to their hometown. That is why the foundation of the 360 home churches was necessary. Blessed families were sent out after having formed a relationship with True Parents centering on the foundation of the home church. That is how the position of tribal messiah can be distinguished from the position of Adam and Eve who started with the Fall. This is because the position Adam was in when he fell was the completion level of the growth stage, but families who have received the Blessing are at the stage where they can go beyond that point to the completion level of the completion stage, centering on True Parents in the era of restoration. That is why they could be sent out to their hometowns in a position where the families of Satan's realm cannot attack them. [62]

Tribal messiahs must return to their hometown, based on the foundation of having restored the Cain realm (people they have met in the neighborhood and environment), and restore the Abel realm tribe (biological children, husband and wife's relatives, blessed central family spiritual children), go through the realm of the eldest son and have sons and daughters from both worlds. Only then can they be restored to the realm of parents. By restoring the realm of the parents centering on the tribal messiah, the land of the original hometown can be set up. Next, by establishing the tribal messiah as the axis, the realm of kingship can be connected and the nation can be connected. True Parents sent the tribal messiahs so that they could return to their hometowns corrupted by the Fall and re-create them as hometowns where Heavenly Parent and True Parents can come. They were sent out to re-create. Tribal messiahs must return to their hometown and fulfill their mission of liberating their ancestors, their hometown and Heavenly Parent.

> What are the three important missions of the tribal messiah? First is to restore the ancestors. Second is to restore the hometown. Third is to live with Heavenly Parent, because God also was exiled due to the Fall of Adam and Eve, the first ancestors of humankind. These are the three missions of the tribal messiah. [63]

The era of returning to the hometown refers to the era when the tribal messiahs must find the nation and the era when True Parents will return to their nation. Until now, humankind could not have the land of the original hometown, so they could not have the nation of the original hometown. The Lord at His Second Advent comes to this land to absolutely find the land of the original hometown. What will he do after finding the land of the original hometown? He will organize the brothers of the hometown in that place, engraft them to the tribe and people, organize the people and form a nation to restore the world into the nation of the original hometown.

1) Tribal messiahs are the new ancestors of the tribe

Tribal messiahs must return to their hometown and become the ancestors. The ancestors we are referring to here are not the ancestors born of the satanic world but the original blessed families who have started out with the good lineage centering on Heavenly Parent. That is why they must live for the sake of the tribe with the same loving heart as a parent who has the original standard of heart. We must go with love and complete the position that Jesus tried to reach but was unable to.

> The term "messiah" is the same as ancestor of the hometown. It means to stand in the position of second parents in the place where the horizontal tribes are living. "I was sent out as a tribal messiah centering on True Parents" means that you have the responsibility to save the tribe. You must save the tribe, and then you can rise to the position of Adam. [64]

It is important for tribal messiahs to return to their hometown and proclaim before their relatives, "I am the tribal messiah!" We must proclaim ourselves as the messiah for our tribe, no matter what the reaction of our tribe members is. If we say, "Our family will sacrifice more than our conjugal love and children's love and all our possessions and we will guide our tribe to become a heavenly family, so please accept us!" then they will accept us. Then Satan will fall to the side, and the ancestors will come to the family, act as the host, and cooperate. Heaven will support and spirit world will cooperate. [65]

> I gave you the title of messiah. All you have to do is become messiahs, and then you can inherit the mountain of treasure and

all things. Just like water flowing from a water pipe, you will come to inherit everything. If you fail with regard to inheriting these valuable things, then your descendants will criticize you. [66]

Without finding Cain, we cannot enter our hometown. The elder brother tribe remains in the satanic world, so we must save them so that they can come within our tribe. Therefore, we must find Cain and Abel and embrace them and establish the standard of the parent. When we get to that position, we can connect the hometown where the parent who is not connected to the Fall was born to the hometown of the heavenly nation. The tribe of the hometown is the Abel tribe. When the tribal messiah can be victorious in the position of the original Adam, he can appear with the original seed.

Going to find your hometown means to plant new seeds. Adam and Eve's seed became a problem, so through you, a new seed can be planted and new roots can emerge. [67]

We must begin with at least three spiritual children. Every person has two types of children. In other words, there are your biological children, who were born through you, and the three spiritual children. God also has the first, second and third Adams, who are in the position of direct children, and He also has human beings in the position of adopted children. Salvation means to have three spiritual children and have them unite with our own biological children. That is the principle. [68]

If we have one spiritual child and one biological child, God will pour down infinite love. Heavenly Parent is waiting for tribal messiahs who can bring the Cain tribe and Abel tribe together and cooperate with Heaven's providence in the position of parents.

2) Witnessing and building a tribe through the Blessing

Home church, in the era of restoration of the Cain realm, was a movement to establish 360 families into home churches individually. Tribal messiahs have received the Blessing, so they must witness, bless and restore 120 people—not individually but on the level of blessed families.

> To fulfill your responsibility as tribal messiahs, you must go to your clan, establish 12 disciples and bless them. Next, you must establish 70 disciples and 120 disciples. You must rally no less than 120 people in total. I have indemnified the 36 couples and 72 couples, who are the center, and I have indemnified 120 couples all at once, so all you have to do is add 120 people to that. Then you can indemnify everything vertically and horizontally. That is why you have the responsibility to go to your tribe and rally 120 people. [69]

Restoring 120 couples is a condition that completes spiritually and physically the responsibility that Jesus could not fulfill. Tribal messiahs must fulfill the responsibility that Jesus could not complete and stand as representatives of True Parents. We must witness to 120 people and help them get married. Then when we go to the spirit world, the gatekeeper will not say, "Who are you?" but rather he will say, "Come in!" and we will be able to travel in all four directions and come and go through the twelve gates of Heaven day and night as we please.

To put this into practice, we must be ready to put our life on the line. If we put our life on the line and fulfill the mission, the dawn of the new nation will come and cast the morning sunshine in the direction of the east. If we witness to 120 people and they put up True Parents' picture and the Unification flag, that tribe becomes part of the heavenly nation. We must go to our hometown, hold a revival rally for our tribe and establish the lighthouse of the Word. We must light the lighthouse of the Word for the sake of the unification of east and west and the unification of north and south. We must light the lighthouse with the determination to become the wick and oil and spread the word through prayer and offer jeongseong. [70]

What must we do after we go to our hometown? As the tribal messiah who was sent out, we must find a way to bring the tribe members in our hometown to unite with us. The way to do this is to show them an example by practicing the Word in our daily life. We must become the educator who is the first to practice the heavenly tradition and pass it on to them. We must demonstrate to the parents of the village, "If you do this, this will become a heavenly village." We must teach them how a husband should love a wife, and vice versa, and how a parent should love their children, and vice versa, by creating a united family through love, and use that as a textbook, passing it on to the people.

3) Restoring the authority of the parents

The mission of the tribal messiahs whom True Parents spoke about for the first time in 1968 and sent out in September 1991 was not simply a movement to save the Abel tribe. It is connected to the providence of finding the authority of the parents that Heavenly Parent lost because of the Fall of Adam and Eve. On September 1, 1989, during the time when the home church movement was being carried out worldwide, True Parents declared Heavenly Parentism in Kodiak, Alaska. The Heavenly Parentism proclamation made it possible for True Parents to regain the authority of the parents from Satan through True Parentism.

On July 1, 1991, True Parents had the blessed families register as tribal messiahs, and on September 1 they appointed them as tribal messiahs and sent them out to their hometowns. [71] This was based on the foundation of having achieved the restoration of the authority of the eldest son on a worldwide level through Soviet President Mikhail Gorbachev in 1990. Through this, it was possible to register tribal messiahs on July 1, 1991, and through that registration, the authority of the parents could be set up.

Blessed families returned to their hometowns following True Parents' direction. Church leaders, people working in church organizations and businesses, and even people working in the outside world—all blessed families without exception—received this direction to return to their hometown. Second-generation members took the positions left open when the first generation departed. They had to give up their humanistic way of evaluating things and follow the strict command of Heaven unconditionally.

The first-generation blessed families voluntarily gave up all their foundation, followed the direction and returned to their hometowns. Blessed families followed this direction to go back to their hometowns with absolute faith, absolute love and absolute obedience. It was a demonstration of absolute faith, absolute love and absolute obedience that is hard to find in any religion or any country in the world.

Based on the foundation of blessed families having returned to their hometowns, in November 1991 True Parents returned to their hometown in North Korea. They met and embraced North Korean leader Kim Il Sung, who was fulfilling the role of parents in place of Satan, formed brotherly ties and restored substantially the authority of the parents. Based on that foundation, from July 6 to 9, 1992, True Parents made the Proclamation of True Parents at the national level throughout Korea. Following that, on the worldwide level on August 24, True Father proclaimed, "My wife, Dr. Hak Ja Han, and I are the True Parents of humankind, the Savior, Second Advent and Messiah." [72] In 1993, they proclaimed the True Parents and the Completed Testament Age, and on August 1 that year, they proclaimed the Unification Church as the True Parent church. [73] On that day, based on the foundation of returning to the hometowns, they proclaimed the

Day of Returning to the Original Homeland. [74]

In this way, based on the foundation of the tribal messiah movement, True Parents could proclaim the restoration of the authority of parents, which is important in the providence of Heavenly Parent. No matter how small, the absolute faith, absolute love and absolute obedience of the blessed families in returning to their hometowns and the foundation of the providence of tribal messiahs meant that God could move forward with the providence of the restoration of the authority of parents. Blessed families embraced their Cain tribe and Abel tribe, restored the authority of the parents, and came to enjoy the benefit of the era by participating in the era of restoration for God's Kingship, following True Parents' declaration of the preparation for the era of restoration for God's Kingship in 1996, after which they had sent out national messiahs to 185 countries worldwide. The national messiahs were sent out on the foundation of the tribal messiahs.

> The mission of the tribal messiah is expanding to 120 to 160 and even 180 families. Jesus' era was centered on 120 clans, but the tribal messiahs of the era of the Second Advent, as head of the tribe, can restore at least 160 families. [75]

The peak of the tribal messiah activities that were carried out focused on the goal of 160 families was the Preparation Blessing Movement that began in the period before *Chil Pal Jeol* in 1997. The movement to find 160 families, carry out the holy wine ceremony, and hold preparation Blessings was connected to the proclamation of *Chil Pal Jeol* and the inception of hoondokhae.

3. Hoondok family church and the era of realizing the ideal of the internal and external Cheon Il Guk

1) What is a hoondok family church?

On February 17, 2005, True Parents proclaimed the hoondok family church during their speech at the closing ceremony of the Cheon Il Guk Leaders Conference. They established a new headquarters for the hoondok family church and said that Korean members must create between 7,000 and 12,000 hoondok family churches in their hometowns.[76] They designated *Cheon Seong Gyeong* as the hoondok textbook for hoondok family church and gave them out to all the leaders present. Copies of the *Cheon Seong Gyeong* were stamped with the words "Sun Myung Moon, Commemoration of the Coronation Ceremony of the King of Cosmic Unification and Peace" and given to leaders. In September 1997, True Parents proclaimed the Realm of the Fourth Adam, in which those who stand in the position of Adam and Eve who have not fallen will live after perfecting their families. If blessed families can gain that qualification, they can bring that realm of fortune into their era. True Parents said that all blessed families, as the fourth Adam, must gain the qualification to live a life of true love that realizes an ideal family in the position of

Adam and Eve before the Fall. To do that, True Parents established the tradition of hoondokhae in November 1997.

What is hoondokhae? Hoondokhae is a new tradition of changing from "the era when the best thing was to know the Principle" to "the era where lifestyle is the priority." [77] The character *hoon* in hoondokhae combines the Chinese characters for "word" and "river." River means the source of life, has eternal value, and something that flows beyond national boundaries. [78] The character *hoon* means True Parents' word is eternal, has life and transcends national boundaries. *Dok* combines the characters for "word" and "to sell" and means "to sell the word." In conclusion, hoondokhae means "the source of eternal life, a meeting where the Word, which flows freely wherever there is a space, is given and lived."

What is home church? The era of home church began in 1978. It was an era when the salvation of the individual was emphasized, because it was the era of the restoration of the authority of the eldest son. Hoondok family church began in 2005. In Korean, the same term, *gajeong kyohwe*, was used for both home church and hoondok family church. The word *gajeong* is used to mean both "home" and "family." When the Family Federation for World Peace and Unification was established in 1996, the word *gajeong* also was used, with the meaning of "family" rather than "home." On July 1, 1997, at Belvedere, True Father wrote "Belvedere Family Church" on the chalkboard and translated it himself to English as "Family Church." [79]

What is a hoondok family church? A hoondok family church is a gathering of all the people and relatives who until now have been connected to us through the home church and tribal messiah work. They gather in one place where they can read the Word together. Centering on the hoondok family church, the relatives can gather and read the Word and take the time to converse with God. It is also a time to find, within the conversation with God, the nutrients of life needed to live day by day. The hoondok family church is a place where we can put into practice the things that we have decided within our conversations with God, report and live day by day.

2) Become the true parent of your family and relatives

Based on the foundation of the providence to unite the Cain tribe and Abel tribe through the tribal messiah mission, True Parents said that all blessed families should establish hoondok family churches. The core point that True Parents have emphasized through the hoondok family church is to find our family and relatives and bless them. They said that from now on, centering on the last name of our parents and on the last name of our blessed couple, we must find our relatives and family and guide them. We must find our family and relatives, guide them, bless them and educate them at the family church and assimilate them within the realm of the heart of True Parents. [80]

> When you go back, if your family is the Kim family, you must become the savior, messiah, returning lord and then the true parents of the Kim family. All of this is being bequeathed to you.

I am saying that you must bring your family together and become a clan that can enter the heavenly nation and establish a nation. Once you establish a nation, then you must save the world. And if you save the world, then you must know that you have the responsibility to liberate Heavenly Parent and the heavenly world. To achieve this goal, you will move forward with one heart, one body and one determination to develop and grow. [81]

True Parents said that when blessed families enter Heaven, they will do so by leading their family and relatives. They will lead their relatives and enter the heavenly nation. They said that Heavenly Parent cannot accept us living in the same house with brothers and sisters who have not received the Blessing. Until now, the reason that it was permitted for blessed families to live with brothers who had not received the Blessing was because it was a period for them to live together and realize how different they are.

Heaven is the nation and world where the family and relatives of people who have received the Blessing, established a family and attended Heavenly Parent will enter. You must have a family. That is why you must participate in the Blessing ceremony in which the spirit world and physical world can become one and you can have a family. Then you can open the door of Heaven, which was closed, and abolish hell. There you must complete the kingdom of heaven on earth and in heaven. [82]

Following True Parents' direction, the church structure was reorganized into a system of hoondok family church. Families who until then had established a foundation, little by little, through the home church movement and tribal messiah activities could naturally make their homes hoondok family churches, find the members of their families, bless them and educate them. Those who were not able to establish sufficient foundation to form a tribe during this time should join forces with other families to establish hoondok family churches and begin activities.

If we accomplish our mission of tribal messiah, we restore the position of the original Adam and inherit the authority of the parents. The parent of the tribe, as the teacher and owner of the tribe, comes to have the authority of kingship in their tribe. The tribal messiah providence was to prepare to enter the realm of the royal family of heaven through hoondok family church.

3) Hoondok family church activities and the restoration of the authority of the king

Heaven always makes great advancements to the providence based on the foundation of the humble jeongseong of blessed families. Following the Enthronement Ceremony for God's Kingship in 2001, True Parents' King of Peace Coronation Ceremonies were carried out on eight occasions from 2003 to 2004. King of Peace Coronation Ceremonies were held on four occasions vertically (first, second, third, fourth Israel) and four occasions horizontally (tribe, nation, world, cosmos). The first coronation ceremony held vertically was one held on the tribal level. It was a ceremony in which clan delegates representing 120 last names out of the 286 last names that exist in Korea gathered and recognized True Parents as the king of peace of each clan, held coronation ceremonies and presented crowns. The participants received True Parents' Blessing. It was a ceremony in which people representing those with 120 last names in Korea attended True Parents as the new father of their tribes and the king of peace.

Hoondok family church was proclaimed right after the Coronation Ceremony of the King of Cosmic Unification and Peace, which was the last coronation ceremony. During the time when the hoondok family church movement was being established, the Cheon Jeong Gung Entrance Coronation Ceremony was held in 2006. This coronation ceremony was held on the basis of Heavenly Parent and True Parents having achieved oneness. Cheon Il Guk was declared through this Cheon Jeong Gung Entrance Coronation Ceremony. Through the preparation process, seven years later in 2013, the era of the substantial Cheon Il Guk began. Even through the small foundation of the tribal messiahs and hoondok family church, Heavenly Parent was able to lead an amazing providence.

Section 4 A New Age for Heavenly Tribal Messiahs Who Attend Heavenly Parent

1. What is a heavenly tribal messiah?

True Parents proclaimed the role of a heavenly tribal messiah for the first time on March 22, 2012 (3.1 on the heavenly calendar). A heavenly tribal messiah is a messiah who attends Heavenly Parent in his family and tribe. He has authority of dominion over his family and tribe who have entered Heavenly Parent's lineage. A heavenly tribal messiah also should build a family and tribe that resemble Heavenly Parent. He should allow Heavenly Parent to rule his tribe directly through his physical body. Therefore, a heavenly tribal messiah needs to lead an exemplary life of mind–body unity and create an environment in which his family and tribe can attend Heavenly Parent. When Heavenly Parent directs him to do something, a heavenly tribal messiah should take action immediately.

After the ceremony for the Foundation Day of Cheon Il Guk, True Mother elaborated on the meaning of the heavenly tribal messiah mission. True Mother explained that the character *shin* in *shin jongjok* messiah was not the character for new (신: 新) as in a "new tribal messiah," which would be a reference to the failure of blessed members to fulfill their responsibility as tribal messiahs. The *shin* character that is used here is the one that means God or Heaven [신: 神], as in a "heavenly tribal messiah," to encourage members to become tribal messiahs who attend Heavenly Parent. Heavenly Parent and True Parents united in heart for blessed members to be reborn as heavenly tribal messiahs whom they acknowledge. [83]

The era of Cheon Il Guk is the era in which families and tribes unite in attendance to Heavenly Parent. It also marks the time to search for heaven's citizens and expand to restore the nation and the world. First, heavenly tribal messiahs should strive to become exemplary families of the three great kingships and the four great realms of heart by attending Heavenly Parent and practicing hoondokhae with their biological children. When they succeed, they create the ideal that Heavenly Parent most desires to live in. This ideal is a family that rejects self-centeredness and instead exists to live for the sake of another. Here, the husband and wife unite with Heavenly Parent's heart and love, the children become one centering on their parents, and siblings have an affectionate bond with one another. A heavenly tribal messiah should establish that standard and approach their tribe to engraft that model to them. It is better to perfect one's own family before building one's tribe, but, practically speaking, we need to carry out both responsibilities simultaneously. The perfection of one's family is attained through the perfection of another family by fulfilling their needs and educating them. In this process, one's family changes as you strengthen your skills while supporting and helping others.

We are not yet confident that we perfectly embody a life in attendance to Heavenly Parent. However, we have learned the laws and principles of that attendance. Through the efforts of perfecting another tribe, one's own family can be perfected. The family can be considered to have accomplished perfection as Adam's original family when one's tribe members say, "You and your spouse are authentic and righteous people. You have a perfected character. You are the parents and the messiahs of our tribe." Up until now, there has not been a single family that has achieved that. However, only through True Parents, who have established the position of heavenly tribal messiahs, can we take the path of becoming one. From now on, we need to live a life that accumulates one by one the qualities a heavenly tribal messiah should have.

At Foundation Day, the principle was that if the whole family attended the Blessing, they would enter Cheon Il Guk. However, there was not one person who deserved it. Instead, True Parents carried the cross of love in our places. They allowed blessed families to enter if they had faithfully followed True Parents and promised to fulfill the condition in the future. True Parents took responsibility for us, and Foundation Day was filled with their unreserved grace.

True Parents revealed their hearts by unconditionally bestowing this message to blessed members, "From now on, you should complete your mission, build Adam's restored family, and become messiahs to your tribe." Therefore, by completing our mission as heavenly tribal messiahs, we can repay the grace of True Parents of allowing us to become Cheon Il Guk citizens.

2. Lay the cornerstones of national restoration through restoring 430 families

We do not receive the position of a heavenly tribal messiah by having necessary and sufficient conditions as a blessed family. Starting now, heavenly tribal messiahs need to establish Adam's family to its status before the Fall by attaining specific results in our lives. This is Heavenly Parent's hope. Heavenly tribal messiahs need to combine their strength with their tribe members to bless 430 families and nurture them through hoondokhae. In their mission area and town, the heavenly tribal messiahs need to expand Cheon Il Guk's territory and sovereignty with citizens who attend Heavenly Parent. If we can only accomplish that, we will be able to restore a nation while True Mother is still on earth.

Even if we have not taken part in the providence of tribal restoration related to the advancement of the providence of restoration through home church, tribal messiahship, hoondok family church, and heavenly tribal messiahship, now is the time to start. Each blessed family needs to complete its mission as heavenly tribal messiahs of giving the Blessing to 430 families, even if they have not completed their responsibility in a home church, the mission of a tribal messiah or the will of a hoondok family church era. The last stop to perfecting a blessed family is returning to Adam's original family.

The work of heavenly tribal messiahs is not exclusive to the earthly realm. Now is the age to cooperate with Heavenly Parent in heaven, our ancestors and the spirit world. If we establish even a tiny condition here on earth, Heaven wants to work endlessly with us. Signs of this began with the realization of amazing miracles on the tribal level and clan level in Asia in 2016, which spread to Africa in 2017. Miracles through spiritual works are occurring all over. All a heavenly tribal messiah has to do is testify to Heavenly Parent and True Parents, and leaders in the Cain realm will take the lead and governments will initiate heavenly tribal messiah activities.

Heavenly tribal messiahs need to transform their mindset. They need an attitude that believes that they will restore Adam's original family without fail. They must firmly believe that they will unite and restore the Abel tribe and Cain tribe and, on that foundation, become the parents of the tribe and restore the authority of the parents. They should repeat over and over their resolve to accomplish this, pledging, "I will achieve it at any cost!"

3. The providence of perfecting Adam's original family in the garden of Eden

The heavenly tribal messiah's mission is to perfect Adam's original family in the garden of Eden. Perfecting Adam's original family is a principle that applies to all people equally. The following is a summary of what we have learned about heavenly tribal messiahs.

First, as people in the position of Abel, blessed members should be the ones to initiate extending their love to those in the Cain position. The order of restoration begins with loving Cain, then restoring the authority of the elder son, the authority of the parents, and the authority of the king through activities in a home church, tribe church, hoondok family church, and as heavenly tribal messiahs. The core of this is to gradually embrace and love Cain in stages. Thus, the work of the heavenly tribal messiahs simultaneously completes the efforts toward the providence of the tribe throughout history.

Second, a Cheon Il Guk environment was created in which Heaven can carry out great providential works on the foundation of small victories by blessed members. The providence can work simultaneously to restore the authority of the elder son through home church, restore the authority of the parents through the era of tribal messiahs, restore the authority of kings through hoondok family church, and restore the authority of the royal family through heavenly tribal messiahship. Even if blessed central families failed in the past to restore the authority of the elder son, the authority of the parents, the authority of the king, and the authority of the royal family, they may still claim victory by restoring everything during the final age in which each level progresses in parallel.

Third, the mission of heavenly tribal messiahs is a providence that blessed families should complete. If a family does not complete this mission while on earth, their future generations will have to fulfill it. The greatest legacy a couple can leave to their descendants is the tradition of inheriting Heaven's lineage by establishing the unfallen realm of Adam. By doing so, they will be born freely into the garden of Eden to grow and live in happiness. It also creates the finest spiritual environment for the people of their lineage to pass between the earthly world and the spiritual world. The path to achieve this is the heavenly tribal messiah mission.

Fourth, for the first time in human history, now is a period of the greatest grace, with which we can complete our mission while breathing the same air as Heavenly Parent and True Parents here on earth in physical bodies. Through hoondokhae, we can enter Heavenly Parent's essence, breathe and meditate with nature, and raise Abel children and Cain children to perfect a parental heart. The experience of feeling a parental heart manifests as hyojeong (filial devotion), and Heavenly Parent, True Parents, and a heavenly tribal messiah unite based on a parent's heart.

Lastly True Parents said, "Go and work in the field! We will be with you! We will take responsibility!" We actually will have a taste of their amazing grace and miracles in the field.

The prayers of those who understand Heavenly Parent's heart are a fearful and serious thing. If we do not convey the Word to the people we meet, we have no idea what will happen to them when they leave. If those people were not some strangers but our parents, our older brother or older sister, what would we do? If we are aware of Heaven's historical hope, and the issues on which human beings can recover from life or death, what would our siblings think of us if we did not tell them? Heavenly tribal messiahs should tell lost and wandering people who their true original parents are and help them achieve an ideal family. That ideal family, in turn, should love both the Cain tribe and Abel tribe as their children to build a standard of one family and take the path to becoming heavenly tribal messiahs and ultimately true parents.

Section 1 The Blessing of Perfecting My Family

The path of a heavenly tribal messiah is the path to perfecting one's family. To attend and live with Heavenly Parent is to achieve the original ideal. Moreover, it is the path on which our direct children and clan of Abel's realm and the children of Cain's realm achieve harmony in heart. These brothers who were separated in the garden of Eden can discover one parent and live together. The original garden of Eden is also recovered to form our homeland and begin the utopia of the kingdom of heaven where Satan cannot accuse. The more we practice true love in such a place, the more we will be able to feel the greatest grace and appreciation for it. If we begin heavenly tribal messiah activities, we will experience our family growing and becoming happier. We also will be able to form Adam's original family. Through heavenly tribal messiah activities, we will become Heavenly Parent's absolute partner by forming Adam's original family through the process of restoring the authority of the elder son, the authority of the parents, the authority of the king, and the authority of the royal family. The absolute partner of that love represents oneness with Heavenly Parent. This oneness transcends time and space to experience Heavenly Parent, share our hearts, and connect us to the spirit world.

1. Family messiahs are the foundation for tribal messiahs

Heavenly Parent's dream is to live as one with human beings. When human beings perfect an ideal family, His desire is to enter that family and live together with them joyfully. Originally, Adam and Eve should have attended Heavenly Parent and perfected a family with unity between parents and children, husband and wife, and brothers and sisters.

If this had happened, Heavenly Parent would have been able to seek out perfected, ideal families and substantially perfect a parental heart by living among human beings and feeling their happiness and joy. Human beings also would have attended Heavenly Parent, experienced His unchanging parental love and heart, and perfected the three great kingships and the four great realms of heart. The happiness of humankind is tied tightly to a family attending Heavenly Parent. Heavenly Parent cannot feel love without human beings, nor can His unchanging parental heart blossom.

The base for Heavenly Parent and human beings to live together in joy is the family. This is because a family can fulfill the three great kingships and the four great realms of heart. The center of the universe is also the family. Let's compare the universe to an onion. The universe has several layers. If you continue to pull off the outer layers, you will discover a core, which is the root of the universe. The same goes for an actual onion: If you peel each of its layers, there will be a core. The expansion of that core creates an onion. The core that builds up the universe is not the individual but the family. The family as the universe's core expanded and created this world. Therefore, Heavenly Parent is happy when the family, created as the core of the universe, achieves perfection.

All things start from one, divide into many, and ultimately come together again as something larger. In other words, one divides into many and then unites again as one. From there, it divides again and is integrated into something even larger. This process is repeated continuously. Families also come to exist through this process of integration, and the structure of the family never changes. The family is where the relationship of husband and wife is established, the place where one man and one woman become as one. The clan brings families together as one, and the tribe is a place that brings the clans together as one. Tribes combine to form one nation. The family, however, is always at the center. The horizontal expansion of humanity comes about based on the family. [1]

Parents feel happy when they visit their children's homes. Likewise, heavenly tribal messiahs should have families that will bring joy and comfort to Heavenly Parent when He visits. Therefore, we need to put a priority on perfecting ideal families. An ideal family has a father, a mother, a husband, a wife, brothers and sisters. It has sacrificial love. The parents' love is alive in the family. Love flows between older siblings and younger siblings. There is thickly layered love between children, and between nearby relatives. All these relationships and connections are tied with a love that perfects and lives for the sake of one another. Everyone interacts with longing and affection. Moreover, a person's life is formed based on the family, not the individual. Heavenly Parent resides in such a family.

> An exemplary family is the haven in which parents and children unite with love and respect, a husband and wife unite with mutual trust and love, and brothers and sisters unite with confidence and reliance. [2]

True Parents stress that the responsibility of heavenly tribal messiahs is primarily establishing Cheon Il Guk families that attend Heavenly Parent in their lives. In other words, heavenly tribal messiahs need to build true families that Heavenly Parent is proud of and ideal families that True Parents acknowledge are examples to the world. The first priority is to build beautiful families whom Heavenly Parent and True Parents can visit freely at any time.

> To seek out and establish Cheon Il Guk families that attend the eternal God in a family in which three generations—grandparents, parents, and grandchildren—live as one is the responsibility of heavenly tribal messiahs, the mission of ambassadors for peace and the hope of Heavenly Parent. [3]

Before saving one's tribe, a heavenly tribal messiah should become a heavenly family messiah who makes his family happy and attends Heavenly Parent together with them. Heavenly Parent automatically will take the shortest path and naturally reside in a Cheon Il Guk family that has perfected the three great kingships and the four great realms of heart centering on true love.

2. Heavenly Parent's reciprocal partners of love

1) Ideal couples are Heavenly Parent's reciprocal partners of love

True Parents said that human beings could unite with Heavenly Parent if we become His partners of love. We would be able to feel Heavenly Parent's presence on our skin, hear His heartbeat, and breathe the same breath.

Yet how can we create that kind of love? We experience love not on the individual level but on the couple's level. That is because the action of love needs two persons, not one. Even if there are two persons, it does not work between two men or two women. It is possible only when a man and a woman are present. Only then can procreation occur. The gears can mesh and turn when there are negative teeth and positive teeth.

Heavenly Parent is love. True love has a central hue. True love's central hue is harmony, unity, peace and happiness. Heavenly Parent is attracted to that hue and resides there.

When a couple unite with Heavenly Parent and they live together as one, that place becomes the center of the universe. [4] The center of the universe is also the root of the universe. Heavenly Parent, the Creator, can move the universe when a man and a woman whom He created become one body through true love. This position becomes the root to which conjugal love and children's love can fuse.

> This would become the focal point of the entire universe, the directional orientation of all cells in the universe. All the spirits in the spirit world would be focused on this point. Moreover, they would protect this position so that no one could invade it. If this place were to be destroyed, it would be catastrophic. For true love to be protected and preserved, it would need to take on some kind of structure. In the teachings of the Unification Church this structure is called the four-position foundation. [5]

Once it has appeared, the center of the universe does not disappear but continues to exist forever. How can we bring forth the center of the universe, the root of the cosmos? Originally, once Adam and Eve were born, they would have completed each growth stage toward individual perfection, been married by Heavenly Parent, united as a couple with love, become substantiations that resembled Heavenly Parent and become His reciprocal partners of love. Then Heavenly Parent would have resided, vertically, automatically, and in close proximity, within the union of love between Adam and Eve. By residing in this union as one with His object partners of love, Heavenly Parent, the subject partner of love, would have manifested the center of the universe. This is how the center of the universe, the root of the cosmos, would have appeared.

> Why do we marry? In a word, it is so that we may resemble God. God is a united being who has dual characteristics that dwell in union. Men and women are projections of God's divine characteristics. Therefore, the destiny of every couple, as husband and wife, is to form a union as one body, become as one seed, and return to oneness with God's original nature. Whom do we resemble when we become one through married life? Our goal is to resemble God. It is only when a man and a woman become one through true love that they truly resemble God, who created them in His image. It is then, and only then, that God resides in them. [6]

> When they become one body in love and bear the fruits of love, God comes down, and they go up, and they meet in the middle. God becomes the center of this sphere, and spherical movement begins. When husband and wife, who are two bodies who have

become one by revolving in oneness with each other, revolve with God, they form a four-position foundation of love. This is the ideal world of love. Only true love dwells there; false love cannot invade. When a man and a woman are blessed in marriage by God and achieve perfect oneness, God is able to come to them at any time. When they form a four-position foundation of love, they will come to love each other's heart through each other's body, and when they come to love the heart their body will follow. [7]

Men symbolize heaven and women symbolize earth. Therefore, a man and woman in harmony can achieve peace and happiness. Heaven and earth joined in virtue refers to the state of a husband and wife fulfilling perfect oneness centering on Heaven's true love. When a husband and wife embrace in true love, it has the power to make the universe whole. This is what Heavenly Parent's ideal creation originally should have looked like. If a husband and wife unite centering on Heavenly Parent's love, the path to cosmic unification opens. [8]

If Adam and Eve attain perfection as an ideal couple, they will resemble Heavenly Parent, become the substantiation of love, and become Heavenly Parent's partner of love. Heavenly Parent as the subject partner of love can achieve unity with Adam and Eve, the object partners of love. The state of unity between Heavenly Parent and human beings connects the spirit world and the physical world as one. The relationships between Heavenly Parent, Adam and Eve have both a parent–child relationship and a couple's relationship.

> "When I desperately prayed to ask what the secret of the universe is, the answer that came was simple. It is the parent–child relationship. If that parent–child relationship is literally the relationship between parents and their child, it also can be found in the fallen world, a world where parents sometimes sell their children and children kill their parents. Then what kind of a thing would this parent–child relationship be that is the secret of the universe? In terms of the sanctity of love, it would be the same as the ideal relationship between husband and wife." [9]

2) The path to experiencing Heavenly Parent's love

Heavenly Parent's dream is realized when human beings begin to unite and live with Him at the center of the universe. At the center of the universe, human beings will be able to feel joyful excitement forever. True Parents said the following to explain that kind of excitement: "Heavenly Parent will create lightning of joy and thunder of jubilation, even if it means moving the sun and moon with a helicopter." [10]

True Parents made it possible for Heavenly Parent to feel joyful excitement forever. True Parents have experienced Heavenly Parent's love directly. They have told us to become partners of love to Heavenly Parent and experience His love. Through heavenly tribal messiah activities, we should become absolute reciprocal partners to Heavenly Parent's love. What would it be like to have a taste of His love?

"You need to learn about God's love. How can we characterize God's love? It can be compared to an environment of a warm spring day. White clouds gently float in the sky, waves of warm air shimmer up from the ground, insects fly around, ants crawl in and out of their nest to see the world, willow blossoms are in bloom down by the stream, frogs sing new songs of spring, bees swarm, and butterflies flutter. You feel intoxicated by these surroundings. You feel that you are about to doze off; however, in reality you are awake and feel so good that you want to remain in this state forever.

This is how God feels when He finds His ideal partner. It is as if He is in a beautiful flower garden, with butterflies and bees flying around. Does it make you feel good to think of this, or does it make you feel bad? These dull-witted men over here may not understand this. It feels good. When you run into someone whom you are pleased to see, you hold his hand firmly and shake hands. Do you like it when someone grasps your hand firmly? If it is someone you like, then once you grasp each other's hands, you cannot let go. What about these young ladies here? Think of how it will be when you are married and your husband loves you. Will you feel good or bad? If your husband loves you, you will feel as though there is nothing in the world you would rather have. You want to live your whole life just staying by his side.

"Love is eternal. Love is not two; it is one. You become as one. When a man and a woman become a couple and love each other, they are bonded together. Of course, this does not happen literally; yet in heart they reach a level even higher than this. That is God's love. If you live with such love, will you become one or not? Think about it. You are destined to become one.

When a man and a woman fall in love, all sorts of strange things happen, don't they? But if you find a way to really taste God's love, you will see that it cannot be compared to anything in this world. Once you have tasted this kind of love, no amount of difficulty or sorrow can defeat you. Such a realm of absolute liberation does exist. The question is how to find it." [11]

Human beings experience Heavenly Parent's love in stages as we grow. First, when we are loved by our parents, we respond with children's love. Second, while growing up with our brothers and sisters, we experience siblings' love. Third, we receive the Blessing and experience conjugal love. Fourth, after giving birth to children, we experience parents' love for them. The central point of alignment for all four realms of love is Heavenly Parent's love. Then what is the Human Fall? It is love centering on oneself. Selfish love does not allow you to experience the love that flows between the spiritual world and physical world and around the universe centering on Heavenly Parent.

Original true love is in itself complete and does not change throughout the ages. Its original form is true, eternal, unchanging, and absolute. World peace can come about when there are peaceful nations. Peace in the family is required for peace in the nation. Only families that attend Heavenly Parent at the center are peaceful families. We need to form families that live for the sake of one another with true love. Heavenly Parent has called heavenly tribal messiahs to be His absolute partners of love. He hopes that they will shed all vestiges of the Fall and unite as Adam's original family through receiving recognition from the Abel children and Cain children. Heavenly Parent hopes to reside in that family. Thus, heavenly tribal messiahs need to cast off any fallen nature that remains in their family and build an original family. The world of happiness is activated by true original families that attend Heavenly Parent. Wouldn't it be amazing to take a vacation in a world that has experienced Heavenly Parent's love at least once? The starting point begins with heavenly tribal messiahs.

3. Heavenly Parent's partners of heart

1) The family messiah and the perfection of the four types of love

Heavenly Parent has a heart of love. However, He has never had the chance to ignite His love or heart. That is why He has eagerly waited for a partner of heart to appear. When that partner does come, Heavenly Parent will be able to realize His dream and human beings will be able to actually experience Heavenly Parent's heart.

Human beings are blueprinted to mature by learning each stage of Heavenly Parent's true love during their growth stages. Human beings were born out of true love. They grow to perfection by learning to love with true children's love, true siblings' love, true conjugal love, and true parents' love, in that order.

When an individual achieves mind-body unity, that person achieves individual perfection. A perfected man and woman who have achieved mind-body unity can experience true love as a true couple. When this couple connects with Heavenly Parent's true love and give birth to children, they become true parents. Heavenly Parent's true love resides in the center of a true couple's minds and bodies. In this union, the couple will give birth to sons and daughters. Then a whole and ideal family is fulfilled. In other words, human beings were born to become one as a true couple who represent heaven and earth and each of Heavenly Parent's dual characteristics. [12]

A true family builds true life and true lineage and is a training center and school that raises children with true character. A true family is both humankind's wish and Heavenly Parent's dream. Only with the true love and true character that are produced by true families can we have a perfected true society, true nation and true world. The ideal of creation for all environmental realms will be realized. [13]

2) The family messiah and the perfection of the four great realms of heart

The relationship centering on love between Heavenly Parent and human beings is a vertical parent–child relationship. Human beings, who were born as Heavenly Parent's children, need to experience the heart of a child, the heart of a sibling, the heart of a spouse, and the heart of a parent in order to truly feel Heavenly Parent's parental heart.

> "Adam and Eve, who were created as God's son and daughter, were the first to receive God's parental love and experience the heart of children as they grew up. During their growth, they also could feel the heart of brother and sister for each other. Next, after being blessed in marriage by God, they were to become a couple, and by loving each other they were to experience the heart of a husband and wife. Finally, after having children and loving them as true parents, they were to feel the heart of parents and also experience the parental heart through which God loved them as children." [14]

When you are experience Heavenly Parent's heart, you will realize why the fundamental unit of the universe is the family rather than the individual. The heart of a child is the stage in which we can experience Heavenly Parent's heart as a child in the growth stage. We can experience the heart of a sibling in the growth stage through our relationships with our brothers and sisters. We can experience the heart of a spouse through marriage and the process of uniting with our spouse as a couple. We also can experience Heavenly Parent's heart in this stage. We can experience the heart of a parent in the process of giving birth, raising children, and getting them married. In this position, we experience Heavenly Parent's heart. *Unification Thought* calls these the four great realms of heart.

What is different about a heavenly tribal messiah perfecting an ideal family with the four great realms of heart? The perfect ideal family can experience Heavenly Parent's parental heart. After someone experiences the heart of a child, the heart of a sibling, the heart of a spouse, and the heart of a parent, that person will be able to experience and understand the parental heart that Heavenly Parent has toward His children.

Furthermore, when someone perfects the four great realms of heart, that person will be able to experience the love Heavenly Parent has for humankind as their Parent. Therefore, Heavenly Parent created human beings to take the path of His representatives and His heirs. In this way, Heavenly Parent allows human beings to fully experience His heart and bestows the right to participate as equals, the right to equal status, and the right to inheritance and strives to establish human beings in the incomparable position of His representative.

> "The perfection of humankind requires a complete understanding of these four great realms of heart under the true love of God.

> The foundation for this is the ideal family. A family that embodies the four great realms of heart is the smallest unit of humankind that fulfills God's ideal of creation." [15]

When human beings unite with Heavenly Parent, they become the substantiation of the ideal and happiness. A family united with the perfection of the four great realms of heart through true love would be the smallest unit in the universe where God's love is shared. From a human's point of view, its influence may seem very insignificant. However, from Heaven's point of view, no matter how small the four great realms of heart perfected with true love are, they are connected to the universe. The wavelengths emitted from a small family perfected by the four great realms of heart extend across the universe and the spiritual world. This is because both the physical and spiritual worlds exist under the principle of true love.

> "When Heavenly Parent and human beings unite in a parent–child relationship of true love, human beings become the substantiations of the ideal and happiness within the harmony of love found there. The realms of heart accomplished with true love, no matter how small, connect to the universe and the wavelengths emitted from everything that happens extend across the universe and the spiritual world. This is because the cosmos including the spirit world all exist under Heavenly Parent's principle of true love." [16]

If we experience a parental heart through Heavenly Parent's heart, we will face the world with a mindset of a parent. We will treat everything in the world with a heavenly parental heart. True Parents have experienced Heavenly Parent's parental heart. They have lived with a heavenly parental mindset to love all people of the world more than their own parents or siblings and children, even in the midst of clawing their way out of danger or overcoming prison life and horrible persecution.

Although True Parents are a single entity, the wavelengths that emit from efforts centering on True Parents extend to all people and the spirit world. The energy of true love that freely flows from True Parents can envelop the earth and fill the spirit world with some to spare. The wavelengths flowing freely from True Parents can easily embrace to their bosoms the entire spirit world and all of humankind.

The path of true love is the shortest path. A life filled with only self-sacrifice and conscientiousness is a direct ticket down that path. In this era of return to the original homeland, Heavenly Parent is guiding heavenly tribal messiahs on the path to perfect all four realms of heart. Cheon Il Guk family members each should become true parents who practice true love. A couple first should become true parents in their family, true parents in their tribe, and true parents in their nation. When they can set that standard, they can become the true parents who Adam and Eve were meant to become. What should human beings fulfill while on earth? We should perfect the position of the true parents, the position of the authority of parents who have not fallen. The path where this can be achieved is the path of a heavenly tribal messiah. The Messiah is a person who shows the way through example to fallen people who have been lost. The Messiah will appear as the True Parents. Through True Parents' example, we have found the right path. True Parents also directed that we resemble them and go the way of heavenly tribal messiahs. The path of heavenly tribal messiahs is also the path to show an example to our tribe as True Parents have. We should become true parents as a result of going this path.

Section 2 Completing and Blessing My Tribe

Heavenly tribal messiahs have the mission of putting true love into practice for the sake of the happiness of their tribe. The greatest happiness for the tribe is to be guided to attend Heavenly Parent and True Parents and live with them. The mission of heavenly tribal messiahs is also to protect the tribe through the solidarity of the family messiahs and to nurture second and third heavenly tribal messiahs. Through this, the tribe can be expanded into a greater community. Furthermore, that nation can be re-created as Heavenly Parent's nation.

1. The fence that protects the happiness of the family

1) Building the garden of Eden and the object partner realm of the heart

When Adam and Eve lived in the garden of Eden, they were to become the object partners of Heavenly Parent's love and the object partners of His heart. During the period before they completed their growth to maturity, Adam and Eve should have learned about the order and rules of the universe through observing the things created by Heavenly Parent. More than anything else, they should have clearly realized the purpose for which Heavenly Parent had created them. Furthermore, they should have grown through the necessary stages of growth, received Heavenly Parent's blessing, and formed a conjugal relationship in which Heavenly Parent could come down and realize oneness. In that place, a world of joy and happiness could have been realized. Heavenly Parent should have been able to feel the emotions that human beings feel by residing within them and living together with them. And human beings should have been able to feel God's emotions through the harmony of the spirit world and physical world of Heavenly Parent and the universe. There they could have felt the explosive stimulation when the corporeal and incorporeal worlds meet.

True Parents have emphasized that lineage is more precious than life and more precious than love. This is because it is when life and love come together that lineage can be created. Lineage cannot be created if life or love is missing. Among love, life and lineage, lineage is the fruit. This is because lineage is what bequeaths the human DNA to the descendants. Therefore, if human beings had just treasured Heavenly Parent's lineage and preserved it from Satan's invasion, the realization of Heavenly Parent's dream would have been possible.

> "Heavenly Parent's lineage contains the seed of true love, and the body of true life is living there. Therefore, if you are connected to this lineage, then Heavenly Parent's ideal for human beings—in other words, completion of character—is possible and ideal families would emerge and, one step further, Heavenly Parent's ideal nation also would emerge. This is how the kingdom of the peaceful ideal world is built." [17]

Adam and Eve in the garden of Eden, centering on the lineage of Heavenly Parent, should have become the object partners of love and heart and realized an ideal family. Based on that foundation, Adam and Eve's children and descendants would have had no ties to the Fall and would have made Heavenly Parent's dream into the dream of humankind and completed the kingdom of heaven on earth. If that had happened, Adam and Eve's family would have continued on into a world without a trace of the Fall.

> "From now on, we just need to establish family-level messiahs. Then, centering on each of their families, messiahs will continue

on. When that happens, Heavenly Parent who is the center of the cosmos will be able to come and dwell with them whenever He wants. If the tribal messiah continues on from his base as a family messiah and expands the realm of his work, the ideal world will be achieved." [18]

The issue is that Adam and Eve fell and could not become family-level messiahs. Human beings born after the Fall were in a position that has no relationship with Heavenly Parent. Throughout the thousands of years of history, the spirit world and earthly world have become filled with the descendants of the Fall. They continued and expanded the lineage of Satan, which had nothing to do with Heavenly Parent. They filled the earth with people of selfish desires.

Satan established a relationship with human beings on the earth as the subject partner, and his realm has expanded without giving up his influence. Society does not make it easy for an individual, even if he wants to live a good and moral life. The environment of the world does not make it easy for Cheon Il Guk families who want to live a principled life. If Satan sees even a slight crack where he can attack, he will attack. That is why we need a fence that can protect the Cheon Il Guk families. It is absolutely necessary to have a protective barrier that can protect and watch over the Cheon Il Guk families. The heavenly tribal messiahs have the role of creating that fence.

The priority of the heavenly tribal messiah, starting as family-level messiahs, is to establish families centering on Heavenly Parent. They also have to give birth to spiritual children, nurture them and help them to become family-level messiahs. They must educate and cooperate so that the biological children and spiritual children can fulfill their mission of family-level messiah. Only then can a heavenly tribal messiah take root.

If we have the foundation of a tribe that absolutely believes in u, it becomes easier for us to achieve mind–body unity. If we have the absolute foundation of the tribe, it becomes easy for the husband and wife to become one. And upon the absolute foundation of the tribe, the family of the heavenly tribal messiah can be protected. The family can only be protected by the fence of the tribe, the tribe can only be protected by the fence of the people, and the people can only be protected by the fence of the nation. This is the logic of the world.

For example, if a nation goes to ruin, what will happen to the families in that nation? The individuals, families, tribes and people in that nation will go to ruin too. For Cheon Il Guk families to be protected, it is absolutely necessary to have at least a fence of the tribe. Heavenly tribal messiahs should not carry out the work of saving the tribe carelessly for the sake of the family's happiness or practice true love only for the sake of the tribe's happiness.

> The individual's wish is to find a family that can stand on heaven's side. The family's wish is that there must be a tribe realm on heaven's side. The tribe's wish is that there be a people and nation on heaven's side. That is why I am telling you that you must do your best to fulfill your mission as heavenly tribal messiahs. [19]

2) Expansion and the attitude of the family messiah

Heavenly Parent wants to go to all the families in Cheon Il Guk and live together with them. When He goes to find families in Cheon Il Guk, He wants to do so as a parent and not as a guest. There can be a reunion of parent and child in that place, and Heavenly Parent can give the love that He has been waiting to give for thousands of years. When True Parents appointed and sent out heavenly tribal messiahs, they blessed them, telling them to become heavenly tribal messiahs who attend Heavenly Parent. When Heavenly Parent comes down to a tribe and lives with them, that tribe becomes a heavenly tribe. The base for that beginning is the garden of Eden, which becomes the hometown of that tribe. [20]

Heavenly fortune will always follow the tribe that lives in attendance to Heavenly Parent and True Parents. Miracles will occur in pursuing tasks centering on heavenly fortune, and Heavenly Parent will breathe. Blessed families must realize the restoration of the authority of the eldest son up until the realm of the tribe based on the victorious realm of True Parents and prepare a foundation for blessed families as Abel families to attend Heavenly Parent. First, they should attend Heavenly Parent at the center of the family and be the first to form the Abel realm and become a model (blessed family model). Second, they must restore the Cain realm, centering on their own tribe, and bring Cain and Abel together to become one (restoration of the authority of the eldest son and the right of brothers). Third, even those in the Cain realm can change lineage from Satan's lineage to Heavenly Parent's lineage (Blessing ceremony) and attend Heavenly Parent.

Ultimately, blessed families must restore the tribe as the Abel chosen by God. Restoration of the tribe means that blessed families must establish themselves in the position of Abel and love the tribe which is in the position of Cain and realize the restoration of the right of siblings (restoration of the authority of the eldest son). When the restoration of the right of siblings is restored, they can become the parents of the tribe and find again the position of the restored Adam. Blessed families who have become parents must attend Heavenly Parent in their family and realize the restoration of the authority of kingship that has achieved settlement. A nation where 12 tribes that have restored the authority of kingship are gathered comes to take the form of heaven. In other words, Heavenly Parent comes down to that nation, and the original garden of Eden where Heavenly Parent can reside can be realized. When this expands further and nations and the world are restored, Heavenly Parent's nation can be restored up to the cosmic realm. This is the concept of the genuine kingdom of heaven on earth and in heaven.

Then what is heavenly tribal messiahship? It is the providence of blessed families restoring the authority of the eldest son horizontally in their own families and up to the tribe realm, based on the foundation of True Parents having restored the authority of the eldest son (restoration of the right of siblings) vertically in the world and up to the cosmos. It is the providence that expands to the family and tribe centered on Heavenly Parent up to the national realm. The heavenly tribal messiah has been connected to the family level and tribe level, so it will connect to the national level in an instant. The foundation for that is for the Family Federation and the government to work together in unity. [21]

2. The standard of a life connected to True Parents

1) In order to breathe true love

How do you think Heavenly Parent designed the kingdom of heaven on earth and in heaven?

> What kind of place is Heaven? There can be no enmity or jealousy in Heaven. It is a free world where people take care of each other and are taken care of. It is not a world ruled by money, honor or power. It is a world where, when one person does well, he does so on behalf of the whole, and when one person likes something, it is for the sake of the whole, and when one person is happy, the whole is happy together as well.
>
> Heaven is a world filled with the air of true love. It is a world where you live by breathing true love. It is a world filled with life whenever and wherever. It is a world where all those who are part of it are connected to the lineage of the true Heavenly Parent. It is a place where the entire world is like the cells in our body, in an

inseparable relationship. Heaven is a world ruled only by true love, which is the original love of Heavenly Parent. Therefore, Heavenly Parent also lives for the sake of true love. [22]

The heavenly tribal messiah is the one who takes the role of True Parents on their behalf in the tribe. Therefore, they must take True Parents' love and create limitlessly. Creation is possible when, through action, I understand the other person's heart as my heart and, on top of that, have the perspective to see with the love of parents. This refers to the heart that feels pity and wants to give every time it feels that the tribe, the longing object partner, is waiting. Heavenly Parent is the great King of love. He is the one with the heart of love. When He stimulates that heart, there is an explosion of infinite love. In the same way, if human beings had not fallen and come to possess that heart and love, they would have come to manifest the heart of a parent who loves the tribe members at the same stage.

True Parents said that they hear the voices of 7.4 billion human beings crying out every day, "Hurry up and save me!" When they hear these voices, they ask back, "How can I sleep comfortably?" As the True Parents of humankind, who are carrying the responsibility for saving humankind, they are living a life with the perspective that "There cannot be even one person left on the planet Earth with Satan's lineage." We can see them embracing humankind with endless love and working hard on the frontline, even today, to save humankind.

Heavenly tribal messiahs share the world of true love that they have experienced with the tribe members for the sake of the tribe's happiness. They must guide the members of the tribe so that they also can have the same experiences. It is good to also prepare an opportunity for members of the tribe to testify about every time they experience the love of True Parents.

There may have been times when, with the heart of Heavenly Parent, we wanted to do whatever it takes for the happiness of the tribe but couldn't see how to do that. Every time that happens, True Father said we should think about what he did in that situation. True Father said that when he was pioneering the Will of God, there were times when he encountered difficulties and could not see the way forward. Every time that happened, he said that he would remember Heavenly Parent's voice saying, "I am not dead!"

> Time after time I came up against dark obstacles. Whenever that happened, I remembered God's voice when He told me, "I am alive." You would not know that His voice remains in the marrow of my bones to this day. I have not forgotten God's sorrowful situation, which He shared with me when He called me. I cannot forget God's plea to me, "You need to focus only on your relationship with Me; you must not forsake Me." Sometimes I feel sorry for my own situation, but then I remember that God's situation is more sorrowful than mine. [23]

At times when our body and mind are tired and weary, we can

gain strength by hearing the voice of True Parents, who have asked us to "Take responsibility for the happiness of your tribe!" Even when we want to give up, True Parents will not give up; thinking of that will help us to go forward without giving up.

2) Do you believe, do you know, or do you live together?

Heavenly tribal messiahs sacrifice the happiness of their own family and give priority to the happiness of the tribe. By living like that, they become the true parents of the tribe. This is because they know that when they live for the sake of the happiness of the tribe, their family's happiness will be taken care of. Happiness is living together with Heavenly Parent and True Parents. Unhappiness begins when we live apart from Heavenly Parent and True Parents. Happiness is attending Heavenly Parent in the tribe and living together, "coming and going, while eating and sleeping, through the good and the bad."

In 1997 True Parents proclaimed the era of the realm of the fourth Adam and once wrote down on the chalkboard the five stages of a blessed family's life, explaining them one by one. "① Have faith in True Parents, ② Know True Parents, ③ Live together with True Parents, ④ Realize oneness of love with the True Family, ⑤ Begin the lifestyle of the kingdom of heaven on earth." [24] Here we would like to think about the words that True Parents have given us regarding ① Having faith in True Parents, ② Knowing True Parents, ③ Living together with True Parents.

First is to "have faith in True Parents." To have faith in True Parents means to believe in True Parents. Believe that Rev. Sun Myung Moon is my True Father and that Dr. Hak Ja Han is my True Mother and that the two of them, who married in 1960, are my True Parents. It means believing that the two of them together are the True Parents, not believing just one of them to be the True Parent. Members of the Family Federation have received the Blessing from True Parents. They received the Blessing because they had faith in True Father, Sun Myung Moon, and True Mother, Hak Ja Han. Heavenly Parent is the One who decides the position of the True Parents. Human beings cannot change what has been decided by Heavenly Parent. If we say that we have faith, the implication is that we don't clearly know the True Parents. True Parents said that when we come to know them clearly, we no longer believe in them but pass on to the stage of knowing them, beginning a lifestyle of attendance. [25]

The second stage is knowing True Parents. When we do not know very well who True Parents are, we are stuck in the belief stage, but after knowing, we can go beyond belief. After knowing, we can put it into practice. I must take what I know and go through a process of making it one with my lifestyle. The kind of knowing that we are referring to here is knowing through very concrete experiences. It is not knowing from hearing someone else's words but knowing from having experienced it directly ourselves. Since we have come to know who True Parents are, through them we have come to know Heavenly Parent, the universe, the world of love, the spirit world, history and the value of the true family.

Third is to live together with True Parents. True Parents said that when we believe in and know True Parents, we must live together with them. [26] We must attend True Parents, hear the sound of their hearts and live together with them. True Parents are one with Heavenly Parent. Even now, True Parents are calling out to Cheon Il Guk blessed families, "Let's live together." They said that we should open the door to our families so that True Parents can come and live together with our families. They are saying that we should have the same standard of heart as True Parents and live together with them.

It is most important for heavenly tribal messiahs, who live for the sake of their tribe's happiness, to help family messiahs within the tribe to believe in True Parents, know True Parents and live with True Parents. A truly happy family is one that attends True Parents at the center of the family and always consults with them. True Parents are asking, "Right now, in what position are you standing together with me?" How are we going to answer the question, "Do you believe, know or live together?"

- Do you believe in Rev. Sun Myung Moon and Dr. Hak Ja Han as your True Parents?
- Do you know the life course and theology of Rev. Sun Myung Moon and Dr. Hak Ja Han, who are the True Parents?
- Do you live a life of consulting with Rev. Sun Myung Moon and Dr. Hak Ja Han who are the True Parents?

3. Consider whether you have determined the start and

whether you are taking action

1) Only one goal, only one path

"If your start is not clear, your goal is unclear." [27] However, if your start is clear, then your goal also becomes clear. If your start is clear, then you can have a direct path to your goal. The motivation and start of the providence centered on True Parents are always clear. Because the motivation and start are clear, the destination is also clear. The start and goal are clear, so the direction is also clear. That is why True Parents emphasized this to the Cheon Il Guk leaders.

> The path is decided, and the destination is decided. What I would like to ask of you is that you do not miss this opportunity. You are probably aware of this, because you heard the report about the world providence a while ago, but the one thing that God desires at this time is to be together with the True Parents. [28]

First, there is a time when heavenly fortune is with the providence of heaven. True Parents are clearly aware of this time in the providence of Heaven, and they are guiding us. They consult with Heavenly Parent every day and figure out the timing of the providence and decide the goal of the providence. No matter how difficult the reality is, they attend Heavenly Parent and consult with Him, and they do not change the content of the providence. When Adam and Eve fell in the garden of Eden, even Heavenly Parent could not change His plan, so He had no choice but to kick them out. This is because anything that is decided by consulting with Heavenly Parent absolutely must be accomplished.

Second, True Parents do not compromise with the reality regarding the providence that comes from God. The path already has been decided for the destination. There is only one path. It is a single log bridge. We cannot go back by going another path. We can only move forward in the direction of that one path. That is why there is only one goal of Heaven's providence, and the center is only one person. Therefore, what our blessed families should not forget is that when we have absolute faith, absolute love and absolute obedience for the path set by Heavenly Parent and True Parents who are at the center, miracles can happen and the work of the providence can be accomplished. Ultimately, if we establish the standard from our own judgment and position, we cannot attend Heavenly Parent and True Parents on that path and the surrounding good spirits and tribe cannot work together with us. Therefore, it must be simple. The work of the providence, the work decided by Heavenly Parent and True Parents, must be thought out while doing it.

Third, True Parents said that we should not worry, "Will it work or not?" regarding the goal of the providence. They said that because they are deciding the goal of the providence, worrying about whether it will work or not is for them to think about. What the Cheon Il Guk families need to think about is how they will start and take action in their providential mission. They said the issue is whether they did it that way or not. Regarding the methodology, the goal must be reached. For example, when we restore our tribes, they must go through the conditional rules of doing the Divine Principle workshop, holy water ceremony, holy wine ceremony, Blessing ceremony, indemnity stick ceremony, 40-day separation period and three-day ceremony. This is because if we go outside the rules and compromise with reality, then the change of lineage blessed by heaven cannot be realized. Heavenly tribal messiahs should establish a condition of separation by asking themselves whether they have adhered to Heaven's laws or not.

When you shed tears, what are you putting on the line? What are you putting on the line when you offer jeongseong? This is absolutely necessary. There is no need to worry about whether it will work or not. The issue is about how you did it. You cannot be greedy. If I had a heart of thinking about myself, then I would not have been able to come to this position I am in today. Everything would just pass away. [29]

As a heavenly tribal messiah, when we begin by establishing the goal of the providence given by Heaven as our own goal, Satan will not just sit by and watch. Satan will do everything within his power to sabotage us and use different ways to disturb us from fulfilling our mission. The success of heavenly tribal messiahs means the ruin of Satan in the tribe realm, so we cannot escape the attacks of Satan.

Satan is a spiritual being, and at times he would attack directly in a spiritual manner. At other times he would incite his representatives to stage a wide variety of attacks. Satan is the false king who claimed for himself an ephemeral power. He transcended time and space to plot against me and obstruct my work. [30]

What is the secret to overcoming Satan and his attacks? True Parents have said that the only way is to have absolute faith, absolute love and absolute obedience toward True Parents' directions. Fallen human beings became Satan's slaves, forgot their identity and have lived a life of absolute obedience like robots. Therefore, restoration through indemnity means to have more absolute faith, absolute love and absolute obedience toward Heavenly Parent than the absolute faith that we had toward Satan. When we become 100 percent part of God, the realm of dominion can change and human beings can find their original position.

Based on the foundation of True Parents following Heavenly Parent's plan and being the first to put it into action, we should have absolute faith, absolute love and absolute obedience for the words that they give to heavenly tribal messiahs. If we establish that standard, Satan cannot take that away from us. [31] If we hear something that is different from the command of Heaven, we should not listen. If we create a standard of object partner to the sound of Heaven, we will become one with True Parents only. However, if we establish a standard of object partner with another sound, Satan will take that as a condition and enter.

Then what is the path to winning against the enemy? The only way is to practice true love. [32] The archangel Lucifer, symbolized by the serpent, caused the Fall of human beings because he felt a lack of love. Fallen human beings have been born of that lineage, and through that lineage the lack of love and loneliness also have been passed down. If we think of it, all human beings are suffering from a deficiency in love. That is why they want to be recognized, and even if they are receiving more love, when the subject partner loves another person, they come to feel a lack of love. The healing of the fallen nature that was brought about by the Fall of human beings is simple. At the same time that heavenly tribal messiahs are giving parental love to the members of their tribe, the members also should be given the responsibility to love other members of the tribe. In other words, they must be made to experience the love of giving. They must change from receiving love to giving love. Only when they experience joy from giving love rather than receiving love, will their ego disappear. The growth of that experience will lead them one day to stand in the realm of parents. It is through the perfection of that love that they can enter the world of heart of Heavenly Parent and True Parents.

The principle is that human beings' lack of love that came to be because of the Fall cannot be won over by force but naturally subjugated through true love. True love means changing from the experience of receiving love to giving love. Then we can enter the world of love of Heavenly Parent and True Parents, who pour out love unconditionally. When harmony, unity and peace can be realized there, Heavenly Parent will come down and open the world of happiness. That is Heaven.

2) The Blessing of True Parents that completes us

True Parents said that heavenly tribal messiahs should live while thinking about what Heavenly Parent and True Parents will say when they come down to find our tribe. We have to think whether they will hug us while turning around and around and patting our shoulders, saying, "You worked hard! You must have worked so hard! Thank you!" Or will they say, "Why are you still hesitating up to now?" Heavenly Parent and True Parents have earnestly requested that we create an environment in which they can come down to the tribe, overflowing with joy and happiness that makes them want to dance together. They are asking us to create an environment in our heavenly tribe in which Heavenly Parent can come down anytime. This is the same for human parents. For example, think about a family that has lost their children and siblings because of a war. The second son is next to the parents, but the other siblings are nowhere to be seen. His parents would say, "Hurry and go find your elder brother and siblings." That is the heart of a parent who has lost their children.

True Parents have met Heavenly Parent directly and have lived a life of consulting with Heavenly Parent. They look at humankind through Heavenly Parent's eyes and shed tears while looking at the world. Just as True Parents are looking at our heavenly tribal messiahs with the heart of Heavenly Parent, they also wish for heavenly tribal messiahs to enter the world of true love of Heavenly Parent and look at the world with the eyes of a parent.

Heavenly tribal messiahs have the responsibility to become parents of heaven, earth and humankind, preserve the pure lineage of the tribe, and bequeath it. They also have the role of ensuring that the tribe can complete the three great realms by living a life of no shadows at noon and dominate and rule over Satan. They also have the mission to create and dedicate a new tribe that serves Heavenly Parent and True Parents with utmost sincerity. They must do whatever it takes to form a heavenly tribe and return it to heaven's side. That is the path of filial piety for Cheon Il Guk families, as heavenly tribal messiahs, to repay the grace of Heaven. [33]

Before meeting True Parents, we did not know who our parents were. True Parents found us, even though we had lost our value. They believed in us before we believed in them, and they kept believing in us, even though we betrayed them over and over again. They stayed with us until the end. They introduced us to Heavenly Parent, when we were lost and confused as orphans. Even before we were qualified, they gave birth to us again as their children and raised us up to be representatives of True Parents. And they created the spiritual and physical environment, so that we could accomplish the heavenly tribal messiah mission, and they helped us to gain capabilities as well. True Parents have said that from now on, we have to realize Adam and Eve's family before the Fall, restore the garden of Eden from that position of a perfected heavenly tribal messiah and set it up as the hometown.

Then heavenly tribal messiahs, by going through the course of restoration of the eldest son, can go beyond the heart of siblings, bring together the Cain realm and Abel realm and, through that, experience the heart of a parent. Then they can return to the state before Adam's family fell and realize the realm of kingship that attends Heavenly Parent. Furthermore, True Parents want us to enter the world of heart of Heavenly Parent and True Parents and the world of heart of direct children in oneness with God and human beings.

True Parents personally put into practice the truth approved by the spirit world and Heavenly Parent and went through the stage of verification. They proclaimed in plain language the verified truth, which was taught to blessed central families. They taught us new truths in accordance with the advancement of the providence. When they proclaimed the new truth, there were many times when the blessed families showed our limits, but by standing on the frontline, proclaiming it and showing it to the world, we could gain courage.

Despite this, True Parents endured and waited and kept advising us to take action until someone who could accomplish this would step forward. Their words, conveyed with true love, moved our hearts. They made each of our cells shake. They made us shiver. They also made us experience the physical cells and spiritual cells becoming one to experience a state of resonance. When we heard their words, there were many times when we couldn't tell whether this place was the spirit world or the physical world. True Parents are pointing to us and telling us to follow them on the path they have walked.

"This path is the path of truth!"
"It is the path that I have verified!"
"It is a position approved by Heavenly Parent!"
"Walk and follow this path!"
"Let us return to the hometown and live together eternally!"

3) The blessing and grace that will set you free through the Word

How do True Parents want the heavenly tribal messiahs to respond? First, they want us to answer, "I now know the path that I must go, so I will begin!" They hope to hear us respond, "I know the destination, so I will go!" Heavenly tribal messiahs know the path that they have to go. What happens if they know the path they must go but do not take action? It is not polite to not take action even after knowing. We will be ashamed before God.

True Parents have said that there can be no perfection in ignorance. [34] We have been able to escape ignorance by meeting True Parents. Just as the Bible says, "Then you will know the truth, and the truth will set you free" [John 8:32], we are people who have met True Parents, who are the manifestation of the truth. Knowing True Parents who came as the manifestation of the truth means that we know the truth. From there, we can know the path and the goal and gain true freedom.

Then, how can we know True Parents? We can know them if we

absolutely believe True Parents' words and practice them when the words emerge as the truth. If we look at the result of absolutely believing and practicing, we can become free people. Freedom comes from peace of mind. Peace of mind means coming out of the conflicted state that we fell into due to the Fall. Coming out of conflict means a person knows the truth, knows the path, and goes the path with a decided goal.

Second, True Parents want us to respond, "The path to go has been decided, so I will go!" This means we do not have to hesitate about the path that already has been decided. We should not look around us and carry out activities silently. True Parents have said that the heavenly tribal messiah mission is not something that can be done or not done, if we don't want to. They have firmly stated, "If you don't do it, you cannot become perfect!" This is the ultimate and powerful love of the parents. They say that because they see the perfection of their children behind this command. They say this because there is no path other than to return as the direct children, return as a couple and become complete as true parents. This means that heavenly tribal messiah activities will ensure the perfection of my family and the happiness of my tribe.

True Parents have said that if heavenly tribal messiahs know their mission but still hesitate and cannot decide whether they should carry out activities or not, they can be attacked by Satan. True Parents ask us, "Why did Adam and Eve fall in the garden of Eden?" and tell us that we must not listen to the voices around us.

Why did Adam and Eve fall? It is because they could not distinguish between the voices they were hearing. This is because they were listening to the words of Heavenly Parent and the words of the archangel at the same time. And when Eve heard the words of temptation of the archangel, she wasn't able to distinguish whether they were true words or false words and acted from there. That is where the Fall began. [35]

Third, True Parents have said that we should start by confessing, "I absolutely believe the omnipotence and omnipresence of Heavenly Parent!" If we absolutely believe the voices of Heaven and act, Heavenly Parent will mobilize the spirit world and have them cooperate. However, if we don't believe fully, the capabilities we have received from Heaven will cease to be. We can see this if we look at the nine disciples in the New Testament. If we look at Matthew 10, Jesus sent out the disciples to their mission field and gave them "the ability to chase out ghosts, heal disease and make right evil."

However, if we look at Matthew chapter 17, there is a scene in which the nine disciples were shaken up because they could not heal a patient with epilepsy. Jesus answered, "'Because you have so little faith. Truly I tell you, if you have faith as small as a mustard seed, you can say to this mountain, "Move from here to there," and it will move. Nothing will be impossible for you.'" In the Palestine region, the mustard seed is the smallest seed, but when planted, grows 3.7 meters by the next day. The disciples did not believe absolutely in Jesus, so they were no longer able to use the abilities that they had received from Jesus.

Fourth, True Parents have said that we first should proclaim, "I now know, so I will begin now!" When should we start? Right now. They said that it is important for heavenly tribal messiahs to start acting now. They said that this is the best way to serve Heavenly Parent at the tribe level and to dominate Satan. True Parents have emphasized that just as we must receive the Blessing, we must do heavenly tribal messiah activities. True Parents have asked us "earnestly" [36] to do heavenly tribal messiah activities. They especially want us to become filial sons and daughters while True Mother is alive on the earth.

Section 3 For the Sake of Building and Expanding My Nation of Cheon Il Guk

Heavenly tribal messiahs must find a nation that God can come to and say, "This is my nation," a nation that is filled with harmony, unity, peace and happiness. That is the wish of heavenly tribal messiahs and the realization of Heavenly Parent's dream.

1. The nation where Heavenly Parent can reside and rule

1) The nation of Heavenly Parent and True Parents' sovereignty

Heavenly Parent's dream is to create a community of peace and happiness where the ideal of one human family under Heavenly Parent has been realized. For Heavenly Parent to have a position on the earth and reside there eternally, going beyond the family, tribe and people, there must be a nation. That means there must be sovereignty, territory and citizens centered on Heavenly Parent.

> The Family Federation must attend Heavenly Parent. However, the smallest unit where Heavenly Parent and True Parents can live is the nation. It is the nation. [37]

We first must find and establish the standard where Heavenly Parent can come and give His blessing, "This is my nation!" My nation is the nation where Heavenly Parent can be happy and human beings can be happy as well. That nation is one where the sovereignty of heaven has been established.

First, Heavenly Parent and True Parents must become the owners of that nation, and the leaders of the nation must govern it according to heavenly law. In other words, it is the nation of True Parents' sovereignty. Just as the citizens of my nation believe in Heavenly Parent, they must believe and follow the nation's leaders. Heavenly law is law, order and freedom governed by Heavenly Parent. It is a nation where the heavenly congressmen of Cheon Il Guk follow the order and law of Heaven and carry out legislative activities for the true freedom and peace of the heavenly citizens, and the national ideology and constitutional government stand upright. When such a nation can be established, it will continue eternally. This is because Heavenly Parent is absolute, unique, unchanging and eternal.

We will govern the country by consulting with God and centering on God. There will not be a party in power and a party out of power. The time has come when all religious and conscientious people need to unite with our government to defeat communism with Godism and unite our territory and people. That time is now. … Korea will be a bright light in the Orient, illuminating the whole world in the near future. The day will surely come when God governs Korea, and all the people of the world will view Korea as their homeland, just as the poet (Rabindranath) Tagore predicted. [38]

Second, it is the nation where the number of re-created citizens of Heavenly Parent will increase. As parents, the heavenly tribal messiahs, who have been re-created as the original Adam and Eve, give birth to children, realize an ideal family and expand that family. They will realize a community of tribes and expand to the levels of people and nation. True Parents said early on that if there are 12 tribes in one nation that believe in Heavenly Parent 100 percent, the restoration of that nation will unfold automatically. Based on that standard, if it can be connected to the cosmic environment already realized by True Parents, the restoration of the world can be realized. In this way, Heavenly Parent's dream of one family centering on Heavenly Parent, consisting of His direct children, will be realized.

The children of God's direct lineage, having matured through a relationship of love with God, would have formed a true family. If this family had been established, the tribes, nations and world descended from that family would have constituted a world under God's dominion, a nation under God's dominion, families under God's dominion and individuals under God's dominion. [39]

Third, a territory where Heavenly Parent can reside is necessary. That territory can be established by having the heavenly tribal messiahs' joint community restore the people and the nation. The land where the ideal families live will expand and become a land where the heavenly tribes live, and the land where the heavenly tribe federation lives will expand to become the territory of the new nation. Furthermore, the new world and new cosmos will be established, and Cheon Il Guk, the Cosmic Nation of Peace and Unity that Heavenly Parent has dreamed of, will be established. That place is the kingdom of heaven.

Heavenly Parent could not realize that world because of the Fall of Adam and Eve and instead had to work for 4,000 years to send Jesus to establish a nation He could call "My nation." Jesus came and said, "Do not worry, saying, 'What shall we eat?' or 'What shall we drink?' or 'What shall we wear?' For the pagans run after all these things, and your Heavenly Father knows that you need them. But seek first His kingdom and His righteousness, and all these things will be given to you as well." [Matt. 6:31–33] That nation is the nation that Heavenly Parent can call "My nation."

Jesus came to earth in search of God's nation. He came in search of one nation, yet due to the disbelief of Israel and Judaism he could not establish that nation. He came to establish a nation on the physical as well as on the spiritual level, except he could establish only a spiritual kingdom. Therefore, Christianity today still does not have a substantial, physical nation of its own on earth. [40]

During Jesus' time, there was no nation or people that Heavenly Parent could call "My beloved nation," and the base for that nation could not be established on this earth. True Parents also have lived their life in order to find the nation that Heavenly Parent can call "My nation." True Parents wanted to settle in that nation that they could call "my nation," demonstrate that sovereignty, make the citizens free, and they eagerly looked forward to "the building of my nation" that can protect that territory. They lived with the hope that they could live even just one day in that nation before passing away.

Dear members, to this day I have lived without any interest in worldly things. My lifelong desire is summed up in the following statements: "Let me die in the kingdom that God protects. If I fail to live in that kingdom, my entire life will be miserable. Therefore, I will seek that kingdom and live there, even if only for one day, before I die." [41]

There can be no failure on the path of Heaven. Heavenly Parent absolutely must realize the Will of the providence on this earth. Then what is the result of the realization of the Will? It is the world that can call out to Heavenly Parent as a parent and where the citizens can be called the children of Heavenly Parent. It is a peaceful world with the law and order centered on Heavenly Parent. That is why, while True Parents are on the earth, we must find the nation that they can call "my nation." This means we must realize Heavenly Parent's dream on the earth. There can be no compromise regarding this, and we just cannot give up.

What happens if we pass away without being able to dedicate our life to finding the nation that True Parents can call "my nation" here on the earth? Even though we go to the spirit world, we will not be able to have the value that comes from the true love of being a part of the heavenly nation. We must go to the spirit world with the results that we lived within the realm of dominion of Heavenly Parent. When we do that, we can enter the heavenly nation as a citizen of Cheon Il Guk. Then we can go to Heaven without a visa. That is because it is the original blueprint of creation.

2) Overcoming the sorrow of not having my nation

True Parents have said that the reason we are born on this earth is to love the nation and the world. The goal of the providence led by Heavenly Parent until now is also to love that nation and the world. However, what happens if there is no nation to love? There are 200 nations in the world, but is there even one nation that Heavenly Parent can call "My nation"? Is there a nation that can freely love Heavenly Parent's sovereignty and citizens and territory? There is no such nation yet. Therefore, Heavenly Parent is still a pitiful Parent.

> Dear members, what is your purpose for being alive on the earth today? It is to love the nation and the world. God's purpose also has been to love the nation and the world. However, if we remain citizens of a nation without sovereignty, we are pitiful. [42]

There is no nation on the planet to which Heavenly Parent can come down and call it "My nation."

> Think about the unfortunate situation of a people without a nation. They are always exposed to aggression. Helpless to defend themselves, they are subject to repeated attacks. Where can we find the kingdom that God desires? Where can we find the kingdom that can become God's resting place? This is the question. [43]

The first Adam fell and could not establish the heavenly nation, and the second Adam, Jesus, had no nation and died on the cross. True Parents also did not have a nation, so they had to go to prison six times and go through many unjust circumstances. Therefore, the words "Save that nation and maintain justice" are the reason we have to build Heavenly Parent's landing base.

> The kingdom's political system will transcend both democracy and communism. Once established, it will endure forever. Considering these things, isn't it shameful that you have not yet

become citizens of that kingdom? You ought to lament that we do not yet have such a kingdom. You must deeply regret that you are not yet able to live there. We all need to repent for not having established that unchanging sovereignty. [44]

From a young age, True Father lived his daily life learning about the hope, situation and heart of Heavenly Parent. By learning about the hope, situation and heart of Heavenly Parent, he came to know that Heavenly Parent was sad because He did not have a nation. Korea was under Japanese rule during the time when True Father was a student in the 1930s. As a colonized citizen without a country, he could directly experience the sadness of Heavenly Parent, who does not have a nation. He had the mindset to love the people and nation more than food, and it is said that he often spent his days without eating lunch.

During the years I was growing up in Seoul, I did not eat lunch. I thought, "As long as we don't have an independent nation, how can I be worthy to eat three meals a day?" I missed meals many times in my life, but I missed my people more than food. This is the path I chose. I continually resolved, "I will love my people and my country more than food." So, after I left my hometown and moved to Seoul, I did not eat lunch. Such was the life I led. It was not because I could not afford to buy lunch. It was because whenever I had money, I gave it to the poor. [45]

2. Heavenly Parent's hometown and my nation, my homeland

1) True Father's final prayer

True Parents have asked us, "What is the purpose for your having been born on this earth?" And they answer it themselves: "You were born to love the nation and the world. And the heavenly tribal messiah mission is the starting point of finding and loving your nation."

Heavenly Parent's dream was designed to be realized by establishing the heavenly tribal messiah as the foundation of substance. In 2012, in his final prayer, True Father proclaimed, "I have accomplished everything!" in the name of the heavenly tribal messiahs who can represent the nation. True Parents proclaimed the realization of Heavenly Parent's dream through the success of heavenly tribal messiahs.

> I declare that if the tribal messiahs are able to fulfill the calling of national representatives and restore the 387 nations (of the Abel UN and Cain UN), everything will be brought to a conclusion. I have accomplished everything for this. I have completed everything. Aju! [46]

Cheon Il Guk families are said to stand in the position of Abel, because they already know the Principle. That is why Cheon Il Guk families should be able to oppose and fight Satan and separate themselves from the satanic world. True Parents have said that no matter what the circumstances are, Cheon Il Guk families must enter the realm of Heavenly Parent's love. They have emphasized that we must save Cain with the love of the Abel realm. This is the principle of the providence of restoration.

> You must willingly sacrifice yourself to resolve the sorrowful heart of Heavenly Parent and your brothers and sisters who are tied to the satanic world. You have to willingly save them from the satanic world by paying the price with your life and your sacrifice. The providence of restoration advances with the love and sacrifice of Abel. This is the principle that you should remember. This is one stage of the providence of Heavenly Parent. [47]

After Foundation Day in 2013, the environment for Cheon Il Guk that Heavenly Parent had hoped for so long finally was realized. The environment for Cheon Il Guk means an environment that is not in the realm of dominion of Satan. That means within that environment, a true heavenly nation can be established. True Parents have said:

"I have created the best environment in history. From now on, it would be good for Cheon Il Guk families to rise up and move on their own. I have already finished the preparations for spirit world to mobilize and cooperate. The five great saints and the good ancestors will cooperate."

From now on, it is the responsibility of the Cheon Il Guk families to find the citizens of Cheon Il Guk within the environment prepared by Heaven. If the Cheon Il Guk families just move and act, heavenly fortune will be with us and the spirit world will join us and help us.

2) The heavenly tribal messiah mission combines tribe church and family church

Based on the foundation of the home church movement, and through returning to our hometowns in 1991, the tribal messiah movement officially began. True Parents said that a tribe is identified by the last names of the father and mother of its central family, and the husband and wife are the center of that tribe. When we become tribal messiahs, we register our tribe with our two last names as the tribal messiah couple who has formed that tribe. True Parents received the registration of the tribal messiahs on July 1, 1991 and sent them out to their hometowns two months later on September 1.

> I told you to register as tribal messiahs when I proclaimed *Chil Pal Jeol* on July 1, 1991. You will go beyond family messiahs to become tribal messiahs. The tribe joins the last names of the mother and father, husband and wife. So, you will be the messiah of the tribe in which two last names have joined. "Messiah" refers to True Parents. You cannot become a messiah on your own. Family messiahs are candidates for tribal messiahs. The tribe is the joining of two last names, so when they join, you rise up to become a tribal messiah. [48]

True Parents said that the heavenly tribal messiahs must embrace both Abel and Cain. If we look at the providence of restoration, we can say that Abel is the one who is closer to Heavenly Parent and Cain is objectively further away from Heavenly Parent. Therefore, tribal messiahs must embrace both their own family and Cain's family. Our own tribe (Abel tribe) refers to the joining of the last names of father and mother, husband and wife. The Cain tribe refers to the tribe that does not start out with a connection of lineage but has been connected through the home church movement.

Heavenly tribal messiah refers to the combination of the tribe church centering on our family and biological children and the family church created by gathering the Cain realm. Just as Jesus would have been able to stand only on the foundation of the unity of Zachariah's family and Joseph's family, only on the foundation of the unity of the Abel tribe church and Cain family church can heavenly tribal messiahs accomplish their mission.

> Therefore, your family church is the Cain-type foundation for tribal messiahship, and the Abel-type church is your own family. These two must join and unite. Only then can the mission of tribal messiahship be accomplished. Family church will not disappear because I have appointed tribal messiahs. The family church will still be necessary, even if all the billions of people on this earth are restored. Just as the mind and body must unite and all the world has to unite, the family church and tribe church must unite internally and externally. [49]

True Parents have asked that heavenly tribal messiahs bless their families and a tribe and establish a tribe hoondok church (tribe hoondok center) centering on them. They have emphasized that the providential success or failure of one global family under Heavenly Parent depends on this.

> First and foremost, I ask you to give the Blessing to your family and tribe and to establish your tribal hoondok church. The success or failure of the Family Federation, the reunification of Korea, and the creation of one global family depend upon this initiative. [50]

3. National restoration and building Heavenly Parent's nation

1) A nation formed of united tribes

The role of a heavenly tribal messiah is to achieve harmony, unity and peace among his nation's citizens and Heavenly Parent for the sake of his nation's happiness. The heavenly tribal messiah needs to play a major role in connecting Heavenly Parent and his nation's people on a national level to achieve unity and maintain a lasting world of peace. The nation that receives Heavenly Parent's sovereignty will have happy citizens.

When a nation is governed by Heavenly Parent and True Parents, its tribes, families, and individuals are protected. When Heavenly Parent can call a nation His, He can settle within that nation with

True Parents. We also can build true families and complete Cheon Il Guk families. When such a nation is established, it will protect Heavenly Parent, True Parents, true families, Cheon Il Guk families, and humankind. That nation will create the ideal world of peace. On its foundation, the entire world will be restored. [51]

Heavenly tribal messiahs lay the stepping-stones that connect a family to the tribe, a tribe to the people, a people to the nation, and a nation to the world. We cannot restore a nation if we are still on the tribal level. We can build a nation after we connect twelve tribes and build a people. For there to be a nation, at least twelve tribes must unite. When the heavenly tribal messiah is at the top, he (she) can build a nation by uniting the Cain-type family church and the Abel-type family church and then unite twelve tribes.

> The next level needs more than a tribe. You must build a people. A people needs 12 tribes. When 12 branches become one, they can form a nation. [52]

Up until now, Cheon Il Guk has not existed anywhere on earth. Now it will offer humankind the model that shows how a heavenly nation is built and what it should look like. Cheon Il Guk is a nation that is governed by leaders on earth who discuss everything with Heavenly Parent and True Parents. [53] Cheon Il Guk will begin with a single nation and then expand until it has brought everything that exists into Heavenly Parent's sovereignty. For the first time in human history, Cheon Il Guk has appeared, and although it may seem as small as a mustard seed in the beginning, when it is time, it will fill the entire world.

2) The settlement of Cheon Il Guk

Cheon Il Guk (天一國) represents the realization of Heavenly Parent's dream for the ideal of creation. It is a nation (國) where two (二) people (人) become one (一). [54] The first "two people" are Reverend and Mrs. Moon, the True Parents, who represent Heaven. If Adam and Eve had not committed the Fall, they would have become one, centering on Heavenly Parent, and given birth to children whose descendants would have filled the world. However, since Adam and Eve became humankind's fallen ancestors, Cheon Il Guk represents the re-created heavenly world which began with the third Adam and Eve, Sun Myung Moon and Hak Ja Han. Therefore, on the foundation of the unity between Heavenly Parent and True Parents, in 2013 True Parents proclaimed the first year of Cheon Il Guk to mark its starting point. [55] Cheon Il Guk began at the center of the cosmos where Heavenly Parent and human beings are one. Through the Blessing, Cheon Il Guk is expanding to the family, the society, the nation, the world and the universe. [56]

Cheon Il Guk consists of an internal Cheon Il Guk and an external Cheon Il Guk. Heavenly Parent consists of Heavenly Father and Heavenly Mother, yet they are one complete entity. Thus, Heavenly Parent has been perfecting the internal Cheon Il Guk since before the Creation. On the other hand, the external Cheon Il Guk refers to a nation in which Heavenly Parent's sovereignty, people, and territory have been established. Heavenly Parent resides in Adam and Eve when they each fulfill individual perfection and unite as a couple within the right environment. Therefore, when His nation and its righteousness are restored, Cheon Il Guk is fulfilled and a unified heavenly nation is realized.

The internal Cheon Il Guk will reveal itself through the external Cheon Il Guk when the two become one. Then the internal and external will materialize as the substantial Cheon Il Guk. To celebrate the new year, on January 1, 2005, True Parents wrote the motto "Let Us Complete the Ideal of the Internal and External Cheon Il Guk!" True Parents explained that the internal Cheon Il Guk is the vertical Cheon Il Guk centered on Heavenly Parent and the external Cheon Il Guk is the horizontal Cheon Il Guk centered on True Parents.

mind and body become one, a man and a woman become one, a parent and child become one, heaven and earth become one, and everything becomes one with Heavenly Parent. "Internal" refers to Heavenly Parent, and "external" refers to True Parents. [57]

The internal and external Cheon Il Guk create the substantial Cheon Il Guk. [58] The substantial Cheon Il Guk was revealed to the world at the proclamation of the first year of Cheon Il Guk in 2013. [59] The union between Heavenly Parent and True Parents is itself the substantial Cheon Il Guk. The proclamation of the first year of Cheon Il Guk has made it possible for Heavenly Parent to appear to the spiritual world and physical world in a physical form through True Parents. Cheon Il Guk is a nation where Heavenly Parent and human beings can become one and the spiritual and physical worlds can live in harmony. It is the starting point of the garden of Eden at the origin of creation.

Cheon Il Guk positions itself on earth by going through stages of establishment and settlement. Establishment is arriving at the destination, and settlement is beginning a specific lifestyle after arriving at the destination. Cheon Il Guk has passed the stage of establishment and is rushing toward settlement. During the settlement of Cheon Il Guk, heavenly tribal messiahs also should hurry on their given path until the day that Heavenly Parent and His citizens have accomplished harmony, unity, and peace and attained happiness.

Section 1 Heavenly Tribal Messiah Code of Conduct

Heavenly Parent's dream is one global family centering on Heavenly Parent. One of the most urgent issues that blocks the accomplishment of this dream is the conflict between Cain and Abel. Heavenly tribal messiahs are also tasked with solving this issue in each of their tribes. True Parents declared that other-and-I thought, finding a love that harmonizes the needs of others with our own, is the key to solving the root of this problem for Cain and Abel to live together. In this chapter, we will answer these questions: What relationship does other-and-I thought have with true love? How can we understand Jacob's life course from the perspective of a life of other-and-I thought? What is the mission of heavenly tribal messiahs from the perspective of other-and-I thought?

1. Practice true love with other-and-I thought

In the past, True Parents' ideology of peace to "realize a lasting world of peace" has been explained through Godism, headwing thought, Unification Thought, and the ideology of true love. In 1958, True Father pointed out that the ideology of peace centering on human beings and its practice were temporary, not eternal, and therefore advocated for Godism, which is the ideology of peace centered on God. In 1976, in Washington, D.C., they officially proclaimed Godism. [1] In 1963, True Parents' ideologies of peace were integrated and collectively called Unification Thought, and in 1987, Godism was changed to headwing thought.

> I call our Godism movement the headwing movement, in contrast to the left- and right-wing movements. True world peace requires headwing thought, because conventional left-and right-wing theories both are self-centered and power-oriented. Self-centeredness breeds conflicts of interest, and this continuously diminishes our ability to create peace and unity. We need to bring forth a new world ideology that will overthrow egoism. Other-and-I thought emanates only from God's providence of love, because God is the essence of love. The essence of love is other-and-I thought that sacrifices itself to save others. [2]

Godism is an essential ideology in realizing an eternal world of peace. It is a thought or ideology centered on the eternal and unchanging Heavenly Parent rather than an ideology centered on human beings who change constantly. Headwing thought, which is also Godism, does not tilt toward either left-wing thought or right-wing thought but maintains a balanced harmony between the two as the head. Ideologies centering on human beings are self-centered and cannot create the eternal world of peace. If one advocates for world peace only from the left, the right, or oneself, one cannot escape from egotism's frame and genuine peace is impossible.

Headwing thought overcomes these limitations and promotes other-and-I thought, which is selfless and loving, unlike egoism, which is self-centered and pursues one's own interests to the exclusion of others. The essence of Godism is rooted in other-and-I thought based on an ideology of mutual true love. Up until now, we have collectively used Godism, headwing thought, the ideology of true love, and other-and-I thought as True Parents' ideologies of peace. [3]

First, on the foundation of the concept of a "public self," other-and-I living is a value system that promotes living for the sake of another until that person grows to the same level as oneself and engages in give-and-receive action on a horizontal plane. Through this approach, we can examine the meaning of the ideology of peace on a deeper level and learn how to practice it as heavenly tribal messiahs. Is the correct way to love simply giving infinite amounts of love without any standards or conditions? What kind of preparation and stages do we need to give true love to other people? Let's find out the answers to these practical questions.

2. The four main attributes of true love (Heavenly Parent's characteristics)

Just like the New Testament declares, "God is love" (1 John 4:8, 4:16), True Parents said, "Heavenly Parent's essence is true love." [4] Furthermore, they said that Heavenly Parent's attributes and the attributes of true love are the same and stressed that we can understand the attributes of true love if we understand the attributes of Heavenly Parent.

Heavenly Parent exists with four main internal attributes—being absolute, unique, unchanging, and eternal. The first of these four main internal attributes is absoluteness, which represents Heavenly Parent's law and order of mobility. All things in the universe and the natural world consist of a structure that is centered on goodness and cares for and protects others. Moreover, absoluteness establishes the necessary standard of determining good from evil and right from wrong. Second, uniqueness represents the reciprocal parent–child relationship between Heavenly Parent and human beings that gives and receives a unique type of love. Third, unchanging constancy represents Heavenly Parent's love, which has the parent's attribute of unchanging parental love. Although the real world may be fallen, the love of a parent has never changed and remains in the human world. Fourth, eternity represents the world of love that Heavenly Parent designed as an eternal world that connects heaven and earth. If human beings had not affected this world through the Fall, Heavenly Parent and His human children would have created the corporeal and incorporeal substantial worlds. That world would have become the eternal utopia of Heaven. In conclusion, the world of Heavenly Parent's internal attributes signifies a world where His law and order centered on goodness and living for the sake of others prevail, where Heavenly Parent and human beings have a parent–child relationship as unique partners of love, where Heavenly Parent's unchanging parental love is manifested, and where a utopia unfolds in the eternal kingdom of heaven of Heavenly Parent's corporeal and incorporeal substantial worlds.

The four main internal attributes belong to the same area as our minds. Thus, for those attributes to develop in the substantial form, they need to manifest in external attributes. In other words, Heavenly Parent's hope is to have an external form and substance through the external attributes. The four main external attributes are creativity, subjectivity, relationship, and unity. [5]

The first main external attribute is creativity. When Heavenly Parent was creating the universe, He designed His ideas and invested unlimited love and energy. Heavenly Parent repeated the process of investing and forgetting that He invested and invested again until He turned His design into reality. In particular, when He created Adam and Eve, he created them as young children and designed the process of the growth stages for them to reach perfection, unite in matrimony, and live together forever. Heavenly Parent created human beings as His reciprocal partners and His children. Once He finished creating them, He invested His parental heart with the standards of absolute faith, absolute love, and absolute obedience.

He created human beings according to these standards, and as they mature, they should begin to inherit the standards of absolute faith, absolute love and absolute obedience from Heavenly Parent.

The second stage is the realization of subjectivity. Heavenly Parent created one man and one woman and, as their parent and subject partner of love, raised them with quantity, quality, and speed until they became adults. He perfected and raised His reciprocal partners by stimulating and drawing out their hidden individual embodiments of truth. Moreover, Heavenly Parent prepared the environment with everything human beings would need and created them to resemble His subjectivity by passing the stage of the roles of a parent and a subject partner. In this stage, Heavenly Parent repeated the process of investing and forgetting in the position of a true parent, a true teacher and a true owner. Subjectivity indicates living for the sake of another person until that person reaches maturity and becomes Heavenly Parent's substantial object partner. True Parents said that Heavenly Parent has been investing in us, forgetting that He invested, and investing again until He could reside in our physical bodies.

The third stage is the stage that manifests Heavenly Parent's nature of relationships. Human beings, who are raised receiving Heavenly Parent's true love, can have give-and-receive relationships as Heavenly Parent's perfect object partners. When a man and a woman attend Heavenly Parent at the center and join as a couple, they can have a give-and-receive relationship of true love. As true children of Heavenly Parent, those who have become the ideal couple achieve one body on a balanced and parallel state of equality through the give-and-receive action of love. In other words, having a relationship means engaging in a give-and-receive relationship with one's reciprocal partner at the center. The action of striving to perfect one another by supporting each other reveals itself through this type of give-and-receive action.

The fourth stage is Heavenly Parent's nature of unity. In this stage, Heavenly Parent can reside in the vertical position and unite with human beings when one man and one woman unite and are balanced and parallel to one another. In fact, we can say that the realization of unity automatically fulfills itself during the manifestation of the third stage, that of relationships. When a vertical give-and-receive relationship forms between Heavenly Parent and a human being, unity is established automatically. Unity also can manifest in multiple forms and expand from individual mind–body unity to couple's unity, family unity, social unity, global unity, and cosmic unity. [6]

When an ideal human being, Heavenly Parent's object partner of love, appears, Heavenly Parent automatically resides in a vertical position to unite through give-and-receive action. When two unite, one side does not absorb the other side. This unity is the continuous absolute, unique, unchanging, and eternal give-and-receive action of true love between Heavenly Parent and human beings. Even when imperfect people unite, they may succeed for a while but eventually will fall apart. Yet when two people, two nations, or the world and cosmos unite, if they are centered on Heavenly Parent, their unity will last forever. The eternal world of peace will come when human beings accomplish the nature of unity by achieving an absolute, unique, unchanging, and eternal nature centering on Heavenly Parent. [7]

In conclusion, Heavenly Parent's internal and external four main attributes may be viewed as follows: First, the four main internal attributes follow the law and order of existing for the sake of others centering on goodness. Moreover, human beings are Heavenly Parent's unique partners of love as they have a parent–child relationship. Therefore, Heavenly Parent's love is an unchanging parental love. Heavenly Parent has hoped that the corporeal and incorporeal substantial worlds that He created would become an eternal world. On the foundation of these internal attributes, the external attributes can become manifest.

Creativity, one of the external attributes, represents the world of heart that Heavenly Parent created by endlessly investing the standards of absolute faith, absolute love, and absolute obedience until human beings were substantialized according to His design for creation. Therefore, human beings, who were created according to this standard, must mature and live with absolute faith, absolute love and absolute obedience to Heavenly Parent. Subjectivity is the consciousness that matures and perfects one's partner by stimulating and drawing out his (her) unconscious individual embodiments of truth. In other words, the subject partner needs to resemble Heavenly Parent's subjectivity by taking the role of a parent and raise his (her) object partner just as Heavenly Parent nurtured human beings from a position of a true parent, true teacher and true owner. Next, relationship represents the give-and-receive action centering on one's reciprocal partner. Giving and receiving centering on oneself is a way of acting that is part of Satan's realm. The ideology of Heavenly Parent believes that the action of striving to perfect one another manifests through give-and-receive action. Lastly, unity, centering on Heavenly Parent, manifests in multiple forms and expands from individual mind–body unity to couple's unity, family unity, social unity, global unity, and cosmic unity.

Fallen human beings lost Heavenly Parent's characteristics. A restored human being can recover the four main internal and external main attributes and through them fully inherit the original characteristics of Heavenly Parent that He established at the time of creation.

3. Four main attributes of true love and other-and-I living

1) The four main internal attributes and other-and-I living

How can we apply Heavenly Parent's four great internal attributes and an other-and-I attitude to the mission of the heavenly tribal messiah? Heavenly tribal messiahs need to inherit the internal attributes—absolute, unique, unchanging and eternal. First, they need to protect and live for the sake of others, centering on goodness, and maintain the law and order of creation. They need to teach their tribe Heavenly Parent's absolute goodness and how to distinguish good from evil in their lives. In other words, heavenly tribal messiahs should offer a turning point to live a life in awareness of others as well as self. This will help people amend their self-identity and Heaven's attributes to become mainstream.

Second, the relationship between Heavenly Parent and human beings is a unique parent–child relationship. Human beings, who are object partners, need to be trained in building a relationship with Heavenly Parent, their subject partner, through which they can give and receive wholesome love. People need to be attentive to Heavenly Parent's Word through reading the scriptures. No matter what they pursue in their daily lives, they should live a lifestyle attending Heavenly Parent and True Parents at the center.

Third, parental love does not change. Human beings, who are the substantial object partners that resemble the First Cause, Heavenly Parent, also should resemble the attributes of an unchanging, parental heart. Heavenly tribal messiahs should grow as parents in their family and parents to their tribe, and ultimately they need to understand the world of Heavenly Parent's heart. They should perfect their parental heart by becoming one with the heart of Heavenly Parent.

Fourth, if human beings practice true love on earth, when they go to the spirit world they will be able to come and go freely between the corporeal and incorporeal substantial worlds. They will be able to glorify life in the kingdom of heaven. That world will be the eternal world of peace, a world that will exist forever where Heavenly Parent rules. Heavenly tribal messiahs should unite the Abel tribe and Cain tribe, establish the authority of the elder son, receive acknowledgment for their results, and establish the authority of the parents. Through this, they can form the ideal family that was lost in Adam's original family. Furthermore, when they form the authority of the kingship by uniting with Heavenly Parent, heavenly tribal messiahs can establish the authority of the royal family, Heavenly Parent's direct lineage. In this way, heavenly tribal messiahs can perfect each of Heavenly Parent's internal characteristics, even if they approach them through external stages.

2) The external main attributes and other-and-I thought

On a practical level, we can explain Heavenly Parent's four great external attributes as the realization of the four stages of other-and-I thought. Heavenly Parent's four great external attributes develop in stages from creation to completion; thus, when we practice keeping and other-and-I attitude we realize it in stages as well. Of course, these stages may also occur within a short period of time, appearing simultaneous.

As mentioned above, the first stage is the preparation stage to realize creativity. Heavenly Parent's vision for creation is to become someone who can love other people. Therefore, it is a stage to prepare oneself first. The *Divine Principle* explains that this type of relationship is the relationship between Cain and Abel. It is the stage for Abel to prepare himself to love Cain. In other words, the purpose of this stage is not to manifest true love, but to prepare and train oneself in realizing true love.

The second stage is the stage for creativity to manifest subjectivity by giving true love to other people. A subject partner is someone who lives for the sake of his object partner with true love so that his partner can manifest his own value of existence. The subject partner must give true love, forget that he has given, and give again until his object partner can realize his own value of existence. Moreover, he must nurture his object partner until he also can rise to the position of a subject partner. In other words, one's partner should develop the ability to create what he needs on his own. If we substitute this logic to Cain and Abel's relationship, it is as follows: Abel gives endless love to Cain. Cain acknowledges Abel, and Abel continues to help Cain grow until Cain can do the same things as Abel.

The third stage is the stage for the object partner to grow and begin developing a relationship with his subject partner. When the object partner grows through the subject partner's true love, the two partners can have a parallel relationship. Through this, they can create a position of horizontal give-and-receive action. If Cain and Abel form a parallel relationship within a relationship of true love, they can maintain and secure the order of love.

The fourth stage is the stage of realizing unity. Centering on true love with a reciprocal partner, both can achieve balanced and level give-and-receive action. Within this union, Heavenly Parent can automatically reside vertically and attain unity with them. When Cain and Abel become one with Him through love centering on Heavenly Parent, true unity is achieved between them. The result is eternal peace between Cain and Abel.

3) Jacob's life course from the perspective of other-and-I living

To understand an other-and-I attitude in a practical sense, let's apply the Divine Principle's explanation of Jacob and Esau's relationship. The Divine Principle demonstrates how Jacob and Esau, with true love, succeeded at uniting, achieving harmony and unity in front of Heavenly Parent and building a peaceful family. Therefore, based on Jacob's story, we can understand other-and-I living much more clearly.

In the first stage of other-and-I living, Jacob tries to become the elder son to receive the inheritance of his father, Isaac. Jacob barters for Esau's birthright with a bowl of lentil stew and then receives the blessing from his father by impersonating Esau. To avoid Esau's anger, Jacob flees to his uncle Laban's home in Haran. He stays there for 21 years, during which he marries, has a family, and becomes financially successful before returning to Canaan. As Jacob returns to Canaan from Haran, he wrestles with an angel at the ford of Jabbok and wins, thus receiving the name "Israel." This process is equivalent to the first stage of preparing to become the elder son.

The second stage is the stage in which Jacob becomes the subject partner with a heart of true love for Esau. While living in Haran, every year Jacob sends gifts to his parents back home and each time he also prepares something for his older brother, Esau. [8] When Jacob returns to his hometown 21 years later, he bows to the ground to Esau, exclaiming that seeing his older brother's face is like seeing the face of God, and asks Esau to receive the presents he has collected for 21 years [Genesis 3:1–11]. Jacob continues to give true love to Esau, and then Esau lets go of his resentment and accepts Jacob.

The third stage is the stage in which Jacob heals his relationship with his brother, Esau, with true love. Before Jacob meets Esau, as the subject partner he makes an effort to give true love to Esau. Thus, even before Esau meets Jacob, he has already forgiven, accepted and loved Jacob with all his heart. When the heart of love of these two brothers reaches the same level, an other-and-I attitude, seeking mutual benefits, is formed and the give-and-receive action of love can occur.

The fourth stage is the unity stage, during which Jacob and Esau reconcile and become one. The Divine Principle calls this process the restoration of the authority of the elder son and the establishment of the foundation of substance. [9] Heavenly Parent can enter the place where Jacob and Esau reconcile and can perfect His absolute, unique, unchanging and eternal family.

Unfortunately, these stages did not reach the stage of a people. Jacob and Esau should have continued to live in harmony in a balanced and level relationship of loving give-and-receive action. Yet, not long after Jacob returned, the seven-year famine caused great hardships. Then Jacob entered Egypt with his clan upon an invitation from Joseph, his son, the prime minister of Egypt. From the point of view of an other-and-I attitude, Jacob should have taken Esau's clan with him when he went to Egypt.

> Therefore, during the seven years of famine while Joseph had become prime minister, when bringing Jacob's family (to Egypt), Esau's family should have gone too. If this had happened, it would have been the quickest path to establishing the realm of the kingship in the land of Egypt, with no need for the restoration of Canaan. However, this was lost. [10]
>
> If Joseph, the prime minister of Egypt, had moved both Jacob's family and Esau's family to Egypt, it would have put a stop on the 40-year wilderness course that the Israelites had to take with Moses as well as the historical struggle between Cain and Abel. [11]

However, Jacob did not take Esau's clan to Egypt. From an altruistic perspective, Jacob loved his older brother, Esau, and united with him as a family member, but once they each built their own families, which expanded into clans, Jacob was unable to love every member of Esau's clan. If Jacob had focused on mutual benefit in his relationship with Esau beyond the family level to the tribal level, Heavenly Parent's providence of salvation to send the Messiah would have been much easier.

Had Jacob entered Egypt with Esau's tribe, Heavenly Parent could have sent the Messiah to Egypt without the difficult process of leaving Egypt. The 400 years of slavery and the path to seek out the land of Canaan were a search for Esau's tribe. From an other-and-I thought point of view, had Jacob and Esau united and created an environment on the national level, Heavenly Parent could have sent the Messiah.

4. Heavenly tribal messiahs and other-and-I thought

Heavenly Parent is the True Parent of humanity. Parents wish to embrace their children with love and bless them, if they so much as meet the smallest of standards. This small standard that parents desire of their children is to not fight with one another but to live in harmony. Heavenly Parent hopes for humanity to achieve equality and balance, centering on other-and-I thought, and to live together in an equitable world. Therefore, when all of humanity become the children of Heavenly Parent and True Parents and achieve equality and balance, He will wish to come and dwell with them.

How can we understand the heavenly tribal messiah mission from the viewpoint of other-and-I thought? Let us consider it in stages. The first stage is when a blessed central family develops creativity to re-create the Cain tribe. It is the preparation stage in which the needs of the Cain tribe are satisfied. Therefore, it is the stage in which the heavenly tribal messiah becomes the substantial embodiment of the original Adam realm, in order to equalize the Cain tribe and Abel tribe centering on Heavenly Parent. Furthermore, it is the stage in which his or her family leads a life of attending Heavenly Parent, with an absolute standard as a family of Cheon Il Guk, and controls Satan after bringing him to voluntary submission.

The second stage is when the heavenly tribal messiah lives for the sake of the Cain tribe in concrete ways as the subject partner. He or she should be able to give what Heavenly Parent wishes to give, while simultaneously also giving the Cain tribe what it desires to receive, based on the original standard. It is the stage when the tribal messiah gives, gives and gives again and then forgets and gives again, as the subject partner of true love. True Parents say that, in true love, the output is always greater than the input and that true love cannot be consumed. Therefore, you should give what you have and forget, and repeat this process until the Cain tribe has achieved equality and balance with the heavenly tribal messiah, thus re-creating the Cain tribe as second heavenly tribal messiahs.

The third stage is when the heavenly tribal messiah maintains a relationship with the Cain tribe, continuing to engage in give-and-receive action with the Cain tribe. After Cain has achieved equality and balance with you, you cannot say, "It's finished now." Instead, it is important to maintain a continuous relationship with him. This is because the hierarchy of love continues to exist even after achieving balance. Therefore, living for the sake of others with true love and thus creating even greater true love is important. The life course of Jacob reminds us of the teaching that maintaining relationships is important. Heaven does not wish for Cain and Abel to unite only at the tribal level. He hopes for them to expand their relationship further to the levels of people and nation.

The fourth stage is the stage of unity. When Cain and Abel achieve equality and balance and continue to engage in give-and-receive action, Heavenly Parent automatically comes to dwell with them vertically and engage in give-and-receive action. This stage, in which Heavenly Parent, Cain and Abel engage in continuous give-and-receive action, is called the stage of unity. Once you reach this stage, Heavenly Parent always will come to where Cain and Abel are united as one and form relationships with them. Cain and Abel thus experience living at the stage in which they attend Heavenly Parent on the tribal level and can discuss matters of concern with Him.

As the number of heavenly tribal messiahs who practice other-and-I thought on the tribal level increases, one by one, the range of other-and-I thought will be expanded from the tribe to the people, nation and world. When Esau and Jacob go beyond the level of clan in their relationship and achieve unity in their relationship on the level of people, Heavenly Parent will come to them and personally work through them. He will come to places where such foundations are established and expand that unity from the level of people to the level of nation, and from the level of nation to the level of the world. The heavenly tribal messiah should ponder upon his or her mission in relation to Jacob's course from the viewpoint of other-and-I thought, and walk the path of absolute faith, absolute love and absolute obedience while keeping true to his or her position and duty until the moment when God can work through him or her.

5. Principle of Cain's restoration

Only when the heavenly tribal messiah attends Cain as the king, father and elder brother from the position of Abel, will Cain be willing to submit voluntarily. If you cannot go past that stage, he will not wish to do so. Abel must attend Cain with a joyful heart and rejoice in everything he rejoices in. Abel's achievement of love is recognized only when he establishes that standard and goes beyond it. It is only then that Cain will submit with all sincerity. If Abel does not attend Cain with a joyful heart, he cannot be said to have truly attended Cain. Only after that process is completed, can Abel command Cain. When issuing commands, Abel first must give commands that work to the benefit of Cain, for only then will Cain obey them. When a king commands with authority, "Serve me for my sake," his subjects will revolt rather than serve him. However, when he issues commands for the sake of the subjects, they will obey with joyful hearts.

In principle, when a father teaches his children or an elder brother teaches his younger brother or a teacher teaches his or her students, the former never seeks to teach the latter to become inferior to himself. If a teacher does not teach his or her student to be better than himself in spite of that original principle, this teacher-student relationship would be problematic. You need to overcome this limitation.

The heavenly tribal messiah should not pray for Abel himself and instead be able to pray for Cain. He or she must walk a path that Cain can acknowledge. When True Father was in Heungnam Prison, he did not pray for himself and instead prayed for the members. When he learned that some members had left, he called out each of their names and prayed for their safe return.

Parents who are raising children should not feel it is all right to raise their voices just because they are the parents. Even when a baby soils its clothes, parents should clean it with caring hands and love it, for only then will their child acknowledge the parents' love and attend them when he or she grows up. For whom do parents exist? They exist for their children. The position of parents cannot be maintained without children, just as the position of teacher cannot exist without students. Similarly, the position and value of a king are determined only when his subjects esteem him and call him their king.

You cannot tell the Cain realm what to do just because you are Abel. Such a leader can never be revered. You must offer early-morning jeongseong with sincerity, praying for Cain, and follow a path on which you set an example of love before Cain. Even when Cain retreats, Abel cannot retreat. Since Cain is in the position of the archangel, he has real power. Before the Fall, he was the one with real power whose task was to share out all love equally as instructed by Heavenly Parent. After the Fall, he continued to control everything and exercise his power with even more authority. To move the heart of one with such power, you need to recognize his presence and authority and touch his heart through love; only then can he be restored gradually.

The place where Heavenly Parent comes to dwell with us is where Cain and Abel unite as one. Therefore, His Will is realized only when the mind and body, Cain and Abel, and subject partner and object partner unite as one. It will never do for Abel to be alienated all by himself. If Cain and Abel are not united, Satan can invade them and the Will can never be realized.

The principle of Cain's restoration is to respect and love Cain. If you try to make Cain submit by force, he will try to leave always. Forceful submission may restore him externally but not internally. You need to restore him through love. There are limits to achieving complete restoration without love. A person who has lost love is someone who has lost Heavenly Parent. Therefore, when someone has lost love, it is proof that he or she has lost Heavenly Parent. [12] Everything crashes if the heavenly tribal messiah loses love and becomes exclusively a logical and practical person. For this reason, the heavenly tribal messiah must always reflect upon him- or herself. Am I carrying out this work out of obligation? For what am I walking this path? What is my identity as a heavenly tribal messiah? Do I really love people? What parts of me should I reinforce, and how should I act to expand my current motivation of love? These are the kinds of questions we should ask ourselves, and we should patiently fill up the parts that we feel are lacking in ourselves by praying to Heavenly Parent.

Section 2 Visiting Spirits in the Area

The providence of Heaven is carried out by first putting the spirit world in order through the providence of conditions on earth and then joining forces with the reorganized spirit world to put the earth in order. Right now, the providence of putting the earth in order is being carried out with the cooperation of the spirit world. For a heavenly tribal messiah to accomplish his or her mission, it is important to receive the cooperation of the spirit world by making visits to the spirits in his or her hometown and mobilization area. When you make spiritual visits in your hometown and mobilization area, the spirits will be so delighted that they will cooperate voluntarily. Let us consider this by studying the case of the Apostle Paul, who brought about the Christian revolution through the cooperation of the spirit world, and the case of those families who have completed the heavenly tribal messiah mission.

1. The progress of the providence and the cooperation of the spirit world

1) Setting conditions for the progress of the providence

The providence of Heavenly Parent refers to His dispensation. [13] If Adam and Eve had not fallen, Heavenly Parent's ideal of creation would have been fulfilled in stages, and His purpose of creation would have been completed. In other words, Heavenly Parent's dream would have been realized. However, due to the Fall of Adam and Eve, the providence of Heavenly Parent's ideal of creation was suspended and the providence of restoration through indemnity was begun instead. When the providence of restoration through indemnity is concluded, that means it is time for the providence of Heavenly Parent's ideal of creation, suspended because of the Fall of Adam and Eve, to begin again.

In what order is the providence of restoration through indemnity to restore fallen humanity carried out? It is carried out in the following order: first, fulfilling the providence of conditions on earth; second, putting the spirit world in order through the providence of conditions on earth; and third, joining forces with the reorganized spirit world to perfect the earth. [14] When you consider the order in which the providence is progressed, you can see that the place where Heavenly Parent's providence is completed is not the spirit world but the earth. And you also will come to understand that, in completing the providence on earth, the cooperation of the spirit world is indispensable.

To begin with, the providence of conditions on earth is absolutely necessary. The Family Federation for World Peace and Unification refers to this providence of conditions as the providence of restoration through indemnity. The answer to the question of why the providence is carried out through conditions is simple. True Parents said, "You ask that because you don't know the spirit world. The spirit world is much more complex than the earth. Without putting the complex spirit world in order, the earth cannot really be put in order." All activities performed for the providence of restoration in the age of restoration through indemnity, such as the numerous rallies, declarations, Marriage Blessing ceremonies, speaking tours and founding of providential organizations, were carried out as the providence of conditions through indemnity. True Parents told us that the reason for carrying out the providence of conditions on earth is to put the spirit world in order. This is because the spirit world first must be put in order before the earth can be put in order.

After the Fall of Adam and Eve, tens of millions of years passed in the history of humanity. [15] The number of people who lived on earth and passed on to the spirit world during this period is incalculably large. A lot more people than the 7.4 billion living on earth today have gone to the spirit world. And there would be just as many different stories of how those people lived on earth, and the stories of how they died would also be quite complicated. All the spirits who have gone to the spirit world also have something in common, that they did not receive the Blessing. The way to put the spirit world in order is by pairing all spirits in the spirit world into couples of one man and one woman each and blessing them. Based on the providence, the earth cannot be put in order until the complex spirit world that has been continued for tens of millions of years is completely put in order.

2) Putting the spirit world in order and the cooperation of the spirit world

To put the spirit world in order, certain conditions must be set on earth. However, the providence of conditions on earth in itself is not a goal. It is the inevitable providence to put the spirit world in order. This work is being carried out through the separation of spirits, liberation of ancestors and spirit world Blessing at CheongPyeong. The CheongPyeong works are the central axis of the providence of putting the spirit world in order. The spirits who are freed through the ancestor liberation ceremony and the separation of spirits attend a 100-day workshop in the training center of the spirit world. While there, the spirits learn about the Unification Principle and purge themselves of all the wrongdoings they committed on earth, thus ridding themselves of fallen nature. Then they return to CheongPyeong and receive the Blessing through their descendants, thereby eradicating original sin within themselves and being transformed into absolutely good spirits. As the number of absolutely good spirits who have received the spirit world Blessing increases, the spirit world is transformed from the spirit world realm of evil to the spirit world realm of goodness.

Absolutely good spirits refer to good spirits who are rid of original sin and fallen nature. Though they have been transformed into infinitely pure and clean spirits, they have not yet achieved perfection. Since spirits can be perfected only on earth, they absolutely need the help of their descendants on earth. Therefore, for absolutely good spirits to grow and become perfected spirits, they must receive the help of their descendants on earth. Accordingly, the absolutely good spirits, who have attended a 40-day workshop for blessed couples at the spirit world training center after receiving the Blessing, return to their descendants on earth and help them in their work. Then the descendants on earth, the blessed families, practice true love and thus bring about the perfection of the spirits, and when the spirits are perfected, they too benefit by becoming perfected. They go on to help with the progress of the providence being carried out on earth centering on True Parents.

The providence of Heaven in progress right now for the settlement of Cheon Il Guk is no longer a concept but an actuality, and it is not being done conditionally but substantially. Even at this moment, the ancestors of direct lineage who have received the spirit world Blessing are appearing to their direct descendants and cooperating with them. The blessed ancestors wish to live and work together with their descendants, be it night or day. They hope fervently for their descendants on earth to act. They are making pleas to be given a chance to cooperate with their descendants and contribute toward the providence. The ancestors are ready to make a move before their descendants. However, since ancestors can only work through the bodies of their descendants, it is important for the descendants to make the first move.

The leaders of every religion who have received the spirit world Blessing also are appearing to the leaders of their own religion living on earth and cooperating with them. Political leaders are appearing to the leaders of their nations or organizations and cooperating with them. Leaders of all fields, including journalists, communists and educational leaders of every class, are appearing to the leaders in their field of work on earth and cooperating with them. [16] The leaders of every field who have received the Blessing in the spirit world are now waiting, prepared to be the first in line to cooperate when blessed families visit their counterparts on earth and propagate God's Will to them.

Even those ancestors who have not received the spirit world Blessing are hoping for blessed families to visit their descendants, teach them about the Principle, and guide them on the path to the Blessing. Since the ancestors in the spirit world know only too well that the path to their salvation and Blessing is opened by their descendants, they are waiting to cooperate with the activities of heavenly tribal messiahs. Can you hear the pleas the spirits are making to blessed families? They are weeping bitterly. National boundaries have been abolished in the spirit world. Spirits can visit any place in the spirit world and realize where their own quarters lie in it. They also know very well what needs to be done for them to move their quarters to the vicinity of the kingdom of heaven. There is only one way to do so, which is to receive salvation through their descendants. That is the reason why they are appealing to blessed families to go out and work actively.

3) Putting the spirit world in order and the era for establishing the Association to Connect the Earth to the Spirit World

In October 2009 True Parents proclaimed the era for establishing the Association to Connect the Earth to the Spirit World. In other words, they announced the age in which the spirit world and physical world are connected as one in union. In accordance with the progress of the providence, the walls that blocked the spirit world from the physical world were completely abolished. The era in which the spirits in the spirit world can travel freely to and from the earth has been ushered in. The spirit world and the physical world are no longer two separate worlds. They have become one connected world.

> Once the actual era of Cheon Il Guk begins, the spiritual and earthly worlds will connect and come into oneness, and the Association to Connect the Earth to the Spirit World, a new entity that we will establish on earth, will govern all creation. Moreover, we will carry out the providence according to heavenly law and the heavenly way. Elections conducted in a purely secular fashion will disappear from the face of the earth. All people will become one family through cross-cultural Marriage Blessings. We will enjoy tranquility and true love in happiness amid the sacred reign

of peace. Let me say it again: This day is drawing near. [17]

Now is the age of the substantial Cheon Il Guk. In the age of Cheon Il Guk, divinity and truth are connected as one to achieve balance and equality. In short, it is an age when divinity and truth work together. The origin of the truth is not humankind but Heavenly Parent. The source of the truth is not the earth but the spirit world. Since the spirit world is a world of order, it is important to act on earth according to the order in the spirit world.

For a heavenly tribal messiah to go to his or her hometown and rally the tribe and thus complete his or her mission, he or she needs to receive the cooperation of the ancestors who lived in that area before going to the spirit world. There may be ancestors who have received the Blessing in the spirit world. And there may be ancestors who have not received the Blessing in the spirit world. The latter are waiting for the heavenly tribal messiah to return to his or her hometown and begin working.

The important question is whether you have established the standard by which the spirits in the spirit world can testify to you when they are mobilized to help their descendants. The spirit world requires such a standard of you. The spirit world knows about the heart of Heavenly Parent. If there is a prepared figure on earth who has set such a standard, spirits will cooperate with that heavenly tribal messiah on earth. The reason spirits in the spirit world cannot come to earth and cooperate is that those on earth have not laid such divine foundations.

The spirit world must be mobilized. How could the kingdom of heaven be constructed if the spirit world is not mobilized? It cannot be constructed. The kingdom of heaven is supposed to start from True Parents, not the fallen descendants who have lived on earth until now. Just as the cooperation of the angelic world was involved in the creation of Adam, those in the spirit world must come down to earth and cooperate in the work of re-creation. Otherwise, nothing can be achieved. [18]

2. Visiting spirits to create a spiritual environment

1) Creation of a spiritual environment in the physical world

What should you do first when you go to your hometown to complete the heavenly tribal messiah mission? It is important to visit and present your compliments to those who were born and lived in that area before going to the spirit world. Among the people who lived in your hometown in the past before passing, there may be your own ancestors, prominent figures of that area, people who led righteous lives, independence fighters and patriots. Visiting them and courteously presenting your compliments is most important.

True Parents taught that when a Family Federation leader is appointed to take charge of an area, he or she should visit the prominent figures of that area and ask for their cooperation. They said that, in whichever village you go to, you first should visit the elders of that village and greet them. If there is any righteous person in that village who is respected by others, you should go and ask for his or her cooperation. A church leader must visit such people and introduce True Parents to them and ask for their cooperation.

However, though we have visited leaders in the physical world, we did not visit the leaders in the spirit world. Until now, we have treated the spirit world and the physical world differently. Though we visited and greeted elders, leaders or righteous people who were alive in the physical world, many was the time when we were remiss about visiting the elders, leaders or righteous people of the area who had passed on into the spirit world. Perhaps it was because we thought of the spirit world and the physical world as separate worlds. We may not have entertained the idea that the spirit world and the physical world are connected.

It is not only the local leaders you can see with your physical eyes who are important. Those invisible to your eyes who lived in that area as leaders in the past are also leaders. You should remember that the influence of the local leaders who are invisible but who exist nonetheless is much greater. Only when you treat leaders of both the spiritual and physical worlds with courtesy, will they move the area to cooperate with you.

For example, let us say that you visit the grave of a historical figure. When you visit a grave, you should present your compliments courteously, praise all that he or she did for the nation, and explain the reason for your visit. You should report to him or her about the providential dispensation of True Parents. And then you should pray, asking for his or her cooperation. What do you think will happen when you pray to Heaven for a local figure and then go to see his or her descendants? You will be able to converse with them and receive their cooperation quite easily. When you absolutely believe that something will happen and act accordingly, indeed it will come to pass. Even if you feel awkward at first, you soon will feel a great spiritual power emanating from you. You will feel strong spiritually, and you will experience the greater power of the invisible over the visible. True Parents told us of this fact after experiencing it themselves. When we absolutely believe in their words and translate those words into action, we will enter the same realm of heart as theirs.

2) Ancestors in the spirit world and visits to good spirits in the area

A heavenly tribal messiah must liberate his or her clan. What, then, must you do first after returning to your hometown to liberate your clan? True Parents said that you first must visit the graves of your ancestors. They said, "Start out by visiting your ancestors' graves and declaring that you have come to take responsibility for the wrongdoings of your ancestors and to liberate them, so that they can stand in a position where Satan cannot accuse them." [19]

They also said that, if you did not fulfill your responsibility as the eldest grandchild, you should raise tombstones for the ancestors when you return to your hometown in accordance with the Korean custom of attending your ancestors well. You also should visit the garden beloved by your grandfather and grandmother and plant trees, if it is desolate, and make it into an ideal garden. You need to clean up the village and make it into a place that can be praised by the mountains and streams of your hometown. Only then can you become an influential person in your hometown and rise to the position of ancestor. [20]

Your hometown is the base of your ancestors. From a blessed family point-of-view, the ancestors are in the position of the archangel and heavenly tribal messiahs were established in the position of the original Adam and Eve in their stead. Just as the archangel protected and raised Adam and Eve, when heavenly tribal messiahs begin working in their hometowns, their ancestors will follow behind them and help them. If Adam and Eve had not fallen in the garden of Eden and had married, the archangel also would have received the benefits thereof. Similarly, the good ancestors in the spirit world waited for the day on which true Adam and Eve would return to their hometown and begin their work. That is why when heavenly tribal messiahs take the first steps toward their hometowns to restore their nation, their ancestors come down to earth and welcome them in full force. [21] Once you have set such a condition, the tribes you bless will receive the Blessing through the joint work of the spiritual and physical worlds.

Who is a heavenly tribal messiah? He or she is a person who inherits the love of True Parents on the tribal level and plants it and establishes it horizontally in his or her hometown. It is important for you to go to your hometown, meet your clan with the authority of True Parents and act accordingly. Your hometown is the place of settlement where you can raise the spiritual standard higher than any standard of love and put down roots by shedding tears, sweat and blood. By doing that, the base on which Heavenly Parent and True Parents can arrive in the hometown of the heavenly tribal messiah is created.

What is the wish of people who lived on earth and went to the spirit world without meeting True Parents? They harbor bitter sorrow for not being able to meet True Parents while they were alive on earth. The spirits in the spirit world know more about the value of True Parents than the people living on earth. According to the words of mediums who communicate with the spirit world, about 3,320 spirits stay with each person living on earth. [22] Their wish is to devote themselves for the sake of True Parents. If the entire spirit world cooperates with heavenly tribal messiahs, they will be more than able to fulfill their missions.

> Spirits know clearly how they can devote themselves for the sake of True Parents and how they can serve True Parents. All their five senses (sight, hearing, smell, taste and touch) feel the stimulating power emanating from True Parents. [23]

3. Examples of spiritual experiences and visits to spirits

1) The Apostle Paul was struck by spiritual lightning

The age after the Foundation Day of Cheon Il Guk is a new age in which the spiritual and physical worlds are united as one. It marks the coming of the extrasensory age. The past age of attacks on the planet Earth, centered on evil spirits, will pass away, and the age is coming in which the good spirits will attack us in turn. In the past, Satan attacked us through evil spirits, but now the time is coming for the good spirits to affect the earth. True Parents have worked hard to pave such a path. [24] True Mother says that that time has now come.

There is an example of the good spirit world attacking a prepared leader and changing his life 180 degrees. The person who left behind the greatest achievements in Christianity after Jesus was the Apostle Paul. He was Jewish and a well-studied, intellectual man. Though he was such a man, he had become a soldier of Rome and was in charge of catching and persecuting runaway Christians. He was on his way to Damascus to catch the last of Jesus' followers, namely the twelve disciples, when he met the resurrected Jesus. He was so spiritually inspired that he was converted. Paul says that the origin of his gospels is the revelation of the resurrected Jesus. He also visited the spirit world three times. People who had not experienced the spirit world could not understand Paul. They persecuted him most severely, saying that he was too different from them.

How do True Parents assess the Apostle Paul? They assess him as an originally intellectual man, who was then transformed into a spiritual person and who attained the position where divinity and truth were in horizontal harmony. Usually intellectual people are said to be spiritually weak and incapable of carrying out revolutionary campaigns. It is said that the people who achieve great deeds in the religious world are not the intellectuals but rather those people who are simple and consistent and not at all capricious. Such people are spiritual people who think and act as they feel, regardless of how the world may see them. They do things because Heavenly Parent told them to do so. Paul, on the other hand, was a person who had both intellect and humanity and who later gained divinity as well.

> A person like Paul is also an intellectual person. However, after being struck once by the spiritual lightning from Heaven in Damascus, he was completely turned around. Because he had felt that there was an explosive path within him rather than the path of external research, he denied everything and followed that path. By so doing, he became the new standard-bearer of the Christian revolution. That is why a person who questions everything based only on logic cannot become a leader in the religious world of spiritualism. [25]

Based on Deuteronomy 21:23 in the Old Testament, the Apostle Paul, who had understood Jesus' death as "God's curse," came to realize after being struck by the spiritual lightning of Heaven that

Jesus had died most unjustly. That is why he boldly proclaimed, "None of the rulers of this age understood this; for if they had, they would not have crucified the Lord of glory" [1 Cor. 2:8]. The closer you get to the spirit world, the bolder you become. The Apostle Paul saw and experienced the third heaven in the spirit world three times, which motivated him to carry out his mission work untiringly for fourteen years. Heavenly tribal messiahs also need to undergo such experiences.

2) Works of the spirit world and the heavenly tribal messiah

There are families in Korea, Nepal and England that have fulfilled their mission as heavenly tribal messiahs. Their answer to the question of how they were able to successfully complete their mission as heavenly tribal messiahs was simple: "Heaven helped us do it. The spirit world cooperated with us to complete it." One family in Korea went to pay their respects at Paju Weonjeon together with the first, second and third generation members of their tribe, on the Day of Victory of Love, which is January 2, every year for 34 years without exception. Before they went out to meet and witness to others, they visited the Paju Weonjeon to report about their activities to the True Children and elder members who were laid there.

Another family in Nepal visited the burial ground of their ancestors for their heavenly tribal messiah activities, and the ancestors appeared in their dreams and showed them the path to follow in the future. A family in England made a round of their village every day to pray at the holy ground, and whenever they passed the graves of historic figures in the vicinity, they earnestly asked for those figures' cooperation before going about their work.

When you listen to the stories of people who have successfully completed their heavenly tribal messiah activities, you can see that they used various ways to move the spirit world. Before you start your work in a mobilization area, it is advisable to pay a visit to the important spirits in the area. You should find and visit the graves of righteous people of that area, as well as patriots, independence fighters, those who died unjustly, and even people who founded new religions if there are any. In addition to visiting such people, you should find and visit the graves of their ancestors, if there are any. When you meet a witnessing candidate, you also should visit the grave of his or her ancestors.

When you make spiritual visits in your area, you should take gifts most favored by spirits in the spirit world. What gift would the ancestors like the most? It is holy wine. You should visit the graves with the four Cheong Il Guk holy items created by True Parents. Consecrate the graves with holy salt and holy soil and perform the holy wine ceremony. And then explain the reason for coming to that area and ask for their cooperation so that your work can be successfully concluded. When you have witnessing candidates, request the cooperation of their ancestors in particular. By going through such a process, you can meet various people who live in that area.

One person in Korea says that he visits spirits in the area in the manner described above, and if anyone submits an application form to join and become a regular member of the Family Federation, he goes to the Paju Weonjeon and reports, "I was able to witness to this person, thanks to all of your help until now. Thank you for your hard work." And then he goes to the JeongShim Won prayer hall at the CheongPyeong Training Center and dedicates his spiritual child to Heavenly Father, because he has not forgotten that he was not the one who witnessed to that person, but that Heavenly Father mobilized the spirit world to "help him do it."

True Father analyzed that there are two kinds of people: spiritual people and intellectual people. You need to ask yourself, "Am I a spiritual person or an intellectual person?" to know yourself. He also said that you should not lean either way, and instead be able to stand at the center and regulate both the spiritual world and the intellectual world.

> Usually, a spiritually sensitive person can grow spiritually but not in terms of the truth. When one side of you is big and the other side is small, you cannot last. At a certain time, you will roll away and fall. And if you grow based on the truth but your spiritual side remains small, you will not last either. That is why you need to live a life of regulating them. We human beings must regulate the spirit world and the physical world. We need to become people who can stand at the center of the spirit world and the center of the world of truth and regulate them. [26]

True Mother also emphasizes the balance between spirit and

truth. "The Family Federation for World Peace and Unification must march forward with spirit and truth. Lights in the church buildings must be kept on 24 hours a day. You need to offer jeongseong until it becomes a place that not only the members but also everyone else will wish to enter when they see that light. The leaders should be the first to march forward with spirit and truth. I don't know how much you realize about the spirit world, but amazing miracles are taking place. As you can see, both the spiritual and physical worlds are trying to give you every chance. Therefore, you need to be willing to risk your lives with desperate determination." [27]

Section 3 Visits of True Love in the Heavenly Tribe

A heavenly tribal messiah starts out with the goal of perfecting Adam's family, which was the dream of Heavenly Parent in the original garden of Eden, and dedicating it to Heavenly Parent. To achieve that goal, the heavenly tribal messiah prioritizes educating and nurturing with true love the Cain-realm children, the children who become connected to him or her through the activities of home church, tribal messiah and hoondok family church. It is his or her mission to form with them a tribe of harmony, unity, peace and happiness centered on true love and to dedicate it to Heavenly Parent. Then Heavenly Parent receives that tribe with pleasure and comes to dwell there.

You need to unite the Cain and Abel children lost by Heavenly Parent, transform the area where that tribe dwells into the garden of Eden, and make it the original hometown. That dream can become a reality only after you find self-centered and greedy Cains and give them rebirth as your children and raise them until they reach maturity. Furthermore, you should transform them into Abel figures who can participate in the providence and dedicate them to Heavenly Parent. This stage can be explicated in relation to the attributes of true love, an other-and-I attitude, and the principle of Cain's restoration as follows.

1. Finding spiritual children based on creativity

Before a heavenly tribal messiah begins his or her work, there is something that needs to be done first: drawing up a plan for heavenly tribal messiah activities. You should draw up a blueprint containing such details as when you are going to start, when you are going to finish, and how you are going to carry out your work. This blueprint can be drawn up only by the heavenly tribal messiah. Though it is only a concept, you should have a blueprint before beginning your work. Starting out without a blueprint is similar to sailing without a compass. Your goal becomes clear only when you start out with precision.

1) Absolute faith, absolute love and absolute obedience

Heavenly Parent created something out of nothing. Similarly, the process of taking a person tainted by the secular world and giving him or her rebirth may be said to be the process of re-creation. In short, it refers to the process of conceiving a grown child in the spiritual womb and giving birth to him or her again.

At first, you need to go through the stage of absolute faith. Absolute faith refers to the heavenly tribal messiah absolutely believing in the blueprint that he or she has drawn up. You need to have complete faith in the fact that the blueprint you have drawn up most certainly will be realized. This means that you must declare your resolution to complete your mission. Once the blueprint is finalized, the heavenly tribal messiah must plow ahead, with that blueprint in the position of the absolute subject partner, and he or she must become its absolute object partner. The blueprint is merely a concept, but only when you believe in it can you take a firm hold of your impulsive mind and march forward toward your goal. We need to follow this method to resemble Heavenly Parent, for when He created heaven and earth, He created the world of things and the world of human beings centering on His blueprint.

The second is the stage of absolute love. The goal of absolute faith is to attain absolute love. ① In the first part of this stage, you must pray for your candidates with a heart united in oneness with that of Heavenly Parent, the absolute subject partner. At this point in time, you should make visits to the spirits in your area and offer jeongseong. ② You should search through local leaders to find John the Baptist figures. ③ You should hold a seminar and invite the people connected through John the Baptist figures and your own blood relatives, thus creating an atmosphere in which the Blessing ceremony can be held.

The third is the stage of absolute obedience. Absolute obedience refers to the heavenly tribal messiah giving and forgetting, giving and forgetting again, and repeating this process until the blueprint that he or she has absolute faith in and absolute love for is realized. The heavenly tribal messiah invests him- or herself and then forgets having done so, until the spiritual children whom he or she absolutely loves appear in real life. By so doing, you come to resemble the creative heart of Heavenly Parent, who invested Himself and forgot about it, with the standard of absolute faith, absolute love and absolute obedience, until Adam and Eve had appeared in their substantial form in accordance with His blueprint for creation. Therefore, the tribes that are re-created based on that standard should be nurtured to grow to maturity, to establish the standard of absolute faith, absolute love and absolute obedience to Heavenly Parent and the heavenly tribal messiah, and to cooperate with them.

2) Creativity from the viewpoint of the principle of Cain's restoration

The people whom the heavenly tribal messiah meets to organize his or her tribe are in the position of Cain. A characteristic of Cain is that he is self-centered. Cain likes people who are nice to him. True Parents said that the first thing a heavenly tribal messiah should do upon returning to his or her hometown is to hold a feast. [28] They said that you should slaughter a cow and hold a big feast in the village, and that Satan will not be able to drag away those who have prayed and eaten the beef. [29]

When you meet Cain, you should acknowledge his position and praise him and treat him well for safeguarding your hometown in your stead. In addition, "You should carry out cultural activities. For instance, if you plan a screening of a good movie based on the Principle for the Cain-realm parents in your hometown, it will move their hearts and they will say, 'Oh, we didn't know about that.'" [30] When you meet Cain, rather than trying to convey the Word to him right away, you should have an understanding of the things he likes and try to speak to him of the Word based on them.

You need to go through a process of always taking an interest in Cain with a heart of prayer, thinking from his point of view, and understanding things from his standpoint. In witnessing, "Jeongseong is 40 percent, the Word is 30 percent, and taking action is 30 percent." The heavenly tribal messiah is not witnessing alone; he or she should start out by working together with the spirit world and demonstrating creativity and offering jeongseong to give birth to a new child. A person who has never given birth to a child does not know how difficult it is. Similarly, a person who has never witnessed to others does not know how difficult witnessing is. In the same vein, a person who has never experienced the great joy of giving birth to a child does not know anything about it. Similarly, a person who has never witnessed to others can never know how rewarding it is to create a child of Heavenly Parent through witnessing. That is why, though a woman who has given birth knows about the pain of delivery, she prepares herself to have another child because she also knows of the joy brought about by the birth of her child. The same is true for witnessing. The process of giving birth to and raising witnessing candidates involves a lot of pain and a lot of investment. Without going through that process, they cannot be made into Abel-realm children. However, no matter how great the suffering involved may be, when a child grows to become a central figure in the providence, his or her spiritual parents will shed tears of joy.

How did families that successfully completed their heavenly tribal messiah mission manage new people until they submitted application forms to join the Church? The families' answer to this question was simple:

> When I witnessed to young college students, I brought them home and cooked for them, because I know how hungry they can get. Young people like to eat, and at their age they eat and eat and eat, so I invited them to my home and cooked delicious things for them and served them peeled fruits and even bought them ice cream. It always felt like a feast. I didn't buy them meals in restaurants; I cooked feasts at home.

> And I also engaged in cultural activities with them, like watching movies, playing billiards, going bowling and even going to karaoke, to spend a lot of time with them. At first, I did not make them listen to the Divine Principle for a long time. Instead, I dealt with those parts that were simpler and easier to understand. My focus was to first give them what they needed, rather than to

swamp them with the Divine Principle, and by so doing I tried to do things for them that their own parents could not do. As time went on, I grew closer to them and I felt that they were opening their hearts to me. That was when I started to implant the Divine Principle more deeply in them. And I also offered jeongseong while calling out each of their names, one by one.

2. Raising children as parents of true love

A heavenly tribal messiah has to do more than give birth to a baby. The heavenly tribal messiah must take responsibility for the baby he or she has had and raise it well as the child of Heaven. How long should you pay attention to raising that child? When a spiritual child you have witnessed has submitted the application form to join the Church, you must continue to take an interest in that child and nurture him or her until he or she receives the Blessing, has children and establishes the four-position foundation. This is because, once the child has established the four-position foundation, he or she will come to have a stable domestic life and grow even stronger in his or her faith.

1) Principled leadership in the restoration of Cain

A heavenly tribal messiah must educate the Cain children in addition to his or her own children. You must raise your spiritual children, the Cain children, with leadership and have them receive the Blessing. Even after they have received the Blessing, you must look after them until they give birth to their own children and form the four-position foundation. And when your spiritual children have formed the four-position foundation and become family messiahs, you need to also play the role of re-creating them and encouraging them to become heavenly tribal messiahs in their own right.

Heavenly tribal messiahs exercise leadership over their tribes with true love. The fundamental root of true love is creativity. Leadership awakens a person's potential based on creativity and enables him or her to do things. True Parents asked, "When there are several people present, who among them is Abel?" The person who lives for the sake of others based on creativity and serves them is the subject partner and Abel. The person who gives more than others in terms of quantity, quality and speed is Abel. That is also the essence of Heavenly Parent.

The leadership of the heavenly tribal messiah should enable Cain to find what he wants in a more concrete way, based on the standard desired by Heavenly Parent. You also must support Cain as he follows his path. Furthermore, you should be able to give him all that you have received with the price of Abel's blood, sweat and tears. In conclusion, the most important thing is for Cain to be able to accompany his spiritual parents on their path of heavenly tribal messiah. Later on, you can make Cain into an owner who can guide the way with leadership.

You cannot manage all tribe members by yourself. Therefore, you need to educate people who can come up from the Cain realm into the Abel realm as quickly as possible and make them experience managing small groups first. And you need to train them so that they can grow in stages. When they form the Abel realm with a sense of ownership, they should be able to shoulder the burdens of their spiritual parents together and grow by realizing the heart of the elder brother, the heart of the parents, the heart of True Parents and the heart of Heavenly Parent.

The leadership of the heavenly tribal messiah follows the principle of protecting and nurturing Cain to the end. [31] You must take responsibility for Cain's mistakes and protect him, nurture him and take care of him until he grows to be better than Abel. To be able to lead a tribal community, a heavenly tribal messiah needs to have financial power, persuasive power and diplomatic power. [32] This is because the heavenly tribal messiah must stand tall as the true parent, true teacher and true owner of Cain. However, even if you do not satisfy those conditions, you can get past them if you become the central figure of love. In the long run, you may need to train your own children and establish them as your representatives. At the same time, you also will need to find and establish Abel-type leaders from your tribe of spiritual children and nurture and educate them to take over from you and your children. You must continue to educate and take care of Cain until he rises to the same level as the heavenly tribal messiah. You need to raise Cain until he grows capable of doing your work of his own accord.

2) Creating an appealing culture

True Parents said that heavenly tribal messiahs should build temples and schools in their hometowns. They said that, as we now live in an age when the spirit world is cooperating with us, heavenly tribal messiahs should bring their hometowns under control and become their masters, building sanctums and altars in their villages where Heavenly Parent can come to dwell. They also said that temples should be built by the joint efforts of the entire clan, and that schools also should be built to leave behind textbooks that teach one to attend Heavenly Parent and love humanity. The people of Israel built sanctums even while walking through the wilderness. And in their homes, they also built altars where they could offer jeongseong. Heavenly tribal messiahs need to lay down the foundation on which Heaven can come to dwell and build sanctums in stages where all tribe members can offer jeongseong together. And as soon as it is possible to do so, it would be good to join forces and build a school where blessed children can be educated.

> You first need to build a church for Heavenly Parent, and then a school. You should build your house after that. Why should you do so? The second generation of Israelites restored Canaan. The second-generation members from all around the world are on our side. You need to create a foundation where the second generation can become even more loyal subjects and citizens than you, and make it become the foundation of the present and the

foundation of the future in front of Heaven. [33]

In physics, the output is smaller than the input, but in true love, the output is always greater than the input. True Parents assert that true love is never consumed. When a heavenly tribal messiah gives and forgets, and repeats this process again and again until he or she and Cain have achieved balance and equality, Cain one day will rise to the position of the heavenly tribal messiah. True Parents have lived their lives for this goal.

One family that had completed the heavenly tribal messiah mission was asked how they nurtured the people to whom they had witnessed. The answer was simple. "We created a delicious culture like *bibimbab* (rice mixed with assorted vegetables and meat)."

"A heavenly tribal messiah is the parent, teacher and steward of the Cain tribe, he or she must take responsibility and raise the Cain children well. When you start witnessing to people, you need to make an effort to cook for them and create a culture where they can harmonize with one another. You must implant the Divine Principle in them and make them carry True Parents' portrait in their wallet and show and teach them everything methodically. It is important to do your best to make your spiritual children feel happier now than they did before they knew of God's Will.

"Some of my spiritual children were persecuted by their families for attending the Unification Church. You buy clothes for those children, give them an allowance, feed them, and even let them sleep in your home, and thus raise them as their parents. When I showed such grace to young children, they repaid me when they were all grown up. Some of them even gave me an allowance when they graduated from college and got a job. I knew then that, in the world of true love, one never forgets what one receives and always remembers it. I came to realize that, in true love, the output is greater than the input.

"I also learned that, when you raise spiritual children and bless them, you still need to take care of them until they form the four-position foundation. When one of my spiritual children received the Blessing, I had him or her perform the three-day ceremony in my home. I prepared delicious food and everything needed for the three-day ceremony as the parent. You have no idea how joyful and wonderful it is to look upon your child as he or she greets you in the morning after the first night of the three-day ceremony. I felt in my heart that Heavenly Parent would have been just as happy as I was. In the case of Japanese daughters-in-law, I made them stay in my home for three months and had them learn Korean in a language institute and taught them how to act like a daughter-in-law before I sent them to live with their in-laws. When second-generation babies were born, I even named a few of them."

3. Give-and-take action of true love and the perfection of other-and-I thought

1) Relationships from the viewpoint of other-and-I thought

The heavenly tribal messiah must continue to take interest and maintain relationships with his or her spiritual children even after they have received the Blessing. After Cain and Abel have achieved balance and equality, instead of saying, "It is finished now," it is important for you to continue maintaining a relationship with Cain. By engaging in the give-and-take action of living for each other's sake with true love, you create even greater true love. By principle, when you engage in give-and-take action, that action takes place and multiplies and expands. Therefore, it is important not to stop at the tribal stage but to continue to maintain and nurture that relationship until you are able to go beyond the level of people and restore the nation.

The principle of give-and-take action is to give without expecting anything in return. And when you receive something, you give back, adding at least one percent more to what you have received, and you should be the first one to give more in terms of quantity, quality and speed, without expecting anything in return. However, it is not easy to get ahead in terms of the three aspects of quantity, quality and speed. Still, at least making an effort to get ahead in the three aspects is important.

Believing that your spiritual children will grow and reach the stage of balance and equality, you need to continue leading a life of giving first and forgetting it. When Cain children reach maturity and settle down, they will repay you one day. From then on, the relationship of give-and-take action begins to expand in every aspect. That connection centered on Heavenly Parent is maintained continuously. And once Heavenly Parent comes to dwell in that relationship, it will continue to grow in the aspects of quantity, quality and speed.

An other-and-I attitude refers to living with others and sharing true love with them centering on Heavenly Parent. To be able to do so, you need to satisfy the condition of being the first one to show consideration to others at all times. Love is interest and consideration. The heavenly tribal messiah should show consideration to his or her Cain children first, and the Cain children should show consideration to the Abel children first. You live together to satisfy one another's wants and help one another.

2) Continuous relationship

A relationship formed through other-and-I thought does not end in one generation. You will wish to form a relationship that is continued to the second generation, third generation, fourth generation and beyond. This is because Heavenly Parent is always at the center of a relationship centered on other-and-I thought. We learned a clear lesson from the relationship of Esau and Jacob. The providence of Heaven desires to restore the nation through the heavenly tribal messiah. Until the nation can be restored, the heavenly tribal messiah must walk the path of hyojeong (filial devotion) by continuously managing the tribe entrusted to him or her while waiting for the day when Heavenly Parent can make use of that tribe as He sees fit.

True Parents have a special interest in the education of blessed children. They say to the second-generation members, "You are pure water. You are heroes. You are the best since the onset of history. You are the elite troops. You are warriors." They also say that blessed children are in the realm of True Parents' direct dominion. They say, "I am happy because we have the second generation. I wish to boast of you to the world. When the second-generation members unite with True Parents, they can display explosive power. The elite troops must absolutely obey the commands of True Parents." They also say, "You are the best since the onset of history. Don't forget that the blessing and love of True Parents are with you at all times on whatever path you may be following in your effort to achieve your dream." [34]

The expectations True Parents have for blessed children defy imagination, since blessed children are the children born of Heaven's lineage. True Parents spoke of their heart when they looked at the second-generation members, "What words could I say to make you understand a heart like mine? Is there a child who can understand ten or twenty things when his or her parents speak of just one thing?" [35] Even today, they are hoping for blessed children to become warriors desired by Heaven, which is something that can be accomplished only through True Parents, pure love, studying and the Blessing. [36]

The core mission of the heavenly tribal messiah is to perfect Adam's family in the original garden of Eden and dedicate it to Heavenly Parent. To perfect Adam's family, you create the Cain tribe, nurture it with leadership of love until its members form their own families, then you take responsibility for their second generation by protecting and fostering their children. Once you have fulfilled your mission, you achieve balance and equality with the Cain tribe, engage in give-and-take action with them and continue to live in such a way.

What, then, will be the result? Heavenly Parent will come and make use of the foundations of such tribes to advance the providence of the next stage. When a heavenly tribal messiah completely restores his or her tribe and dedicates it to Heavenly Parent, his efforts allows God to partake and that advances the providence of restoring the people, restoring the nation and restoring the world based on the foundation of that tribe.

The ultimate destination of other-and-I living is for the Cain tribe and Abel tribe to achieve harmony and unity and live together under Heavenly Parent. This refers to Heavenly Parent's coming to dwell in the place where people gather and engaging in give-and-take action with that tribe and becoming one with it. [37] Unity signifies becoming one centering on Heavenly Parent, the subject being of true love. At such a place, Heavenly Parent will directly govern over us with true love.

When the heavenly tribal messiah community is perfected, Heavenly Parent will come to that place and form a relationship with it directly, "face to face," and settle down. Then the heavenly tribes will enter the age when they live together with Heavenly Parent in their everyday lives.

2) Expansion of unity from the viewpoint of other-and-I thought

When heavenly tribal messiahs fulfill their missions in their respective bases, Heaven collects all their energies and uses them in restoring the nation. Esau and Jacob were unable to go beyond their relationship as brothers. Though Jacob achieved the restoration of Cain and the realm of brothers, he was unable to take responsibility for his clan. Jacob should have fulfilled the responsibility of taking care of, protecting and nurturing the Cain clan to the end. He also should have played the role of true parent, true teacher and true owner to the Cain clans. If Jacob had done so, Heaven would have been able to restore the national realm. However, because Jacob failed to fulfill his responsibility, the providence was prolonged for an unimaginably long time.

When twelve tribes that have completed the heavenly tribal messiah mission emerge, a people can be organized and a nation can be restored. Then the range of unity can be expanded from the nation to the world.

> Our path has been decided. There is only one path for us to follow. There is no other way. And there is only one destination for us. The smallest unit in which God can dwell is the nation. [38]

We need to restore the nation where Heavenly Parent can come and govern as He pleases. The core mission of the heavenly tribal messiah is to perfect Adam's family in the original garden of Eden and dedicate that family to Heavenly Parent. The perfection of Adam's family is achieved when you create the Cain tribe and take responsibility for it, and nurture it and bless its members until it grows to reach the stage where it can achieve balance and equality. You need to continue engaging in give-and-take action with the tribe members and enable them to live attending Heavenly Parent. By going through such a process, Adam's family that has won the recognition of the Cain realm and triumphed over it can be born.

Section 1 You Inherit Heaven's Creativity and Subjectivity

Today's heavenly tribal messiahs have come about after passing through the ages of home church, tribal messiah, hoondok family church and heavenly tribal messiah. You must fulfill your given mission, which is to achieve the restoration of the sibling realm (restoration of the authority of the eldest son) by uniting the Abel-realm tribe and the Cain-realm tribe. And when you accomplish the Blessing of 430 couples and win recognition as the parent of the tribe, you can return to the original garden of Eden as Adam's family and achieve perfection. Then what blessing did Heavenly Parent plan to give to perfected Adam's family? He planned for perfected Adam's family to resemble His creativity and thus come to have subjectivity over all created things. It was also His design to establish the status and authority by which they can stand in the position of His children and have dominion even over the angels.

> It was not only to prevent their Fall that God gave immature human beings the commandment. God also wanted them to enjoy dominion over the natural world—including the angels—by inheriting His creative nature. To inherit this creatorship, human beings should perfect themselves through their faith in the Word as their own portion of responsibility. God gave the commandment not to the archangel but only to human beings. God wished to exalt the dignity of human beings as bestowed by the principle of creation, which entitled them to stand as God's children and govern even the angels. [1]

1. You come to resemble Heavenly Parent's creativity

1) Harmonizing with Heavenly Parent's wishes, circumstances and heart

When you accomplish the heavenly tribal messiah mission, you become the object partner of Heavenly Parent's love and heart, moving into the same realm of heart as the perfected Adam and Eve. Thus Heavenly Parent's wishes, circumstances and heart naturally become yours and your daily life is connected to Heaven.

When a heavenly tribal messiah accomplishes the Blessing of 430 couples, it brings a feeling of freedom and liberation. The Bible says,

"Then you will know the truth, and the truth will set you free." In other words, it is possible to have freedom only when you know the truth and when you know the path you wish to go. This refers to living in accordance with the Principle to realize Heaven's dream. The human Fall came about because the first human beings did not live according to the Principle. Problems occur when things go against nature and do not function in accordance with the Principle. If Adam and Eve had followed their path according to the principle of creation, there would not have been any problems. If they had lived in accordance with the Principle, the original Adam's family would have earned the authority of parents and perfected the kingship and the ideal world under Heavenly Parent. They would have come to have creativity resembling that of Heavenly Parent, and they would have become fruitful, multiplied and had dominion over all things.

Then what does it mean for a heavenly tribal messiah to have creativity resembling that of Heavenly Parent? The *Exposition of the Divine Principle* says that it is to take part in His great work of creation. [2] That does not mean making things created by Heavenly Parent in the exact same way. It means adding your own creativity to what has been created by Him to create something new. First, it refers to multiplying human beings who resemble Heavenly Parent infinitely. However, problems arose due to the Fall of humankind. From the viewpoint of the heavenly tribal messiah, citizens of Heaven must be created infinitely. You need to re-create fallen humanity, together with the Messiah, Savior and True Parents, and make them return to the position of the original children of Heavenly Parent. You also need to awaken others' potential and satisfy their needs to help them perfect their characteristics as individual embodiments of truth. All human beings have unique characteristics, which make them individual embodiments of truth. Stimulating and developing each person's unique individuality to perfect his or her own unique characteristics is accomplished by using creativity.

Second, how are we to understand creativity in regard to the creation? Human beings who participate in Heavenly Parent's great work of creation must love and protect the third object partner, the created things, and preserve and develop the environment provided for them by Heavenly Parent. The heavenly tribal messiah must make use of the natural advantages of the environment given by Heaven to help the heavenly tribal messiah community grow, develop and engage in interactions. When the human mind becomes enlightened, all things will find their way to their true masters. We are now living in such an age.

2) The joy of becoming parents by re-creating a heavenly tribe

Parents voluntarily develop a sense of responsibility that springs from their original nature, which leads them to take care of their family. This sense of responsibility naturally springs from the base of infinite love. Similarly, heavenly tribal messiahs come to have a voluntary sense of responsibility when they embrace the members of their tribe as their children. They feel a sincere hope that all their tribe members will be embraced in Heavenly Parent's bosom, so that their whole tribe can deeply feel the connection of Parent and children with Heavenly Parent and be reborn as His mature children. Thus, heavenly tribal messiahs come to understand Heavenly Parent's wishes, circumstances and heart, and feel a sense of responsibility that seeks the same standard as that of Heavenly Parent. When you continue to live in such a way, one day you will discover that you possess a parental heart resembling Heavenly Parent's. There also will be people among the families of tribe members who step forward and take the lead to help the heavenly tribal messiah and become one in heart with him or her. Once they start accompanying you, they will come to understand the heart of the heavenly tribal messiah and will grow even more. Thus, they will become the eldest children of the tribe and go on to the next stage, which is to walk the path of heavenly tribal messiah themselves. Then they are reborn as children who understand Heavenly Parent's heart and circumstances.

It will never be an easy task to lead a tribe formed entirely of Cain children. From the moment you accomplish your mission, as a heavenly tribal messiah, of gathering and blessing your tribe, your spiritual responsibility will grow that much greater. You must live for the sake of your tribe with true love based on boundless creativity, and you need to go through the pain of spiritual delivery. Nevertheless, the more you help your children to grow, the greater your position as the parent will become.

2. Attaining the right of dominion over the angelic world

1) The way to exercise dominion over the world of angels, who are spiritual beings

Since the heavenly tribal messiah stands in the position of the perfected Adam's family, he or she is given the right to have dominion over the angelic world. Then how does the angelic world exist? The angelic world is at work both in the spirit world and on earth. Heavenly Parent created the angelic world before human beings. The role of angels was to help in Heavenly Parent's great work of creation. After creation, it was their role to protect and help the human beings Adam and Eve, created as Heavenly Parent's own children, until they reached the completion stage.

However, the archangel Lucifer, in charge of love, seduced human beings before they had reached maturity and caused their Fall. Originally, if Adam and Eve had not fallen and instead had become perfected, they would have had dominion over the angelic world by living for their sake with infinite true love, based on creativity. Angels reach perfection when, based on the results of the help they give to human beings, those human beings who were helped by them acknowledge their deeds and affirm their position in the angelic world. Therefore, when the heavenly tribal messiah returns to the original position of Adam and leads the tribe community, the angelic world should cooperate with him or her. And he or she should acknowledge their work so that the angels can enter Heaven's presence.

Subjectivity is achieved based on creativity. Creativity is exhibited when the subject partner, instead of trying to make use of the object partner, tries to satisfy his or her needs and help him or her to become perfected. That is why an object partner of absolute faith, absolute love and absolute obedience appears in front of the creativity of the absolute subject partner.

2) Restoration of the right of dominion through true love

To the heavenly tribal messiah, the angelic world can be said to include the Cain tribe. According to the traditions of the Family Federation for World Peace and Unification, you are told to witness to three persons and create a protective shield around you after you receive the Blessing and before you start your family. Those three spiritual children symbolize the three archangels. The three archangels who were under the dominion of Satan must be restored so that, when the spiritual parents become pregnant after starting a family, the three can set the condition of praying and offering devotions for the baby in the womb. By so doing, the siblings' realm (authority of the eldest son) can be restored in the spiritual parents' family from within the womb, through their unborn blessed children and the spiritual children of the Cain realm. Thus, this can right the positions of the three archangels created in the beginning. Originally, angels were entrusted with the task of looking after Adam and Eve, the children of Heavenly Parent. However, an archangel made the human ancestors Adam and Eve go astray and gained dominion over them instead. To restore this through indemnity, the archangel must be restored to his original role. The people in the world who are yet to join the Family Federation symbolize the Cain realm representing the angelic world. After that Cain realm joins us, when the spiritual parents' family belonging to Heaven's side conceives a baby, the Cain realm must unite with the conceived child, restoring the Cain realm's position and status through indemnity. Restoration through indemnity thus takes place, and the spiritual parents' family becomes a family that cannot be violated by Satan.

Then how much must the heavenly tribal messiah love the Cain family for Cain to reach the level at which he can love the Abel family of his own accord? You must set the condition of loving the Cain family more than the Abel family. It takes a long time for Cain to understand the Principle and reach the stage where he protects the Abel family, and during that time he needs to be moved by love and have deep experiences of heart. For him to reach that stage and act accordingly, he will need to continue his spiritual training and offer frequent jeongseong.

If the spiritual parents do not love their Cain children before their Abel children, the formula for restoration becomes complicated. Therefore, for a heavenly tribal messiah to complete the mission, he or she must first find and establish the condition of loving the Cain children more than his or her own children. Only when you establish that condition, will the Cain children step forward to help your own children and take part in raising them. When the Cain children grow to a certain level, they begin to feel your heart even before you speak. To help them reach that level, you should have them accompany you when you offer jeongseong or carry out your work, inspire them through hoondokhae and the Word, and touch their hearts by making them look upon the scene of your giving love to others, so that they will think to themselves, "This is a person whom Heaven cannot help but love," and be motivated by God Himself. When the heavenly tribal messiah wins the recognition of the Cain realm, he or she is established in the position of the absolute subject partner. Once you are established in the position of the absolute subject partner, your absolute object partner appears naturally. When all is said and done, everything becomes possible when the heavenly tribal messiah becomes the substantial embodiment of true love.

Then how should the heavenly tribal messiah lead those people in the Cain-realm tribe who are still in the process of being restored and who still assert themselves? There is only one way to have dominion over them. When you first establish three spiritual children of the Cain realm in the position of the absolute object partner, they will testify to their spiritual parents in front of the rest of the Cain children. You then should have them stand at the center of the Divine Principle education and make them the three core disciples who can become the leaders of education, traditions and activities. This is made possible when you become the substantial embodiment of true love with the right of dominion and establish the condition by which the Cain tribe can call you their "parents."

Having dominion through love over Cain who is living on earth is connected to having dominion over the spirit world. If you embrace 430 couples of the Cain realm with true love and receive the title of "parents" from them while you are on earth, when the time comes for you to go to heaven, a miracle will take place in which you will transcend the opposition and accusation of the angelic world, which stands in the position of the parents of the Cain realm. And the heavenly tribal messiah will attain the authority to exercise the right of dominion of love. In other words, you will be able to have dominion over the angelic world with true love rooted in creativity, even in the spirit world. When they were being seduced by the archangel prior to the Fall, the human ancestors Adam and Eve were able to hear both the voice of Heaven and the voices of angels simultaneously. At that time, Adam and Eve should have listened to the voice of Heavenly Parent and exercised discretion against the voice of the archangel. When the heavenly tribal messiah attains perfection, he or she will stand in a position with the power to exercise discretion when he or she hears both the voice of Heavenly Parent and the voice of the archangel simultaneously, and he or she will not set the condition of hearing or heeding the voices of the angels against the wishes of Heavenly Parent.

3. You attain dominion over all things as a true owner

1) Living in interdependence with all things

When the heavenly tribal messiah restores the Adam realm, he or she comes to have leadership centered on Heaven. To have dominion over all things with true love means to realize the principle of give-and-take action in which humankind loves all things and all things return beauty to humankind.

The Apostle Paul says that all things were under the rule of fallen humankind until now, and that all things have continued to hope for the true owners, the sons and daughters of Heavenly Parent, to appear and attain dominion over them. The things did not fall. Therefore, when the original human beings appear and give them love, they will dance with joy. How do you think all things, which have long waited for the true owner to appear, will react when a family that has completely fulfilled the mission of heavenly tribal messiah appears in front of them?

> For the creation was subjected to futility, not of its own will but by the will of him who subjected it in hope; because the creation itself will be set free from its bondage to decay and obtain the glorious liberty of the children of God. We know that the whole creation has been groaning in travail together until now; and not only the creation, but we ourselves, who have the first fruits of the Spirit, groan inwardly as we wait for adoption as sons, the redemption of our bodies. [Rom 8:20–23]

Then what are the conditions for taking complete dominion over all things? The first is to be established in the perfect position of Heavenly Parent's children. The second is to win the title of "true parents" from the Abel realm and the Cain realm. Therefore, fulfilling the heavenly tribal messiah mission refers to more than completing the numerical concept, that is, the Blessing of 430 couples. You need to win recognition from the Cain realm to the effect, "You are the true children of Heavenly Parent, and you are our true parents." And that takes place when you first find and establish the position where you are restored as the original Adam's family.

What does it mean to have good dominion over all things? In the principle of governing all things with love, the stage of learning what all things desire is important. All things are tools that can assist us in realizing Heavenly Parent's dream. The heavenly tribal messiah needs to realize that human beings and nature were designed to live in interdependence, centering on the purpose for which Heavenly Parent created all things. Our existence is acknowledged at the place where we invest ourselves for the sake of all things and forget having done so. Then it will be a pleasure for us to add our creativity to the foundation of Heavenly Parent's creation and help all things to fulfill their respective roles. The heavenly tribal messiah needs to live in such a way that he or she can work the miracle of helping all things to play the roles that give them joy. By going through such a process, the heavenly tribal messiah attains the right of ownership over all things. Then people who possess many things will appear from among his or her tribe members, and miracles will take place in which third parties appear and give large donations as offerings. Many such miracles took place in the early days of the church when True Parents were expanding their providential work. By undergoing such experiences again and again, the heavenly tribal messiah learns to find and expand the path that gives joy to all things. Then all things will find their way to the heavenly tribal messiah, by whatever route there is, whenever he or she needs them.

2) The material world is managed through true love

The heavenly tribal messiah is a blessed member whose original nature has been restored in a Cheon Il Guk family that can hear the voice of the original heart. Therefore, his or her original nature automatically will kick in whenever he or she deals with the material world. As we learn from the Korean saying, "To see is to desire," human beings desire to possess material things when they see them. Material things, however, cannot be taken into possession just because we wish to possess them. That is why a heavenly tribal messiah who has accomplished the mission should use material things in accordance with his or her original nature. That is a difficult thing to do unless we stand in a public position and not a self-centered one. When we manage material things according to our original nature, we will learn through experience that material things naturally will come to us when we need them and leave us when we don't. And when a heavenly tribal messiah, who is a person belonging to Heavenly Parent, needs something for public work, he or she will go through an experience in which things come to him or her in a reasonable manner in the exact amount required. A heavenly tribal messiah, who has been restored as a human being with original nature, plays the role of the medium that moves the things of the world to where they desire to go, and this is how he or she manages the material world through true love.

How did True Father, who came to earth as a human being with original nature, manage the material world? We know how he managed material concerns when he stayed in Busan for three-and-a-half years after he arrived in 1951. When he came to Busan from North Korea as a refugee, he had nothing. And when Rev. Kim Won-pil earned money with great difficulty by drawing portraits of U.S. soldiers and brought the money to him, True Father spent all that money for those in need, so he always felt apologetic toward Rev. Kim Won-pil. However, such days were repeated, not once or twice, but all the time. It was acts like these that ultimately paved the way to today's Cheon Jeong Gung.

True Father knew what the material world desired, and he was very good at achieving balance and equality with the material world and engaging in give-and-take action with it. Though he needed things too, he always sought out people who needed them more and shared them out. He knew that, in true love, the output is greater than the input, and he translated that knowledge into action. He remembered that even matter has eyes. He felt that matter lives and breathes, because it too is a living organism. Heavenly tribal messiahs are people who have restored the original family of Adam, and through their original nature they can hear the voices of material things saying what they desire. They are the people who have advanced to the position where they can hear those voices and carry out give-and-take action to bring those desires to reality.

Section 2 Receive the Wisdom of Heaven, by Which Creativity Is Manifested

What changes would take place in the relationship between a tribe and its tribal messiah who has gone through the ages of home church, tribal messiah, hoondok family church and heavenly tribal messiah and achieved results step by step until he or she was able to completely fulfill the Blessing of 430 couples? What changes would come about in a newly organized tribe when Heavenly Parent comes to dwell with it and governs it with love? What kind of awareness would families that belong to that tribe come to have? Let us expound on the process by which the wisdom of Heaven can be received, in the order of the sense of ownership, sense of responsibility, and creation of new culture, centering on testimonies of leading families that have completed the heavenly tribal messiah mission.

1. Your true sense of ownership for your tribe grows stronger

1) Joy received from the growth of the spirit self

"When I first started witnessing, I did not think much about forming a tribe. I began witnessing to give True Parents joy. I also thought that witnessing is a duty of blessed families. Heaven drove me to such a degree that I physically became ill if I did not go out to witness. The more I witnessed to others, the more interesting it became, so I continued to do it. Heaven guided me to witness to only unmarried, young college students aged 22. I met more than 1,000 people with the purpose of witnessing to them. Only about a tenth of them, about 120 people, received the Blessing as unmarried candidates.

By the time I was about to complete the mission of 430 couples as a heavenly tribal messiah, the second generation, the blessed children of my spiritual children, were receiving the Blessing and the third generation was being born. I guided my spiritual children who received the Blessing as unmarried candidates and also guided and educated their children, the second generation, from the time they were conceived, and now I have an enormous number of spiritual grandchildren. That awakened a strong sense of ownership within me, for I was no longer just a spiritual parent but a heavenly tribal messiah, and as such I needed to guide and protect my tribe for all eternity.

Even from before I completed the heavenly tribal messiah

mission, I nurtured the children with parental love, thinking to myself, 'Spiritual children are also my children, my descendants.' They also multiplied, for they too are my descendants. And so I raised my spiritual children based on the same standard as my own children. As I continued to nurture them with parental love, Heavenly Parent guided them to naturally expand into a tribe. I now have a strong belief that I must preserve, guide and develop this tribe that I have been allowed to form as the heavenly tribal messiah, on behalf of True Parents.

I think that the base of the heavenly tribal messiah is the foundation of the tribe to which Heavenly Parent, who makes us live a life in which witnessing is our main job and our own lives are only a side job, can come and dwell at any time. This tribal foundation is not the foundation of the heavenly tribal messiah but rather the foundation of Heavenly Parent and True Parents. When I accomplished the heavenly tribal messiah mission, I felt a strong sense of ownership well up within me to make this foundation of heaven into a safer, sounder and sturdier community, whose members can multiply most remarkably, and to protect and develop it. I naturally came to have this sense of ownership, which made me want to nurture my tribe to become more solid, so that Heavenly Parent can make use of our tribal foundation in advancing His greater providence. It was not a sense of ownership over a possession. When I say 'a sense of ownership,' I actually mean the mission that one naturally needs to fulfill as the true parent, true teacher and true owner of a tribe as granted by Heavenly Parent."

2) Multiplication of spiritual children and automatic spiritual works

"In the *Exposition of the Divine Principle*, the spiritual energy that Heavenly Parent gives to human beings is called the life elements. The life elements supply the living spirit element to the physical body through the spirit self. When a heavenly tribal messiah practices true love in witnessing to a new person, he or she creates vitality elements and supplies them to the spirit self. Then the living spirit element and vitality elements engage in give-and-take action. [3] And the spirit self grows as a result. The more the spirit self grows, the greater joy a person feels. The more we practice true love, the more vitality elements we create and supply to the spirit self, and then we receive even more living spirit elements from the spirit self and our joy grows that much greater. I too felt that the more zealously I carried out the witnessing work of practicing true love, the greater my joy became. And because I received joy from witnessing, I witnessed to even more people and practiced love even more. As I continued to practice true love through witnessing, I could see that my spirit self also was growing gradually.

I think it is similar to when a mother gives birth to a baby. A mother suffers much every time she delivers a baby. However, only a little while after giving birth, she forgets about the pain of delivery and starts thinking about having another baby. Curiosity about what the next child will be like and expectations for him or her makes you forget the pain of giving birth, and you want to have another baby. I think the mother's desire to have another baby is also applicable in witnessing. When I witness to a person, I meet that person for about six months and give him or her true love repeatedly. However, after about six months, you get tired of giving the same love you gave at the beginning to the same person six months later.

So that naturally makes me want to go out and find someone else. It makes me want to find another person with a different character and dedicate him or her to Heavenly Parent. I believe this heart also comes from Heavenly Parent. As I continued to listen to the voice of this heart and act accordingly, the number of spiritual children continued to grow. In fact, they multiplied automatically. I know that Heaven makes us witness to others by giving us the heart that desires to witness. When the time was right, Heaven also gave me inspiration regarding where to find and witness to new people. All I needed to do was to follow those inspirations and act on them.

I asked myself what I should accomplish as a heavenly tribal messiah. The answer is to find ways by which I can make the phenomena sent from Heavenly Parent even more beautiful. Witnessing is also a work of art. I always thought to myself that I should not stop at the witnessing stage, but that I should create for Him a beautiful world of love that everyone can sympathize with. I think this, too, is the heart given by Heavenly Parent."

2. Your true sense of responsibility for your tribe grows stronger

1) The protective shield of the tribal realm for Heaven's children

"Blessed families are the families of Heaven. [4] Blessed children are Heaven's children. Blessed families are under the dominion of Heavenly Parent, not the dominion of Satan. In short, they are in the realm of the dominion of True Parents. How can Heavenly Parent's families permitted by Him be raised in the fallen environment without becoming contaminated? How can Heaven's children be protected in accordance with His expectations of them?

As a heavenly tribal messiah, I came to have a strong sense of responsibility that my tribe should take responsibility for, protect and nurture Heavenly Parent's families and children, because I am the representative entrusted with the role of true parents in the tribe. At present, Satan's environment is ruling the world. And we must never let Satan take the blessed families and blessed children entrusted to us by Heavenly Parent, no matter what. How pleased would He be if we can stand on His side and take responsibility for and protect them?

When you witness to a fallen person and take responsibility and live for his or her sake through true love, Satan is naturally banished and you can bring that person over to Heaven's side. After accomplishing the heavenly tribal messiah mission, I am focusing on bringing second-generation members to the Blessing. That is why I feel that my sense of responsibility has grown that much stronger, for I need to do a good job of educating the second generation of my tribe, who should grow up to become future leaders.

This sense of responsibility stems from the sense of responsibility of being the true parents of the tribe who should continue investing true love into it, and not from a sense of ownership that makes me think that I own the tribe. I invest and then forget, and because I have no memory of the love I have invested, I invest again. I really feel a strong sense of responsibility for my tribe. I also feel a strong sense of leadership centered on true love. I will take responsibility for my tribe members till the end, and raise them as stainless, pure, clean and innocent children whom I can dedicate to Heavenly Parent through the Seonghwa Festival Blessing ceremony.

True Parents said, 'The one who lives more for the sake of the other is the subject partner,' and that we should live for others' sake and love them. I am only practicing their words. As I continue to practice True Parents' words, there are times when I am so happy that my heart overflows with tears. Whenever I look upon my spiritual children, who are growing up so beautifully, I think to myself that they are so admirable and wonderful. After I witnessed to my spiritual children, I did not leave them as orphans to be raised by others but instead personally raised them as their spiritual parent, and when I see that they have grown up well, received the Blessing, and are living so happily, I too cannot help but be happy."

2) The joy of nurturing Heaven's children and the tribal realm

"Among spiritual parents, there are some who give birth to their spiritual children but leave them as orphans to be raised by others. There are cases in which a person witnesses to someone but is unable to personally nurture him or her. There are other cases in which, after witnessing to a person, one is unable to take a greater interest in that person anymore. When I saw all that, it made me feel strongly that a person needs to have a thorough sense of responsibility to be able to raise his or her spiritual children as his or her own children and not orphans.

And so, in 2017 I remodeled a storehouse where I used to store agricultural equipment and dedicated it to Heaven as a Hyojeong Education Center, and since then I have been using it as an education center for second-generation members. I believe that this Hyojeong Education Center belongs to neither the heavenly tribal messiah nor the tribe, and that it belongs solely to Heavenly Parent. When we dedicated the center, blessed children collected money from their allowance to plant one tree each at the place, for it was where they and their younger siblings were going to be educated.

What will happen if we are able to educate and guide well the first, second and third generations of blessed families? I believe that if we can manage them well until the fourth and fifth generations, that foundation automatically will become the foundation on the level of a people. The problem is whether you are able to continuously provide education for the blessed children. When I witnessed to 120 unmarried people who later received the Blessing, and continued to guide and educate their children with true love, a tribe was naturally formed. I believe anyone can do so, as long as they realize it is not too late and they go out to witness to single men and women, one by one, and thus organize a tribe. I even had the idea that, if you are unable to finish that work in your lifetime, you can ask your descendants through your last words to carry on with it.

I think witnessing is a duty of blessed families, just as giving birth is the duty of the mother. I created my tribe by investing my entire life into it. Thus, I became the owner of re-creation in that tribe. I feel my sense of responsibility growing even stronger as the third creator. I believe that, if I guide well the second, third, fourth and fifth generations born in my tribe, creating a people will not be difficult."

3. Creating Heaven's culture as the owner of re-creation

1) The new wisdom of blessed children

"After each part of the creation was completed, Heavenly Parent exclaimed with joy and saw that it was good. When I looked upon the children of the tribe after accomplishing my heavenly tribal messiah mission with a sense of ownership as the true teacher of the tribe, I felt a little of what He must have felt then. I was so moved that I said to Heavenly Parent at the time, 'Heavenly Parent, thank You! Are

You happy to see them? Are they good enough for You?'

"I went to college campuses to meet young students and make them my spiritual children, then I raised them with true love and had them receive the Blessing, and they gave birth to blessed children who grew up in turn and received the Blessing as members of the second generation and gave birth to their own children and became parents. I watched over them all throughout that process. While doing so, there was one special thing that made me exclaim, 'Thank You!' to Heavenly Parent, without even realizing it. I discovered one amazing fact as I raised blessed children with true love and creativity and leadership I had inherited from Heaven.

It was that blessed children receive new wisdom from Heaven as they grow up, nourished by the true love they receive from their parents. Quite naturally in their everyday lives they receive creative wisdom that comes from Heaven. I discovered the amazing fact that, when Heavenly Parent sees parents and children united as one in love, He gives to those children the wisdom He gave to Solomon. I also discovered that the children received that wisdom and demonstrated new creativity.

In fact, those children received various kinds of wisdom from Heaven. I felt keenly that Heavenly Parent indeed creates each of us as individual embodiments of truth. When parents and children in a blessed family exchange love with one another, the children receive their own wisdom from Heaven. Based on the talents they are born with, they receive new, creative wisdom from Heaven and grow up well, and it is truly a joy and a happiness to watch them grow. I grow to appreciate the taste of Heavenly Parent's love with each passing day as I continue to create a new culture with those children on the tribal level.

We are creating on the tribal level a beautiful culture with the true sense of ownership and with creativity given to us from Heaven. The culture after Foundation Day is called the culture of heart centered on hyojeong (filial devotion), isn't it? I keenly felt that Heaven is making us create a new culture. And I also realized that hyojeong culture is a culture that has not existed until now, for it is a new culture begun from True Parents. Then I came to know naturally that hyojeong culture is rooted in the heavenly kingdom, not on earth."

2) Heaven's culture of heart and creation

"I think the wisdom that the children receive from Heaven is the wisdom from the spirit world. The culture begun from blessed children, who are pure and clean like clear water, is the culture begun from the spirit world. The calligraphic motto bestowed to the Universal Ballet with the words '*Ye Cheon Mi Ji*' (Heavenly Art Creating a World of Beauty!) also speaks of expressing art from Heaven on earth. I know that the best art that has been sent down from Heaven is performed at the Seonghwa Festival. And second- and third-generation children of the blessed families can sense all by themselves that the Seonghwa Festival is a new culture of Heaven that has never before existed in the fallen world until now.

To participate in the Seonghwa Festival held at CheongPyeong every year, in my tribe we hold our own Seonghwa Festival in advance. This has become a living education for my tribe members. This Seonghwa Festival on the tribal level is taking root as a new cultural event created by the joint efforts of first, second and third generation members of the blessed families in my tribe. I feel that we are growing and developing with each passing year.

"As we continue to make efforts to become the object partner of Heavenly Parent's love and heart on the tribal level, I can feel vaguely that Heavenly Parent has come to us to experience the explosion of love. I am experiencing a world of new culture that I was unable to feel during the earlier stages of accomplishing my heavenly tribal messiah mission.

I believe this phenomenon is taking place in my tribe because the culture of heart, the originally created culture, has revealed its true self to us, which is something that could not take place in the fallen world until now. True Mother explains to us that everything by which we practice Heavenly Parent's heart in our everyday lives is hyojeong. I understand that it means building a relationship of affection with Heavenly Parent through filial piety. When you build a relationship of affection with Heavenly Parent through love, you naturally will enter His heart. The culture in which the heart of Heavenly Parent and the hyojeong, the filial devotion, of humankind meet and dance with joy is the culture of filial devotion, and that culture is expressed through the Seonghwa Festival.

When I think that the Seonghwa Festival is a cultural festival in which the heart of Heavenly Parent and the hyojeong of blessed families meet after being separated for 6,000 years by biblical reckoning of time, the realization that this makes it a place where Heavenly Parent experiences an explosion of heart also makes my heart beat fast with excitement. And when you hold cultural events like that on the tribal level, your heart also will pulse with a different beat. I have come to know Seonghwa Festivals to be the celebrations that incorporate all ceremonies pertaining to the birth, marriage and death of blessed families.

I came to realize, as we held Seonghwa Festivals on the tribal level, that the culture the original human beings were supposed to create in the originally created garden of Eden, centering on Heavenly Parent, is none other than the culture of heart and the Seonghwa Festival. I am truly grateful to Heavenly Parent for allowing us to create that Heaven's culture on the tribal level. During our own Seonghwa Festival, I threw a "baby shower" for pregnant second-generation members, I held an engagement ceremony for second-generation members who were participating in the Blessing ceremony, and I also performed a Seonghwa Ceremony because one of our first-generation members passed away during that period. In this way, Heavenly Parent permitted us to experience the value of the Seonghwa Festival, to get a taste of what its atmosphere should be like.

While holding the Seonghwa Festival on the tribal level, I came to appreciate what True Father had meant when he said, 'You should perform your Seonghwa Ceremony while you are still alive!' [5]

From the moment I fulfilled my heavenly tribal messiah mission, I could see with my own eyes that a completely new age was unfolding before us. I am inexpressibly grateful for the fact that True Parents proclaimed this age to be the returning age. In his speech in which he proclaimed the Word as God's embodiment, True Father said, 'On March 16, we celebrated our 52nd year of marriage. On that occasion, I brought to a close the Era before the Coming of Heaven, which was marked by sin and indemnity, and proclaimed the Era after the Coming of Heaven, through which a new heaven and new earth will be realized by returning to true love.' I read those words thousands of times in hoondokhae and came to understand the Seonghwa Festival to be the greatest work of art bestowed on blessed families from Heaven, in this age of returning to true love."

Section 3 You Enter Heaven's Realm of the Royal Family

The ultimate conclusion of the heavenly tribal messiah mission is to enter Heaven's realm of the royal family. If Adam and Eve had not fallen, only members of the royal family of Heaven would have inhabited the planet Earth. Due to the Fall, it became impossible for Heaven's royal family to appear on this planet. When the royal family centered on True Parents is manifested, the age will come in which all humanity can enter the realm of the royal family. Human beings who were restored to original human beings will enter Heaven's realm of the royal family. In short, the greatest gift given to a person who has completed the heavenly tribal messiah mission is the permission to enter Heaven's realm of the royal family.

1. Ways to become a member of the royal family

1) Human beings were originally created as a royal family

If the human ancestors Adam and Eve had not fallen and instead had perfected the four great realms of heart and the three great kingships, Adam's family would have become Heavenly Parent's royal family right away. Adam and Eve were born as Heavenly Parent's children from the moment of their birth. Adam would have lived as the prince and Eve as the princess. They would have perfected the three great kingships and the four great realms of heart, and their children naturally would have gone on to become Heavenly Parent's royal family. Based on this logic, Adam and Eve would have become the first human ancestors as the prince and princess of Heavenly Parent, and all people born on earth would have been their direct descendants. Then all humanity would have been born as members of the royal family, and they would have lived as the royal family. Then, after their lives on earth drew to an end, they rightfully would have entered the kingdom of heaven and attended Heavenly Parent as they lived in eternal peace and happiness in the kingdom of heaven in heaven. We can go to the kingdom of heaven in heaven only after we have lived as the royal family on earth before passing into the spirit world. [6]

However, due to the Fall of the human ancestors, Heaven's royal family never came into existence, either on earth or in heaven. Heaven's royal family is different from other royal families that appeared in the course of history. A requisite of Heaven's royal family is, first, that they are born as original human beings. The second is that they need to perfect the three great kingships and the four great realms of heart. Whereas human beings before the Fall were born as Heaven's princes and princesses and all they needed to do was to perfect the three great kingships and the four great realms of heart, human beings after the Fall must first be restored as original human beings through the Blessing of True Parents. Only when we are reborn as original human beings, can we earn the right to enter the realm of the royal family.

That is why heavenly tribal messiahs are important. We need to receive the Blessing and form ideal families. However, our families cannot become ideal families and be perfected on their own. Our family is perfected when we perfect the world of our object partners. To put it another way, we need to love our tribe members with our own family as the central starting point of love, and thus walk the path by which we can win their recognition. First, the heavenly tribal messiah must be recognized by the Cain realm as the true parent, and second, the heavenly tribal messiah's own children must be recognized by the Cain realm as elder brothers and sisters. Only when that standard is firmly established, can our family win complete recognition from the Cain realm and, at the same time, can we be allowed to stand in the position of the original Adam. Then our family will settle down as the original ideal family. Therefore, the heavenly tribal messiah has to do more than secure the designated number of couples. We need to educate them and make them into citizens of heaven and help them form true families, so that they too can walk the path of the heavenly tribal messiah and become perfected.

2) The originally created human beings and I

Human beings born after the Fall are not born as the royal family. Therefore, they have neither the environment nor the right to perfect the three great kingships and the four great realms of heart. The heavenly tribal messiah is the person who can create that environment. To begin with, one needs to be born as an original human being through the Blessing and perfect the four great realms of heart centering on one's family. When three generations of that family follow that path, they can achieve the three great kingships. [7] Everything is concluded when that family follows the path by which it can reach perfection through the heavenly tribal messiah mission.

For fallen human beings to be born as originally created human beings, they need to receive True Parents' Blessing. By receiving the Blessing, they establish the principle through which they can be recognized by True Parents. And to restore our true selves as original human beings on that foundation, we need to rid ourselves of fallen nature. The core of fallen nature is self-centered greed. It also can be referred to as self-centered awareness (a mentality centered on one's own interests). To rid ourselves completely of this self-centered awareness, we need to practice true love. In giving love, however, we must establish the standard of loving someone else more than ourselves. That goes beyond what we ordinarily would do for other people in the world. To be able to sacrifice ourselves completely, we need to have the heart of parents. And it is only possible to have that parental heart when we have adopted the Cain realm as our children and given them rebirth and raised them as our own. Even fallen parents invest everything they have unsparingly for their children and treat them with love, for such is the culture of the relationship between parents and children. Therefore, the course of the heavenly tribal messiah is to walk the path of nurturing the Cain children from the position of the parent, thus winning recognition from those Cain children as their true parent.

Fallen human beings need to perfect the four great realms of heart through the Blessing and thus experience the heart of Heavenly Parent. And they also must perfect the three great kingships and win recognition as the originally created human beings in order to perfect the ideal family of Heavenly Parent. Then they can restore their tribes and enter the realm of the royal family. In the originally created world, everyone lives as the royal family.

> You thus form a direct relationship with the king, horizontally and vertically. The Divine Principle refers to this as the four great realms of heart and the three great kingships. Based on the principle that you cannot enter the kingdom of heaven unless you become a member of the royal family, in order to enter the kingdom of heaven, you need to become part of the royal family by establishing the position of the three great kingships, centering on

your grandfather, your father and yourself, and lead a life of inheriting that foundation on behalf of the royal family. The place you can enter after perfecting that and forming a family united in oneness centering on Heavenly Parent's love is the kingdom of heaven in heaven. [8]

To enter Heaven's realm of the royal family and live attending Heavenly Parent, we must be in resonance with and resemble the divine character of Heavenly Parent in order to live a life of complete harmony and assimilation with Him. A core part of the providence being carried out by the Family Federation now is the organization and management of a genealogy of blessed families by the CheonBo Won genealogy center, because it is directly relevant to the organization of the realm of the royal family.

2. The principle of restored human beings for the formation of the royal family

1) The original human being is born after seven vertical generations

People born as fallen human beings can join the realm of the royal family and live as citizens of the kingdom of heaven only after passing through seven vertical generations. In the case of blessed families, the original human being is born in the seventh generation of descendants. In other words, human beings of this age, who are the products of humankind that has lived in the fallen environment for 6,000 years by biblical reckoning, cannot be transformed into original human beings right away after receiving the Blessing. This is because the results of the Fall, such as original sin, hereditary sin, collective sin, individual sin and fallen nature, are continuously inherited to the descendants.

The Family Federation for World Peace and Unification teaches us that original sin was eradicated through the Blessing. Much of the hereditary sin has been purged through the CheongPyeong works. Collective sin will be eliminated when national restoration takes place. Individual sin (violation of others' hearts, failure to maintain lineage, embezzlement of public funds) must be eliminated individually. The problem is fallen nature. Fallen nature is self-centered awareness. Self-centered awareness includes Satan-centered awareness of others (transfer of responsibility), self-centered awareness of the self (judgments and decisions based on the self), personal awareness centered on personal purpose (prioritizing personal matters before public matters), and material awareness in which one always considers one's own interests first (not taking any action unless one's own interests are involved).

When can self-centered, fallen nature be completely eradicated? In a blessed family that practices faith in the ordinary way, original human beings can be born in the seventh generation of descendants. And it is only possible when all those seven generations practice their faith most earnestly, even to the point of putting their own lives at stake. That also means that the first generation, the ancestors of that family line, inevitably will end their lives on earth without being restored as original human beings. In short, the tribe finally can be properly registered only after seven generations, which also means that the ancestors must be registered after their descendants of the seventh generation.

> Family, all things, husband and wife, and the tribe. … It goes up to the tribe. The nation is not included. It is only up to the tribe. I declared that registration should be done after blessing the tribe for seven generations and dedicating it to God. Everyone in the tribe—the children, wives, husbands and parents—must be registered as people belonging to Heaven. Otherwise, there is no way for them to return to their original state. [9]

2) The key to securing the seven vertical generations with one horizontal generation

In faith, preparing well for the future is important. The purpose of faith is to make good preparations on earth, so that one does not have any problems when one goes to the spirit world, which is the eternal world. It is similar to a baby inside its mother's womb developing in preparation for its life on earth. People on earth, however, wish to receive some guarantee about the next world while they are still living on earth. This is more so for members of the Family Federation, who know only too well that they must establish the standard of perfection during their time on earth. The fact that an original human being can be born in a blessed family only after seven generations of descendants is very important. What, then, is my position as a first-generation blessed member living on earth? If I cannot be born as an original human being in my generation—because that will come about only after seven generations—what am I supposed to do? These are the questions you may be asking right now.

True Parents' answer to that question is, "There is a key to achieving perfection in one generation, depending on your portion of responsibility." This is the key by which even first-generation members of blessed families can be restored as original human beings while they are still living on earth. True Parents also taught us about the method quite clearly. They say that what we need to do is to fulfill our responsibility by connecting the seven horizontal generations representing seven vertical generations. Then members of a blessed family can be born as original human beings during their lifetime. What is this method, then? When seven vertical generations are expanded horizontally, they become relatives to the twelfth degree. In short, what a blessed family needs to do is to witness to relatives to the twelfth degree and have them receive the Blessing, and thus form a tribe during their lifetime.

> If not for the Fall, seven generations would have lived together, spanning 120 years. That is why tribal restoration involves seven generations. When you compute the degree of kinship in seven generations, it goes up to the twelfth degree. That is a principled

number. If you cannot achieve that, you cannot be registered and you cannot enter the kingdom of heaven. It is more important than the trinity. [10]

Centering on the three generations of your ancestors, you need to make a resolution that new grandparents, parents and grandchildren be born in your lineage. And you need to hold a resolution rally for your family, at which you first need to make resolutions as individuals and then all together as a family. After that comes the resolution of the clan. You need to have seven generations of relatives to the twelfth degree participate in it. Only then can you go on to the number thirteen, which connects to the ideal of family. This is all in accordance with the Divine Principle. Therefore, you must hold a Blessing ceremony on the tribal level. You must bless your own mothers, fathers and brothers, no matter what. [11]

Even in the case of blessed families that have been restored as original human beings, they absolutely need the protective fence formed by their tribe to be kept safe from the fallen environment as they endeavor to perfect their family. That is why the seven vertical generations of a blessed family were converted to seven horizontal generations and the number of 430 couples was determined. Even if you are the first generation of a blessed family, when you witness to 430 couples on earth and bless them, you can be born as a family that has restored the realm of heart of the original human being who originally would have been born after seven vertical generations.

We now entering the age of the realm of God's direct dominion. Ladies and gentlemen, the D-Day declared by Heaven is less than two years away. I hope you will bear in mind that we have entered the age of the realm of cosmic Sabbath, in which you need to make even your family members in the spirit world return to earth and attend the Original Divine Principle workshop, and in which eight generations of a family must live together in one home. Aju. [12]

Thus a family that has been horizontally expanded, both on earth and in the spirit world, lives together. These seven generations living together signify that a horizontally expanded tribe has formed one great family and is living together, both on earth and in heaven.

3. The realm of the royal family and the path of heavenly tribal messiahs

1) From seven vertical generations to one horizontal generation to the twelfth degree

A heavenly tribal messiah who has completed the Blessing of 430 couples by going through the process of home church, tribal messiah, hoondok family church and heavenly tribal messiah can win recognition for seven vertical generations in one horizontal generation. A clan with relatives to the twelfth degree was computed to be made up of 430 couples. Then it leads to the number thirteen. The number thirteen represents the number that Jesus could not restore because he was unable to become one with his twelve disciples. In other words, it is the number by which the hill of Jesus' bitter sorrow can be crossed, the bitter sorrow of failing to marry and instead being forced to bear the cross. Winning recognition for completing the heavenly tribal messiah mission by blessing 430 couples has the same value as winning recognition for being born as the original human being, which otherwise can come about only after seven generations.

The heavenly tribal messiah follows the path of perfection through the providence of restoration of recovering the authority of the elder son, the authority of the parents, the authority of the king, and the authority of the royal family, which were taken from Heavenly Parent by Satan through the Fall of Adam and Eve. While following that path, he or she also organizes the tribe of Heaven and thus participates in the process of re-creating its members as perfect human beings and perfect ideal families in front of Heaven. A heavenly tribal messiah who has participated in that process of re-creation inherits Heavenly Parent's great work of creation and becomes the owner of creativity. In short, he or she becomes the second creator, who is the true owner of the providence and who has done his or her part for the providence by laying the foundation of faith and the foundation of substance. Even if you may not understand all the wishes, circumstances and heart of Heaven, when you follow right away, with absolute faith, absolute love and absolute obedience, the instructions you receive, you will find that you have perfected your position as a heavenly tribal messiah without your knowing it. The functions of a messiah may be said to be that of salvation, being the true parent, connecting people to True Parents who were sent to earth as the Messiah of humanity, and establishing the parent-children relationship with Heavenly Parent. The one who carries out these functions in the tribal realm is the heavenly tribal messiah.

Heavenly Parent guided us, knowing what our destination was going to be from the time He used the term "tribal messiah." It was His blessing to us to allow us to restore the status of original human beings by completing the seven vertical generations in one horizontal generation. Heavenly Parent showed the way by which blessed families can be restored as original human beings, in the form of the gift called the heavenly tribal messiah mission. Heavenly Parent has guided blessed families to walk the path of heavenly tribal messiah with His fervent hope for them to enter the realm of the royal family and live together with Him.

As a heavenly tribal messiah continues to struggle to accomplish his or her given mission in accordance with the progress of the providence, he or she comes to discover that the concept of "self" gradually disappears and that vacant space is filled with Heavenly Parent and True Parents. In other words, he or she appears in this time and place in the form of the original human being, though originally it would have taken seven vertical generations. Heaven, therefore, can permit him or her the grace of joining the realm of the royal family.

2) The blessing of being included in the realm of the royal family

When a heavenly tribal messiah completes the mission of blessing 430 couples, he or she enters the realm of the royal family together with the tribe. The realm of the royal family refers to Heavenly Parent's own children. The fact that a heavenly tribal messiah has fulfilled the mission signifies that he or she has earned the right to enter the realm of the royal family. True Parents say that we should go to our hometown and become the ancestors of our tribe to teach them the way to enter the realm of the royal family. The term "hometown" also may refer to mobilization areas where tribes can be newly born. That is to say, they are the places where the environment of the garden of Eden before the Fall has been created and the tribes have been re-created and perfected. We have been told to become ancestors who can bring Satan to voluntary submission at that place and move Heavenly Parent to tears. In fact, we need to make Heavenly Parent say to us, "Thank you!" with tear-filled eyes. [13] Furthermore, True Parents gave us a blessing, saying that we should become the parent, teacher and owner of our tribe.

The royal family of Heaven, which has never existed in the fallen world, begins from True Parents' family. If Adam and Eve had not fallen, they would have become the royal family of Heaven and the first ancestors. All people on earth would have been their direct descendants. All human beings would have become members of the royal family and formed one family of humanity centered on Heavenly Parent.

Then how can all humanity join that royal family? The first way is based on the fact that the royal family originates from a clan. And the only way to join that clan is by marriage. The second way is to enter the realm of the royal family as stated in the third verse of the Family Pledge. Even if we are not born as a member of the royal family or married to one, there is a way for us to enter the realm of the royal family. This is because the realm of the royal family includes all blessed families. Though we need to be of direct descent from True Parents or married to one of their direct descendants to be a part of the royal family, the gates to the realm of the royal family are open to all blessed families. All blessed families that fulfill their responsibility of blessing 430 couples as heavenly tribal messiahs can enter the realm of the royal family. This can be interpreted to mean two things.

One is that, when we witness to 430 couples and attain the authority of parents, the fallen nature that remains in us is eliminated completely and we can be said to have been re-created as an original human being. It means that, through our own efforts, we have rid ourselves of fallen nature in one generation when it is supposed to take seven vertical generations. Because we have continued to live as the parent of our tribe members, we have been in accord with True Parents' heart and our life has been in accord with Heavenly Parent's characteristics, and we thus have been transformed. Above all else, this becomes evident when our own tribe members recognize us as their true parent. Once we set that standard, it is also acknowledged that our mind and body are united as one. With that medal pinned to our chest and armed with the testimonies of those who have attested to us, we can enter the realm of the royal family together with our tribe.

The other is that we have formed our own tribe and attended Heavenly Parent through our own efforts. The tribe we have organized is our foundation of substance, no matter what anyone might say. There is no freedom without results, and no one can take those results away from us. Those results are proven by the fact that the foundation has been laid on which Heaven can go beyond the family level and work as He pleases on the tribal level.

We will come to know about the heart of True Parents, who wish to embrace all 7.5 billion people in the world, down to the last person, within the realm of the royal family. The heavenly tribal messiah activities must be expanded beyond the level of tribe to the level of people, then to the level of nation, and then to the level of world, so that the providence of Heaven can be carried out automatically.

Section 1 The Perfection of Parentism by the Heavenly Tribal Messiah

1. Everyone wants true love [1]

What is most important and necessary to a human being? It is not money, power or knowledge. It is love. When all is said and done, human beings do things hoping they will result in love, so everything they do is for love. Then how is love generated?

First, love can be generated only when there is an object partner. If love were something that we could generate alone, this world would not have been created as a world of relational beings. And Heavenly Parent would have had no need to create the world of human beings or things.

Second, love is generated when we accommodate our object partner. The action of love takes place when we know about our object partner's needs and wants and accommodate them. The problem is that, when we try to make our object partner accommodate us, a fight will break out instead. Only when we accommodate our object partner first will he or she instinctively feel our love and try to accommodate us in turn. Therefore, the principle of the action of love is such that we need to walk the path of endeavoring to accommodate our object partner. Our object partner will accommodate us when he or she is moved by love to do so. Hence, the subject partner must make sacrifices until both the subject partner and object partner can accommodate each other and the action of love can take place.

Third, the size of love is not limited. The original heart of human beings aims to expand their world and the world of love infinitely, because it resembles Heavenly Parent's creativity. The only difference is whether that direction is centered on goodness or on individualistic egoism. Therefore, to generate true love, the heart that desires to live for each other's sake should be put into operation.

Fourth, love does not begin on the premise that the subject partner will receive something in return; instead, it grows when he or she gives something to the object partner and sees the joy it brings. Therefore, a trait of true love is to give and forget. When the subject partner sees the object partner's joy in return for the sacrifice he or she has made, he or she progresses to the stage of true love of giving and forgetting, and giving and forgetting again.

Fifth, the results of love lie in the object partner's growth and happiness. Depending on how much the object partner has grown, the subject partner also becomes pleased and happy. And when the object partner returns beauty, through it the subject partner finds the meaning of all that he or she has invested. Therefore, in true love we walk the path of receiving joy from enabling our object partner to reach perfection, for then we too can become one who perfects love.

Sixth, love is generated when we see our object partner with the eyes of a parent. If an older and more knowledgeable person we don't like and have trouble forming a relationship with has committed a mistake, we still can pity that person when we look upon him or her with a parental heart. Then we will be able to embrace him or her with love.

Seventh, sincere true love travels through the shortest route, opens hearts and achieves unity. True love makes us understand our object partner right away by sharing the truth, it opens our heart, and it has the power to unite us with him or her. Therefore, it is the original heart centered on the conscience that lets us be moved by true love, which is generated through transparency.

As can be seen, everyone likes and desires love, but they live their lives without knowing how to satisfy that love evenly. Moreover, the right way to begin love is by giving for the sake of our object partner, but the greed of the human Fall, which desires to begin by receiving, prevented true love from beginning at all. Human beings feel joy when the purpose and results of their lives appear as love. This principle of true love may be said to be the motivation behind Heavenly Parent's creation of human beings, as well as the motivating power that enables Him to carry out the providence of salvation.

Love originally was begun from Heavenly Parent. That is why when we examine all the beings in the universe, we find that they all exist in pairs. Love is something we never can receive by ourselves; in contrast, when an object partner appears, everything can be connected through love and be included in it.

The life principles of heavenly tribal messiahs begin from Heavenly Parent's ideal of creation. The original human world is trying to return to the original state and principles, by which it can resemble Heavenly Parent and engage in give-and-take action with Him. Similar to how Heavenly Parent invested Himself for human beings and forgot and felt happiness from doing so, the parental love that is generated within our family comes to have significant meaning. This is because the origin of all kinds of love is parental love. Human beings who grow up receiving that parental love expand its range as vertical and horizontal love, that is, the love of children, the love of siblings, the love of husband and wife, and the love of parents.

Accordingly, heavenly tribal messiahs must perfect the four great realms of love and make them appear as the love of their tribe communities. Families of the tribes must be educated and trained to attend Heavenly Parent at their center and perfect the four great realms of love. Furthermore, all tribe members need to attend the heavenly tribal messiah as one family, and thus make their tribe into an expanded family community. Then it will become the heavenly tribal messiah's small nation that was formed through true love under Heavenly Parent.

The owner of love is the object partner. When we pave the path that gives joy to our object partner, love grows and expands. Therefore, we need to treasure our object partner and live for his or her sake with parental love that resembles the love of Heavenly Parent. This is the basic value that a heavenly tribal messiah couple should attain.

Moreover, the principle for the perfection of true love is such that, though at first it begins with a perpendicular relationship of love directed from the subject partner to the object partner, the result of that perfection appears in the form of vertical love directed from the object partner to the subject partner. When the perpendicular relationship of true love continues to rise in level vertically, in the end it reaches the top that is the position of Heavenly Parent, the "King of true love." In that position, everything is united, embraced, harmonized and brought to fruition. That is why all beings in the universe desire to live in true love. In life, we are born for love, we live for love, and we die for love.

Not only people but also all things desire true love. Human beings, therefore, should love all things, and they also have the responsibility to love all things, for they are the lords of creation. All things are looking for such an owner. All beings exist in their position together with their object partners, but they all wish to follow the principle of being absorbed into the higher level of love and thus become elevated. In other words, minerals desire to be absorbed and assimilated by plants, plants by animals, animals by people, and people by Heavenly Parent. By thus rising to higher levels of love, one can ultimately rise to the position where one can receive the love of Heavenly Parent, who is the origin of love. In short, the ultimate destination of all beings is the position of true love.

Among those beings, the most precious being of all is humankind. This is because we were created as the object partners of Heavenly Parent. True love is not a term that anyone can use, for it appears only in conjunction with the structure by which Heavenly Parent's creativity is manifested in accordance with His principle of true love. His ideal of creation follows the principle by which one becomes perfected by enabling one's object partner to reach perfection. We need to know that, though everyone desires true love, it can be generated only when one lives for the sake of one's object partner. Only by living for each other's sake can action take place, results be achieved, and the generation of love be continued. Another principle of love is that it is expanded by the object partner, depending on how much love the object partner has received. By nature, an object partner desires to belong to the subject partner, depending on how much the heart of that object partner has been moved by the love received from that subject partner. That is why humanity desires to belong to True Parents, who have invested all their love unsparingly for the salvation of humankind, and why humanity also tries to return to Heavenly Parent, the original Parent. In contrast, egoism and Satan's stratagems lurk at the place where people tell others to live for their own sake first, rather than giving love first. Satan disguises himself with false love, but the result is that he only uses human beings as his tools. And false love only works once, for it is all used up after one use.

2. The place where true love settles down

Heavenly Parent can be found at every stage of human beings' growth. He looks upon them and invests Himself and feels joy, because human beings, who are His object partners of love, are the greatest beings that perfect His love. It is similar to how, when a being you love appears in front of you, you treasure that being millions of times more than yourself and try to approach that being with love.

Heavenly Parent invests Himself, then forgets, then invests again and forgets for the sake of the one who is more precious than Him. In fact, if a child becomes perfected and stands in a distinguished position, his or her parents will think that they won't mind working as servants under their child. That is what happiness is. In this way, the essence of true love makes us erase ourselves. The perfection of our object partner equals our own perfection. When we give and forget and repeat this process over and over again to rise to a higher level of love, in the end we will be connected to the position of Heavenly Parent, who created that principle and the structure of true love. That is the very structure of the world where everyone lives for the sake of others, as has been desired by Heavenly Parent and all humanity around the world since the beginning of time.

Heavenly Parent, the origin of true love, created us human beings as His sons and daughters. Children are the fruit of love, born of the combination of their parents' love, life and lineage. If Adam and Eve had not fallen, they would have received the education of true parents and become the model of true conjugal love. Humanity would have resembled that model and received the education of love. Moreover, their children would have been married to their spouses by their parents. We need to think about how large a role parents in today's society play in their children's weddings. Since the Fall was nothing but a wrong wedding performed in the garden of Eden, now the True Parents must marry their children in the right way and thus rightly establish the institution of marriage once again. Through True Parents, the original true love, true life and true lineage centered on true love should be recovered so that the true parent-children relationship can be restored. Similarly, the position of heavenly tribal messiah signifies returning to the position of the original Adam's family. That is why heavenly tribal messiahs are entrusted with the authority to personally marry and bless not only their own Abel children but also their Cain children.

As a result, the owner of the model of true love in the eight stages, which is Heavenly Parent's ideal of creation, is perfected. By passing through the age in the womb, babyhood, age of siblings, adolescence (age of engagement), age of husband and wife, age of parents, age of true grandparents and age of true king and queen, the traditions of eternally unchanging true love are established. In short, the model of true love of the parent–child relationship is perfected. Heavenly Parent's love, life and lineage are inherited as the model centered on true love, which is absolute, unique, unchanging and eternal for generations to come. That is the place where true love settles down.

3. Experiencing the love of Heavenly Parent [2]

The perfection of true love signifies the perfection of the kingdom of heaven on earth and in heaven. Earth is the world where we experience and create love, and heaven is the world where we feel and live with perfected love. If human beings had not fallen, they would have lived in communication with the incorporeal Heavenly Parent. In other words, the incorporeal Heavenly Parent would have entered the body of human beings and experienced human love by giving and receiving it in substantial form. At the same time, human beings would have entered the world in Heavenly Parent's incorporeal space and experienced it, and thus prepared themselves for the world after earth. With the corporeal and incorporeal worlds united in such a manner, Heavenly Parent and human beings would have traveled to and from the two worlds and experienced life in the kingdom of heaven, where heaven and earth are united in harmony.

True love refers to Heavenly Parent's love, and Heavenly Parent is love itself. The spirit world is a world where we live, seeing the color of true love and tasting the taste of true love. When we harmonize with that true love, we can even feel the feelings of the universe. Though this may be difficult to believe, not only the human world but also the invisible microscopic world lives by forming relationships with the entire universe.

Though Heavenly Parent is love itself, how can we know this incorporeal Heavenly Parent whom we cannot see? Though we cannot see Him with our eyes, we can come in contact with Him. We can feel Him if we are in a relationship with Him and connected to Him. Though the body is visible, the mind is invisible. However, the world of the mind connected to the body can be seen and felt. This is also the case in knowing Heavenly Parent. We can feel Him when we have prepared the environmental conditions through which we can form a relationship with Him within our living environment.

4. The results of jeongseong and love [3]

When we offer jeongseong, we should have the heart that we are doing so as a representative of humanity and on behalf of Heavenly Parent. After living on earth, we pass on to the next world and meet Heavenly Parent. At that time, it would be a problem if we went there without knowing the heart of Heavenly Parent, who devoted Himself for the world to carry out the work of the providence of restoration. We need to set a condition that proves that we received the Blessing of Heavenly Parent and fulfilled our duties as His children. To do so, we must go through the process of standing in the position of Heavenly Parent and True Parents and experiencing their hearts. That is why we need to do something that proves that we have offered jeongseong and stood the test in experiencing the heart of True Parents and Heavenly Parent for the salvation of humankind. That is the reason why we need to become heavenly tribal messiahs.

While leading their tribes, heavenly tribal messiahs go through many difficulties in their position and experience many hardships from their Cain children. If, at such times, we endure those difficulties only as our own sufferings, Heavenly Parent cannot come and be with us. When we are in a difficult position, we need to connect to the heart of Heavenly Parent and True Parents, who have endeavored to find us. Then when the heart we experienced is connected to the heart of Heavenly Parent, our position as the parent can be recognized by our tribe members. Thus, we become the work companion and consoler of Heavenly Parent, who wishes for the kingdom of heaven on earth and in heaven.

When it rains, one or two drops of water flowing down the ravines are as nothing, but they come together as they flow down and become a stream of water, which then is connected to the great ocean. The water that comes from the mountains flows into the sea, then evaporates to become vapor and returns to the mountains, and the realm of liberation is brought about through this cycle. Though it sounds like a simple concept, wouldn't it be a very difficult process in reality? Only when we connect the stream of love through endless prayers and jeongseong can we be connected as original descendants and not fallen descendants.

An unprepared person will drift away. An unprepared person cannot become the heir. We can win the recognition of our tribe members only when we offer jeongseong again and again, endeavor to live for the sake of others again and again, and try to love others again and again. On the path where we have won our tribe's recognition, Heaven will show us compassion. From then on, we will be given the authority of parents and Heavenly Parent will start to be involved with us in earnest. Miracles will take place when we win the recognition of the Cain realm and Satan loses the right to accuse us. Therefore, we need to establish the standard by which the Cain realm can become our object partner and we can engage in a fulfilling give-and-take action with those in the Cain realm of our tribe.

The way to rid yourself of the Fall is to perfect your object partner, thereby perfecting yourself. You need to perfect the path where you can bless those in the Cain realm, move their hearts through love, and thus be recognized by them as true parents. When you stand on that standard, you can inherit the original realm of Adam and attain the kingship of your tribe. Then you can finally reach Heavenly Parent's realm of the royal family and become His own children. Thus, you will ultimately become original human parents who live as representatives of Heavenly Parent.

We are now in the age of great, historic transition. It is the age of transition when the earth, from its starting point to its final edge, is completely overturned. The original recovery is the last path by which this side can return to that side and fill the original position. Since the people who had lived in the world of darkness until now have followed True Parents to the side of light and achieved the realm of liberation, they have attained the form with which they can return to the natural flow of things. When we make all the preparations to connect to Heaven, our clan will inherit that prepared connection to Heaven. That is why we have been told to pray and love and offer jeongseong.

Moreover, we cannot complain on this path. When we say things like "Oh, I'm so exhausted! True Parents don't appreciate me," hoping that others will appreciate how much jeongseong we have offered, we will block the way to greater miracles. Even if others do not appreciate us, we need to let the flow of the works unfold automatically. Similar to flowing water, we will meet it when we reach a certain stage. Water flows, and so does air. As they flow, water and air fill empty spaces without exception. Similarly, when the time comes, the flow will fill even the crevices of the sufferings endured by heavenly tribal messiahs with love.

We need to know. How deep would the crevice of bitter sorrow be in the center of Heavenly Parent's heart? In terms of air, how often would He have fluctuated between low pressure and high pressure? He is covered with the traces of His desperation and anguish for human salvation. Then what can fill those wide and deep crevices? It is the love He will receive when He welcomes back human beings who have been returned to their original state. When the restored Adam and Eve become true parents and flow into the heart of Heavenly Parent with a heart of love, the crevices of His bitter sorrows and sufferings will be filled. That is the greatest jeongseong and love that heavenly tribal messiahs can offer Him to fulfill their duties as His children. There is nothing more blessed and joyful than that. When that time comes, Heaven will appreciate the value of people who have made efforts. The people who prioritize filling the crevices of wounds on their parents will go through an experience in which their own crevices of wounds are filled through the automatic flow of the works.

That is why heavenly tribal messiahs must walk the path of loyal citizens, which is on a level higher than that of filial children. Loyal citizens are the people who love and offer jeongseong for the entire nation. Saints are the people who love and offer jeongseong centering on the world rather than the nation. And holy sons and daughters are the people who love and offer jeongseong centering on heaven and earth.

Such has been the life of True Parents. Though a wretched and difficult one, it was a path that Heavenly Parent had no choice but to follow. True Parents led a life based on the resolution to follow in the footsteps of Heavenly Parent, who was walking a path of suffering and anguish, and to comfort Heavenly Parent. They stood in a position of even greater suffering than the suffering of their subject partner. That is where wails of lamentation break out. In the rest of the world, people usually stand in the position of the object partner and look to their subject partner, but the path of True Parents has been one where they looked upon others and lived their lives from the position of the subject partner. That is why they were able to pioneer their way to the place of liberation by investing themselves and forgetting, over and over again, in order to finally reach the realm of liberation of Heavenly Parent after billions of generations in the eternal world.

When Adam and Eve fell, they planted the roots of anguish in the deepest part of Heavenly Parent's heart. To pull those roots out, we need to go down even deeper and feel that heart. We need to be of the mind that we cannot pull them out unless we too stand in a position of anguish, hundreds of times greater than that of Heavenly Parent's heart at the time of the Fall.

In offering jeongseong, it is very important to be clear about what we are offering jeongseong for. It does not do to worry about how things will turn out. In an argument over whether we are going to do something or not, we first need to make a decision and then make our way forward. Another problem is whether we have become a person who misses other people. A leader in the church should be someone who, after he or she parts with the members and returns home, hopes for the members to come again even before he or she has passed the threshold. The heart of love should be connected continuously and never be severed.

The path of righteousness is the path of jeongseong we follow so that our jeongseong never ceases. That is why we need to report on the life we have led and declare how we are going to live in the future. We should say, "Heavenly Parent, I will do this today," and when we have done it, we should report, "I have achieved this today." Heavenly Parent's vertical heart should be on a horizontal level with us, and once we have achieved that, we should make reports while standing on the vertical standard once again. Such jeongseong lasts eternally.

When we achieve balance on the vertical standard, we can stand on a level horizontal line. Once we have done so, we try to achieve balance vertically once again. The value of our standing at the center and achieving balance is recognized after we report on it to Heaven and try to observe that standard for all eternity. A person who has followed such a life course will come to live in a horizontal world in the eternal world, the width of which will depend on the standard of balance he or she established in life. On that standard, Heavenly Parent will work together with us, and the Cain realm will find its way to us to become one with us.

In True Parents' experience, the stronger our jeongseong, the more and more we imbue love into our object partner. That is why they tell us to hold hoondokhae every day—to put our jeongseong into hoondokhae. A person who says that the taste of hoondokhae is even more delicious than food can develop infinitely. The words studied in hoondokhae contain scenes from serious situations in True Parents' lives that have been compiled in the best of words to be declared, and so they hold a certain standard. They also contain the record of victories won against Satan. That is why if a heavenly tribal messiah stands on the standard of those words, even when he or she is in a serious situation, he or she can inherit the standard established by True Parents on the base of their victory and find the way again. By reading the record of victories won against Satan, he or she can learn about the standard to establish and the direction to follow as a heavenly tribal messiah.

The way to go as near to True Parents as possible in the spirit world is very simple. It depends on how much effort we made to comfort the heart of and liberate Heavenly Parent, and how much we loved, based on that standard. Heavenly Parent's heart has been overwrought with the desire for human liberation from the time of creation. Therefore, a heavenly tribal messiah must be able to find the lost brothers and sisters and to find and establish the position of the original Adam. We should never forget that those are the duties we need to fulfill and the life we need to live as the child of Heavenly Parent.

The age has been opened in which, when we offer jeongseong on the expanded level of the universe for the Will of the providence, our object partners naturally will come to follow us, depending on how much jeongseong we have offered. When we stand in the plus position, those in the minus position will always follow us. Heavenly tribal messiahs need to offer devotions and work with such a heart in their old villages or in places where their tribe members live. We need to be able to say, "There is not one person in the areas connected to me who has not received the Blessing. There is not one place or home where I have not left a connection of love behind." Only when we satisfy the condition of having shed light on an area as that area's subject partner, can the realm of liberation be achieved.

The path we walk is left behind as a record. Hence, we need to work with a heart of absolute joy. We should work joyfully when we go out in the morning and return home with happiness in our heart. Only when we practice leading such a life at home can we continue living such a life, no matter where we may go. It is only then that we can create positive energy, through which we can help others shed the shadows of darkness and move them to the world of light. We need to train others to like the most what they hate the most, so that they can climb up from the place of darkness to the bright aboveground world. Therefore, we need to be able to harbor Heavenly Parent's heart in our own, even if we sometimes cannot feel the appreciation that is coming from that heart. When we become a person with a heart of jeongseong and love who can be remembered in Heavenly Parent's heart, we will never drift away, even if we shed many tears in the course of our work.

5. Realizing the one tradition, the one lineage, and the one resemblance [4]

Though lineage is continued vertically, love and life are connected horizontally. Therefore, lineage can be connected only through sons and daughters. Children are the union of their parents' love and life. Adam and Eve were supposed to form a family of three generations, the first generation being Heavenly Parent and the second generation themselves, but they fell and Heavenly Parent was left with no children. Instead, Satan became the first generation and took possession of the realm of three generations, and the descendants of Adam and Eve inherited his lineage and came to have original sin. That which has been created by the false parents can be resolved only by the True Parents. Everything that belongs to Satan must be severed and be connected and grafted to the True Parents' true love, true life and true lineage. To make a wild olive tree into a true olive tree, it must be grafted to the branch of the True Parents. Because the wedding that took place in the garden of Eden was wrong, the Family Federation for World Peace and Unification performs this grafting through the Marriage Blessing. Heavenly Parent can dwell with us only at the place where the one tradition, the one lineage and the one resemblance have been realized.

First, what is most important is the tradition centered on Heavenly Parent. That tradition from before the Fall is most important. Lineage stems from that tradition, and True Parents inherited that tradition. Through True Parents, the tradition of true husband and wife and true parents has been realized for the first time in human history.

Second, it is the ideology to establish the standard of pure lineage and to help one another grow and reach perfection centering on an other-and-I attitude. At the place where people try to help one another to reach perfection, only absolute faith, absolute love and absolute obedience can exist. Absolute faith refers to leading a life of the settlement of noon together with Heavenly Parent, whom we believe is our Parent. Absolute love refers to living for the sake of others. Absolute obedience refers to absolutely obeying our object partner, for he or she is the one who perfects us. Then the original action takes place when Heavenly Parent comes to us to make us grow and reach perfection, and our brothers and sisters around us also try to satisfy our needs and perfect us. That is the tradition of Heavenly Parent.

Third, it is the lineage. Do you know about the true lineage? Presidents, vice presidents and ministers all come from different lineages; how can they be made into one? The lineage centered on True Parents comes only from the one line. Only when the lineage centered on Satan is severed and connected to the lineage of Heavenly Parent can we be restored as original human beings. The way to bring the lineages together as one is to have people receive the Marriage Blessing internationally and cross-culturally and for them to participate in the holy wine ceremony.

Fourth, it is that a true mother, a true father and their sons and daughters resemble one another. They follow the same tradition, they come from the same lineage, and they come to resemble both the internal and external aspects of their parents. We need to resemble Heavenly Parent's attributes internally and inherit Heavenly Parent's tradition externally, in order to live in accordance with the purpose of creation with which we were created. When this world finally ceases to be a fallen world, sons will say they want to marry women who resemble their mother, and daughters will say they want to marry men who resemble their father. This becomes possible only when the parents lead a life of reporting to the Heavenly Parent and observing Heavenly Parent's traditions together.

In conclusion, the first is tradition! The second is lineage! The third is to resemble True Parents! True Parents brought together and married people from 387 nations (194 nations of the Abel UN and 193 nations of the Cain UN) around the world inter-religiously.

All of them became brothers and sisters. True Parents have also created a special textbook for them, so that they can take after Heavenly Parent's attributes and see with their own eyes the heavenly kingdom. All of this was to enable the tradition, the lineage, and the resemblance to Heavenly Parent. The textbook was so that all of us, as sons and daughters can resemble the form of True Parents. Although this book is not long, it is something you cannot exchange even with your entire wealth or your entire nation. When you hold hoondokhae at the same time as True Parents and Heavenly Parent for three years, you can create an environment in which they can live together with you.

Section 2 Spirit World Citizens Who Have Reached Perfection on Earth

People who have accomplished the mission of heavenly tribal messiah must prepare to live on a level utterly different from the one they have lived on till then, with the mindset of "I am starting now" rather than "Now I am finished!" They need to create a new culture in which they live naturally discussing matters face to face with Heavenly Parent. Until the day when humanity living as one family centered on Heavenly Parent can be realized, they need to pioneer the path by which they can live as His representatives. Therefore, heavenly tribal messiahs must become "spirit world citizens who have reached perfection on earth," in order to create a world where true love occurs automatically.

1. Life armed with spirit and truth

1) Achieve balance through spirit and truth

The purpose of life is to live in preparation for the spirit world. If there is a person who wishes to be glorified on earth, he or she would be the most foolish person. The glory we receive in the spirit world is much greater than the glory we receive on earth. However, the position of glory in the spirit world is determined through our life on earth. That is why human beings need to thoroughly prepare for life in the spirit world while they are still living on earth. True Father said, "No matter where you are, when it is or what you are doing, you must never forget that the ancestors in the spirit world are with you at all times, and you should live your lives keeping pace with the spirit world. You should communicate with the spirit world through jeongseong and prayer and become spirit world citizens who have reached perfection on earth." [5]

To become spirit world citizens who have reached perfection on earth, we need to know about the spirit world. We need to know about its structure and its relationship with the earth. Not only the small number of people who have been specially trained to do so but also heavenly tribal messiahs should develop the ability to know the spirit world. We must be well aware that the spirit world was cooperating with us until we were able to fulfill our mission. To become spirit world citizens who have reached perfection on earth, it is important to have a sense of balance between divinity and truth. Jesus also emphasized that we should worship with divinity and sincerity.

> The Family Federation must go forward in spirit and truth. The lights must be burning at the church 24 hours a day. You have to offer jeongseong so that when the members, and even other people see that light, they will want to go inside. You need to go forward in spirit and truth, beginning with the leaders. I don't know how closely you feel what is happening in the spirit world, but miraculous things are happening there. Many fantastic opportunities are being prepared for you. You must work with a life-or-death determination. [6]

> But the hour is coming, and now is when the true worshipers will worship the Father in spirit and truth, for such the Father seeks to worship him. God is spirit, and those who worship him must worship in spirit and truth. [John 4:23–24]

Among people, if there are those who lean toward the spiritual side, there are also others who lean toward the physical side. A balanced person does not lean toward any one side. An intellectual person studies something with the truth and accepts it if it is reasonable and tries to deny it if it is not. A spiritual person gets a grasp of things through his or her spiritual sense rather than reason. These two kinds of people are different from each other, but it is necessary to achieve the balance and equality of both sides. Heavenly tribal messiahs lead a life that requires standing at the center of divinity and truth and maintaining balance and sense.

A person who has led a life that brings joy to the spiritual cells because he or she has a bright divine side continues to live multiplying the true love virus. When a heavenly tribal messiah practices true love and reveals the truth that has been piled up in layers, the divine world also moves. Originally, human beings who had not fallen were able to see their spirit selves while they were still living on earth. Therefore, they were able to lead a life in which they could check what their spirit selves looked like in advance while they were still on earth, for they were going to go to the spirit world and live in those forms. When a human being is reborn in the spirit world, he or she appears as the most beautiful, handsome and wonderful version of his or her appearance on earth.

A life of divinity and truth originates from a life centered on love and the conscience, which resides in the human mind. Conscience is something that Satan could not take, even after the Fall of human beings. It can be said to be the basic value that arises from Heavenly Parent's heart of creation. When we continue to expand that conscience, it will meet up with love. The world of love appears as a place where both the spiritual and physical worlds are included. In other words, the substance inhabited by the incorporeal Heavenly Parent and the substance of human beings who live on earth resembling Heavenly Parent with their creativity combine through love and appear as one. At this place, not only the oneness of the spiritual and physical worlds but also the union of divinity and truth takes place. The spirit world is a place where there are no compromises when it comes to its principles. Heavenly tribal messiahs must know about the workings of not only the corporeal world but also the incorporeal world and live in accordance with that standard.

2) Developing the "heart field"

When a heavenly tribal messiah offers jeongseong, the grace of Heavenly Parent is bestowed upon him or her. When we lead a life of prayer, we feel that a great and mighty power is with us. We receive that grace and love when our conscience is established in an upright manner and the love of Heavenly Parent has a firm hold of us. That power is why the eyes of a person who prays can see not only the physical world but also the spirit world. Heavenly Parent stimulates the essential feelings of human beings to connect them to a line that reaches beyond the physical realm. When a human being establishes the standard of conscience for that connection and offers jeongseong in addition, the gates to the spirit world are opened and he or she can see through them. [7] True Parents say that if we want to experience the spirit world in person through jeongseong, we should establish the standard of conscience, stand in line with the gates of the heart, and develop the heart field.

> What do you need to do to experience it? You need to be in line with the gates of the heart and develop the entire field of your heart by tilling it. There are people with a spiritual side and people with a truthful side. [8]

From the moment of their creation, human beings already were born with a heart that can be in accord with Heavenly Parent. However, due to the Fall, the heart that connects them to Heavenly Parent lost its power and could not play its role. Human beings can live as original human beings only when their relationship with nature, their original relationship with other human beings and their original relationship with God, which were severed because of the Fall, are all connected again. We need to engage in an action by which they can be linked. To be able to connect those relationships again, we need to rightly establish the conscience and till the field of heart to develop our divinity or our heart field in stages. The purpose of developing our heart field is to be able to personally experience the spirit world.

The first stage in doing so is the stage of indirect connection. In relation to the mind, this refers to setting the zero base of the mind. In other words, it means horizontally balancing our body and mind. When the body and mind are horizontally balanced, the zero base is set and we can experience even Heavenly Parent and the spirit world. It is a position in which we feel like we are not there even though we are, and we feel like we are there even though we are not. When we clear our mind through the horizontal balance of our body and mind, we can meet the gates to Heavenly Parent's mind. When we are in that state, we can understand the teachings of the spirit world and Heaven through indirect connection. [9]

In the second stage we can see dream revelations. We receive dream revelations when our mind is in a state of resonance. It refers to a state in which we can hear voices from or feel the spirit world through our five senses. It signifies the state in which our mind enters the realm on the spiritual level where it can be in resonance. Then we will sense that "my mind and I are two separate beings." When we pray, we can even converse with our mind. You are conversing with a being that is you but not you. You can converse with each other through the wavelengths of the mind. You also can smell your mind. In this stage, your mind should be yearning for something. [10]

The third stage is where phenomena, such as revelations and instructions, occur. Instructions are teachings that come directly from the spirit world. When Heavenly Parent teaches us through revelations, sometimes it may be through giving us spoken instructions, and at other times it may be through showing us visions. That is why we always need to interpret revelations. Such phenomena are the works of Heavenly Parent to develop our field of heart. [11]

The fourth stage is the stage of direct revelations. It refers to actually experiencing the spirit world directly. We can experience direct revelations by entering the spirit world and traveling through it all day long. It is a stage in which sometimes we can personally experience the spirit world, not just for a day but for days on end. We can even reach the realm of feeling Heavenly Parent in our everyday life. [12]

The purpose of spiritual works is to enable our spirit self and physical body to engage in a fulfilling give-and-take action, so that we can achieve the perfection of our character and form an ideal family desired by Heavenly Parent. The spiritual works themselves are not the purpose, but that which help us to practice true love in concrete ways in our daily life. That is why we need to develop our heart field through the gates to our heart by going through the process of indirect connection, dream revelations, revelations and direct revelations. Their purpose is also to help us gain a clear perception of the direction of life Heaven desires of us, so that we can follow it in our daily life. Spiritual works can remain on earth only when the foundation of substance is laid by practicing true love. If we do not practice it, spiritual works will be nothing more than a passing incident. Above all else, if we fail to achieve the balance of our intellectual side and spiritual side and instead tend to lean toward the spiritual side, problems will arise. Therefore, we need to achieve balance in the practical aspect of our life by reading True Parents' words in hoondokhae, offering basic jeongseong, and carrying out activities continuously. Furthermore, if we cannot stand in a position in which our mental side can control our spiritual side, it would be advisable not to engage in spiritual works at all.

2. Life in which the spirit world and physical world are connected

1) Life principles in the era for establishing the Association to Connect the Earth to the Spirit World

In 2009 in the United States, True Parents proclaimed the era for establishing the Association to Connect the Earth to the Spirit World. They said that it is an association that brings together the spirit world and the physical world as one. In short, they opened the age in which the spirit world and physical world, which were divided due to the Fall, can be linked together as one, and Abel and Cain can live together in oneness centering on Heavenly Parent. Then what is the meaning of the era for establishing the Association to Connect the Earth to the Spirit World?

First, what does it mean to "Connect the Earth to the Spirit World?" It means to link the spiritual and physical worlds, connecting them as one. Due to the Fall of humankind, Heavenly Parent became estranged from human beings. Moreover, human beings also became estranged from other human beings as well as from all things in the world. The severance of all relationships centered on Heavenly Parent is nothing other than the Fall. Connecting the earth to the spirit world means that Heavenly Parent and human beings—and human beings and all things—can now be linked once again through the original relationship of true love in the original garden of Eden, with Heavenly Parent at the central axis.

Yeong Yeon Se Hyeop-hae (the era for establishing the Association to Connect the Earth to the Spirit World) brings us together in front of Heavenly Parent's knees! Do you know it? It can connect the spirit world and the physical world. It will link together the satanic world where Abel and Cain are united as one. The Chinese character for "union," *yeon* (聯), is made up of the characters *yi*

(耳), meaning "the ear," and *sa* (糸), meaning "thread," and it brings the two together. It is not the character *yeon* (連), meaning "to attach," but *yeon* (聯), meaning "to link." It signifies that everything that was severed from God will be linked together as one, so that they never again can be severed from Him. [13]

Second, what does *hyeob-hae* (association) mean? "The Chinese character *hyeob* (協) is used in the word *hyeob-hae* (association), and it is made up of a cross (十) and three characters meaning power (力) next to it. What that means is that it is a world of the cross where Heavenly Parent, Abel and Cain are united." [14]

Third, which *shi-dae* (age) are we talking about? It is the *shi-dae* referring to the providential time when the Association to Connect the Earth to the Spirit World is declared. It is an age when the spirit world and physical world are linked together as one, and all their citizens, who are beloved by Heavenly Parent, will be elevated to the position of value higher than that of the people of goodness before the Fall. That is why it is named the Association to Connect the Earth to the Spirit World. [15]

That is why I have named it the *Yeong Yeon Se Hyeop-hae* (the Association to Connect the Earth to the Spirit World) under Heavenly Parent. I created an eternally unchanging association that attends Heavenly Parent. Since the time has come when the lineage and nation of peace cannot be separated, these words can be included in the book *Owner of Peace, Owner of Lineage*. [16]

The Association to Connect the Earth to the Spirit World is not simply an organization that unites the two worlds as one. Its purpose is to connect the spirit world and physical world as one at the place before the Fall, so that all beings living in them can be taken to the garden of Eden before the Fall to live together. For Heavenly Parent to realize the goal of the Association to Connect the Earth to the Spirit World, Heavenly Parent, Cain and Abel must become one centering on the cross.

We are now in the age of substantial Cheon Il Guk. Heavenly tribal messiahs do not differentiate between the spirit world and physical world. We need to recognize that they are one world. Through the Association to Connect the Earth to the Spirit World, True Parents are governing the entire universe through the laws and ways of heaven. Heavenly tribal messiahs need to become people who can unite Abel and Cain as one and form the realm of the original Adam to attend Heavenly Parent.

2) A world of endless creativity and the oneness of God and humankind in love

If human beings could travel freely to the spirit world while still living on earth, they would wish to visit it at least once. To be able to do so, it is important to live a life of conforming oneself to the standard of the spirit world.

What the Apostle Paul saw and experienced in the third heaven

in the spirit world motivated him to carry out his mission work untiringly for 14 years. You need to undergo such experiences. I too have a standard I require of myself. Though I did not tell you about it, there is a firm root of belief in me that says, 'I will do such and such a thing.' With such a conviction within me, I will plow my way through till the end. As long as this conviction is not broken or destroyed, I will continue to make my way forward, no matter what hardships or troubles come my way. [17]

The concepts of heavenly tribal messiahs who live their lives knowing about the spirit world should not be limited to the life of the flesh; instead, they need to live their lives to perfect their spirit selves. Though human beings live on earth in their physical bodies, they need to perfect their spirit selves through the work of their physical bodies. Heavenly tribal messiahs must lead a life of giving generously to and living for the sake of others until the moment of their death, in order to perfect their inner selves. We need to add our creativity to what has been created by Heavenly Parent to create something new, and then add another part of our creativity to what we have created to create something even more novel. By thus creating our object partners repeatedly, we need to experience the taste of creation and become a true parent resembling Heavenly Parent.

Heavenly Parent's work of creation is being continued even today. When the Creator and humankind become one, human beings' experience of creation together with Heavenly Parent will unfold infinitely. Though human beings face limitations when they stay in their physical bodies on earth, they will know no bounds when they are in the spirit of Heavenly Parent. The Association to Connect the Earth to the Spirit World ultimately aims for the cosmic life in which the spirit world and physical world are connected as one and where we have achieved oneness of God and humankind in love.

Section 3 Human Beings on Earth Who Resemble Divine Character

Heavenly Parent's wish is to unite as one with human beings and live together with them in a Parent-child relationship. This would make it possible for Heavenly Parent to share love and become one with human beings who were created in His image. In short, it is to live together in the original Eden where the ideal of oneness in love of Heavenly Parent and humankind has been realized. Heavenly Parent, who exists as an incorporeal being, comes down to earth and experiences the corporeal substantial form, and the corporeal human beings enter the incorporeal Heavenly Parent and experience the incorporeal world. With human beings as object partners of love, Heavenly Parent comes to dwell there and unite with them in love. For a heavenly tribal messiah to meet Heavenly Parent, he or she must be at the zero point. The zero point refers to a place where neither the Fall nor the self exists. It is a place established centering on the conscience. It is the place where we live a life of the settlement of noon with Heavenly Parent, centering on the conscience. It is the place where a heavenly tribal messiah meets the heart of Heavenly Parent after perfecting his or her parental heart by nurturing Cain and Abel children. It is the place where the union of parental heart takes place, and where we meet Heavenly Parent's ideal of creation. At that place can be found the union of will, the union of heart, the union of love, and the union of sacrifice where we desire to live for the sake of others as the parent. It is the standard that the heavenly tribal messiah must try to resemble.

1. Heavenly tribal messiahs are human beings who resemble divine character

When we unite our characteristics centering on Heavenly Parent, human beings naturally become the children of Heavenly Parent. When the human character of a human being meets the divine character of Heavenly Parent, that human being comes to have the status of the second Heavenly Parent. Consequently, Heavenly Parent is connected to human beings and becomes a Being of human character, and human beings are connected to Heavenly Parent and come to resemble beings with divine character. Divine character and human character were designed to work together as one, based on the common denominator that is true love. Thus, the corporeal and incorporeal worlds are connected as one world, in which the incorporeal Heavenly Parent can experience the corporeal through human beings and the corporeal human beings can experience the incorporeal. The Fall of humankind resulted in the severance of the connection between the corporeal and incorporeal worlds.

If Heavenly Parent and a human being had been able to understand each other's wishes, circumstances and hearts, Heavenly Parent would have been manifested as a Being of human character through that human being and given love to humankind. Human beings, in turn, would have overcome their physical limitations through the nurturing of the incorporeal Heavenly Parent, thus perfecting their spirit selves and preparing themselves for the eternal spirit world.

Why did Heavenly Parent wish to become a Being with human character? It is because alone, it was not possible to engage in any action. Without action, love cannot be generated, and if love is not generated, Heavenly Parent cannot be fruitful or multiply. Without a physical form, Heavenly Parent would not have been able to have dominion over the created world. Therefore, He created human beings who resemble Him so that He could operate through them, by entering their bodies to love, multiply, have dominion and experience being in substantial form.

> The Parent of the Cosmos is the incorporeal God, and the Parents of Heaven and Earth are the substantial Parents. Only when these two sets of parents unite as one, can they become the personal

Parents and then go on to become the Parents of the Cosmos, the Parents of Heaven and Earth, and the Parents of Heaven, Earth and Humankind. Unless God becomes a personal God, He cannot become the True Parent. God needs to become a personal God so that He can assume a body and give birth to sons and daughters. [18]

Human beings who help Heavenly Parent to become a Being of human character are the object partners of His love. Only the children in substantial form who resemble Heavenly Parent can stand in that position. For human beings to come to resemble His divine character in the fallen world is a revolutionary event, and as such it requires revolutionary change in character. To be created with human character that has an equal status as divine character, we must be born again. And we can only be born again through True Parents, the Messiah and Savior, who came to earth as His representatives. We need to unite with them and learn about the original form of human beings before the Fall. We must go through a process of self-creation centered on Heavenly Parent's attributes. Only when we trust and love True Parents 100 percent can we be transformed and re-created. That is the path of the heavenly tribal messiah.

God certainly exists. True people are those who resemble God. To realize the world in which true people abound, not a social or political revolution but a revolution of character must take place in human beings. This character revolution is to transform people into true people who will come to resemble God. This character revolution is to uplift human beings' character and bring it closer to God's own character. God, who is already omniscient and omnipotent, does not need any more knowledge or power, but even He needs His object partners of love, man and woman. [19]

Heavenly tribal messiahs must be born again through the love of Heavenly Parent and True Parents so that, once they reach the destination of love by giving birth to and raising sons and daughters of the Cain realm and the Abel realm, they can return to the world of oneness of God and humankind in love where they can live eternally with Him. When all is said and done, human life begins with love, matures through love, and is harvested as the fruit of love. Parental love also is perfected through it. At the end of that parental love, human beings can meet and live eternally with Heavenly Parent, who is the origin of everything. The death of a person signifies being harvested as the fruit of love and returning to the world of Heavenly Parent. Since that person's human character makes him or her the object partner of Heavenly Parent, he or she then becomes a part of the incorporeal world as the second Heavenly Parent.

Because we received our parents' love, shared conjugal love and loved our children, all of Heavenly Parent's love that was sown in the internal world of love is brought to fruition and harvested through our lives, after which we go to the next world. Therefore, when we become completely united as one in love, we come to resemble Heavenly Parent. When a husband and wife go to the spirit world after completely fulfilling these three stages of love, they become the eternal substantial object partners of Heavenly Parent, the eternal subject partner. That is what happens when a husband and wife who are centered on true love pass away. In short, they are begun from Heavenly Parent and they come to their end as substantial embodiments who resemble Heavenly Parent. [20]

When heavenly tribal messiahs are in accord with Heavenly Parent, they also receive the teachings of the spirit world. If people live righteously and piously to resemble Heavenly Parent's divine character, they can be shown what they are asking for in advance. If they continue night and day to offer jeongseong and share love with others, Heavenly Parent even makes their wishes come true. Among the people who were praying for the second advent of the Messiah in Korea, there was a person who spiritually attended True Father and received guidance from him even before he was born. [21] Two thousand years ago, Simeon and Anna, who were endeavoring to resemble divine character, also knew of Jesus' birth beforehand, and they testified to him as soon as he was born. [Luke 2:25–38]

When a heavenly tribal messiah comes to resemble divine character through his or her life, he or she may emanate the fragrance of Heavenly Parent or appear with a face that incorporates Heavenly Parent's love. The heart of Heavenly Parent is the heart of parents, sometimes appearing with the masculine heart of the father, and sometimes with the heart of the mother. The maternal part of

Heavenly Parent is manifested in substantial form as True Mother.

The maternal heart desires to give birth to children and raise them well. Because every delivery is so painful, the mother sometimes pledges never to give birth again after so much suffering. However, after time passes, she forgets ever having such thoughts and rejoices after giving birth to another child with a different character.

The heart of a mother is like the sea. The sea can take all impure things and absorb them to purify them and make them clean again. Like the sea, the maternal heart has the power to embrace the innumerable people living in the world in the maternal bosom and absorb them through love to re-create them as people who resemble divine character. The people who have completely fulfilled the heavenly tribal messiah mission could also be said to possess this maternal heart.

The father, on the other hand, is responsible for educating the family and supporting it financially. He establishes the vertical standard, together with Heavenly Parent, and guides the family down the right way. Though he may look as strong as a rock, he treats his children with deep, gentle love that comes from within. If a mother's love is the sea, a father's love is the mountain. Spring water flowing down the deep ravines serves as life-giving water to thirsty people and animals. And the thick forest creates shade where people and animals can rest. Oxygen emitted from the deep mountains provides air, which is needed by everyone. These aspects of parental heart that resemble Heavenly Parent's heart are reflected in the hearts of human parents, and it is Heavenly Parent's wish that they remain in continuous operation through heavenly tribal messiahs.

2. Humankind living together with Heavenly Parent

True Parents say that heavenly tribal messiahs must never stop growing but must grow continuously. They say that is the best conclusion in the world, for heavenly tribal messiahs must expand beyond Korea, beyond the world, and even beyond the ancestors in the spirit world. Only when heavenly tribal messiahs expand this far, can they bring the world under control and make it a world of order. Heavenly tribal messiahs need to have the warmth, speed and order that resemble Heavenly Parent, in order to experience all of His love. Heavenly tribal messiahs carry out the true love movement, together with Heavenly Parent, to rightly establish the world order as the original order. [22]

What would be the ultimate wish of heavenly tribal messiahs? They need to unite the Cain realm and Abel realm as brothers and become their true parents, and thus be victorious in the position of true parents. They also need to realize the kingship, so that the substantial form of Heavenly Parent can rule over this world. Next, they should enter the realm of the royal family, which is the position of Heavenly Parent's own children, and live eternally with Heavenly Parent while traveling to and from the corporeal and incorporeal worlds. To do so, they need to attend True Parents, who were manifested on earth as the substantial embodiments of the incorporeal Heavenly Parent. They need to form ties of lineage with True Parents and be reborn by receiving the Blessing. After establishing that standard, they should live as the parents of the Cain and Abel realms.

Heavenly tribal messiahs must re-create their tribe members every day as the children of Heavenly Parent by paying them visits with the Word, visits of life, visits of true love and visits of culture.

True Parents said to us, "Let us live together," while reading during hoondokhae the speech given at the Cosmic Assembly for the Settlement of the True Parents of Heaven, Earth and Humankind Who, as God's Embodiment, Proclaim the Word. They are asking us to live together with them in the ideal world of the kingdom of heaven, a place where all thoughts can be made into reality and where we all can dance together, sing together, eat together and create a world of culture together.

> If there is nothing to eat, you can draw it and enjoy it while looking at it. You can eat with your eyes and your mind. Knowing that, I hope that you will make the grand resolution to live together with us. Let us live together! All who memorize the speech of the Cosmic Assembly for the Settlement of the True Parents of Heaven, Earth and Humankind Who, as God's Embodiment, Proclaim the Word and translate it into action can live together. Simple, isn't it? All those who can do so are the people of our home, the people of our nation, and our brothers and sisters. It is simple. 'Let us live together!' Let us live together in a world where everything is possible, a new world where we can fly to the sky or delve underground, a world where we can dance, sing and create a world of culture at the residence Rev. Moon built for God! [23] (Applause!)

Section 4 Free People Living in Accordance with the Voice of the Conscience

A person who has received Heaven's decree responds with results. A person who responds to the commands of Heaven with results earns freedom. We earn true freedom by fulfilling our responsibility and achieving results. What kind of freedom would that be? A person who listens to the voice of the conscience and acts accordingly is a naturally free person. Responding naturally to the commands of Heaven is what we do in the world of the unity of heart. Heavenly tribal messiahs are free people who have been trained to act immediately upon hearing the voice of the conscience.

1. The conscience is the original heart's program that manages me

What is the conscience to me? It is the vertical me connected to Heavenly Parent by lineage. The conscience is the being that exists inside me, which is me but also another me. It is the vertical mind connected to Heavenly Parent through lineage. The conscience is alive within me, and it commands me on behalf of Heavenly Parent. From within me, it breathes together with me and operates in my subconscious as my parent, teacher and owner to guide me on the decisions I need to make. [24] Heavenly Parent approaches me as my conscience, and thus controls and intervenes in my actions.

Every human being has a conscience. Though human beings fell, they still can have dominion over themselves by listening to the voice of their conscience. When they listen to that voice, they attain peace. However, when they become centered on their greed and earthly desires, though they may attain things externally, they lose true peace. When the voice of the conscience rings out and we ignore it, what remains of our conscience is destroyed and becomes hidden. After that, our character deteriorates, and we suffer the indignity of falling to the level of an animalistic human being. When the balance between the internal and external aspects is broken, serious problems arise. The conscience heard through the internal voice is the only attribute of Heavenly Parent that is still left to human beings, which helps them to go to His presence even though they fell, and the tie that connects them to Him. Though human beings fell, they can live their lives without making big mistakes if they listen to the voice of their conscience and act accordingly. Anyone who listens to the voice of the conscience and translates what it says into action 100 percent can meet Heavenly Parent. The conscience also grows. When we carry out good and right deeds, the attribute of Heavenly Parent that guides the conscience is stimulated, which leads to its gradual growth. As a result, it makes the power of love work upon us and guides us down the path that leads to the recovery of our original nature. The best way to have dominion over ourselves is to live in accordance with our conscience. As a matter of fact, the root of the conscience was begun from Heavenly Parent's attribute. The conscience is the vertical self that is connected to the Heavenly Parent through the original lineage. [25]

The conscience is the medium of the attribute sent to me from Heavenly Parent. It plays a role within my body similar to that of a basic operating program saved on a computer. It plays the role of receiving information sent from headquarters and conveying it to me, and when a virus tries to invade from outside, it creates a defense system for me so that I can return to my basic self. If I make good use of the conscience sent to me by Heavenly Parent as His representative, I always can advance toward Him. When I expand my life centering on my conscience, Heavenly Parent wishes to be in contact with me at all times. That is why the conscience plays the role of a compass that is necessary in finding my way to Heavenly Parent. [26]

Deciding on my daily schedule after listening to the voice of the conscience and executing it to the letter is the way to have dominion over my own self. However, if we aim to satisfy the desires of our body rather than listen to the voice of the conscience, though our body may like it at first, we will fall deeper and deeper into a trap centered on ourselves. Our sense of responsibility will dwindle, and we will guide ourselves to where the comforts and desires of our body lead us. As a result, even our mind will become tired and we will be unable to feel true freedom. That is why we need to live in such a way that we "go, come, eat, sleep, like or dislike" based on the voice of our conscience. When we do so, we automatically can become a free person and have self-dominion and achieve the unity of body and mind. True Father said, "In your life, you need to unite your body and mind, no matter what. When I first became determined to walk the path of Heaven, I started out with a fierce resolution under the motto, 'Before seeking to dominate the universe, first achieve dominion over the self!'" [27]

When we pay attention to the voice of the conscience and listen clearly to what it says, and lead a life in which we absolutely obey that voice and practice what it tells us, our body and mind most certainly will unite as one and we will live in resonance with the voice of Heaven. Thus, we will experience the unity of mind and body. [28] Then how can we hear the voice of the conscience? It is something we can just feel and know. Heavenly tribal messiahs, who were born again as human beings before the Fall, can develop the sense with which they can hear the voice of the conscience. Heavenly tribal messiahs need to listen to the voice of the conscience and act accordingly, thus ridding themselves of fallen nature and becoming people of divinity. If acting in accordance with the voice of the conscience is the way to have dominion over ourselves, self-dominion begins from keeping promises we make to ourselves.

When heavenly tribal messiahs live in accordance with the voice of the conscience, they become free. If they don't, their own actions will imprison them. In the fallen world, there are cases in which people deceive their own conscience and say they become free by doing so. However, living a life of deceiving our conscience only makes us distressed and conflicted. When we deceive our conscience, we cannot listen to our original voice and we will make all decisions based on what others say.

2. The key to becoming a truly free person

What is the root of Heavenly Parent's creation? It is the blueprint of creation. In it are included the role of Heavenly Parent and the role of humankind in the realization of Heavenly Parent's dream. We call that blueprint of creation the principle of creation. the principle of creation teaches us three things. First, it explains why God created all things and humankind. Second, it explains how He intended to perfect humankind and what He wished to have them do. Third, it tells us what kind of world will unfold when humankind is perfected.

What, then, would be the value of the blueprint of creation and Heavenly Parent? While drawing up the blueprint of creation,

Heavenly Parent was the subject partner. In the process of perfecting that blueprint, He could make changes if He so desired. However, once the blueprint of creation was finished, it became something that not even Heavenly Parent Himself could change, because it had become the principle, order and formula that even He had to absolutely observe. Thus, the blueprint of creation became the absolute subject partner to Heavenly Parent. The being to whom the principle of creation is applied first, even before humankind, is Heavenly Parent. He came to stand in the position of the absolute object partner in front of the blueprint that He Himself had created. Examples of this principle also can be found in the human world. Before becoming parents, a couple draws up a blueprint for having children. The parents can decide whether to have children or not. Therefore, they can exercise the right of the absolute subject partner before they conceive a child. However, once they become pregnant with a child, based on the blueprint they drew up for having children, in the world apart from the Fall, the parents cannot change the blueprint. Everything after that is done to accommodate the children.

At the time when Heavenly Parent drew up the blueprint of creation, there were no other beings in the spirit world or the physical world. That blueprint is Heavenly Parent's self-made promise, pledge and law. There is no one to say anything, even if He does not keep that promise to Himself. However, if He were to break that promise, Heavenly Parent Himself would be in violation of the fundamental spirit with which He established the basis, order and law of goodness. In other words, if the absolutely perfect Heavenly Parent were to break the order and law of goodness, that would mean their spirit had not been imbued in the blueprint from the very beginning, and He would not be able to appear as the absolutely perfect Parent. And any created things in which the spirit of that order and law is not established would be born as beings that cannot abide by that law and order. Therefore, breaking the order and law that He Himself established cannot be permitted. This is because the principle of creation was begun on the standard of the declaration that it is absolute, perfect, faultless and unchanging. [29]

What is the meaning of keeping one's promise to oneself? No matter what difficulties and agonies Heavenly Parent may face, it is His self-dominion to hold fast to the principle of creation. Only when He keeps the promise He made to Himself can the self-dominion of Heavenly Parent become the model for His object partners and His authority be demonstrated. We need to keep the promise we make to ourselves, even if there is no one there to watch us. That is the reason why Heavenly Parent started out from the origin of the conscience. Because He had to keep the promise to Himself, Heavenly Parent was unable to interfere even when He saw His beloved son and daughter eat of the fruit of the knowledge of good and evil and fall. It was to protect the absoluteness and absolute perfectness of the Principle of Creation. Human beings had to pass through the growth period and earn the authority to have dominion over all things by fulfilling their own portion of responsibility, and Heavenly Parent's interference would have impeded the perfection of humankind. That is why Heavenly Parent practiced self-dominion based on the principle of creation, even when He was in a position of such unendurable anguish and sorrow that it was almost as if He were being bent double and His bones were melting down and breaking into a million pieces.

What was it like for True Father? He heard the voice of Heaven in the year he turned 16. He received Heaven's decree, "Save the people of the world, who were born of the fallen lineage as parentless orphans and have been wandering for thousands of years, and bring them back together with you." [30] True Father determined this decree from Heaven to mean the liberation of Heavenly Parent, the salvation of humanity and the realization of a world of perpetual peace, and he kept that promise, even though he was forced to stand on the brink of death seven times during his lifetime. That promise was something that only True Father himself knew. True Father archived that promise to himself under the law of the conscience. While listening to the voice of Heavenly Parent resounding from that conscience, he fulfilled his portion of responsibility and lived his life as a free person.

Then what was it like for True Mother? From a young age, she led a life in which she discussed matters face to face with Heavenly Parent. When she heard the word "father," the first person she thought of was Heavenly Parent. She made the resolution and promise to herself, "I will end the restoration through indemnity in my lifetime." And she did keep that promise. That is not all. On the third anniversary of True Father's Seonghwa, she proclaimed the content of the promise she had made to herself.

> Those of you gathered here today, what do you want to say to True Father? I want to say to him, "Father, don't worry from now on. We will fulfill our responsibility at all costs. Therefore, Father, I pray that you will live with freedom and glory in the eternal original homeland, and be a source of comfort to God, our Heavenly Parent, who has been lonely until now." [31]

True Mother declared her promise to herself to all of heaven and earth. To keep that promise, she is working at the forefront, even as we speak, with inexpressible words cherished in her heart. She is working for the providence not only because she made a promise to Heaven but also because she made a promise to herself. True Mother is now working to make that promise a reality. To keep the promise that she made at the third anniversary of True Father's Seonghwa, that she will take responsibility for the fulfillment of the providence, she is working late into the night even now. Responsibility is in line with the conscience. And by making the promise she made to Heaven come true, she can become free.

The best way to practice self-dominion is to kill the self. What that means is to kill the concept of ourselves, by investing ourselves and forgetting in order to live in accordance with the blueprint that Heavenly Parent has shown us. To keep the promise we made to ourselves, we should continue to invest and forget. What is the difference between heavenly tribal messiahs and ordinary blessed families? It is that the heavenly tribal messiahs do not change the blueprint they promised Heavenly Parent in the middle of the process. This is because they know that it is the key to resembling Heavenly Parent and True Parents and nurturing the conscience through responsibility and becoming free. We are looking at a blueprint that has gone wrong due to the Fall, and the people who can still find the way they need to go are indeed happy people. So how should people who walk the path of heavenly tribal messiahs live their lives? True Mother says, "We have only one purpose. Our path has been decided. We have only the one path to follow. Heaven is together with me, the True Mother. Then how are you going to live your lives from now on?" [32]

What she actually is asking is, "Do you believe that the providence being carried out through True Mother will be realized without fail? Do you know the meaning of that providence, and will you work together with us?" She also is saying, "In advancing toward the established purpose of the providence, you should not worry about whether it can be achieved or not. That is my responsibility as the person who declared that goal. What you need to do is to stay in your places and fulfill the mission of heavenly tribal messiah. All you need to do is to fulfill your responsibility." She is saying that, from now on, we should clearly recognize what our mission is, and she is telling us, "You should draw up a blueprint for it and worry about when you should execute it." She also is asking us to become truly free people whose bodily suffering is rewarded through the happiness of the heart by fulfilling our mission.

In conclusion, for heavenly tribal messiahs all parts of the providence are taking place at once: restoration of the authority of the eldest son through home church, restoration of the authority of parents in the age of tribal messiahs, restoration of kingship in the age of hoondok family church, and restoration of the realm of the royal family in the age of heavenly tribal messiahs. Even if blessed central families were unable to carry out the restoration of the authority of the eldest son, restoration of the authority of parents, restoration of kingship and restoration of the realm of the royal family when those parts of the providence were in progress in the past, they have received the blessing by which they still can prevail in the final parallel age.

Therefore, heavenly tribal messiahs should live a life of constantly checking their spirit selves through endless prayers and jeongseong and the practice of true love. We need to perfect our human character to meet the divine character and make our spirit self within us appear in its most luminescent form. We also should feel the love of Heavenly Parent bestowed on us every day and perfect our dominion over ourselves. We need to expand love based on the conscience in order to embrace the Cain children and Abel children with true love and thus perfect the parental heart. Thereupon, the parental heart we experienced and the heart of Heavenly Parent can come together, and the original Parent and children can meet at the place of hyojeong.

Endnotes

Introduction

1   Family Federation for World Peace and Unification, *Pyeong Hwa Shin Gyeong*, (Seoul: Sung Hwa Publishing, 2009), 283.

2   True Mother, 2013.08.15, Cheon Jeong Gung.

3   Editorial committee for the Collected *Sermons* of Sun Myung Moon, Ed., *Collected Sermons of the Rev. Sun Myung Moon*, vol. 306 (Seoul: Sung Hwa Publishing, 2003), 232–36. See also, including the day of the proclamation, *Sermons*, vol. 306, 232–36, given as 1998.09.23. FFWPU, True Parents' Life Course 10, (Seoul: Sung Hwa Publishing, 2001), 98.

4   Full return refers to the state in which fallen human beings surpass the stage of restoration and return to the state of Adam and Eve when they were born. If restoration is the process of

solving original sin, full return is going back to the point before the commandment not to eat the fruit of the tree of the knowledge of good and evil was given. In the place of full recurrence, there is no self-awareness or fallen nature. Special speech by True Father, True Parent of Heaven, Earth and Humankind, 2012.4.21, CheongShim Peace World Center.

5   Family Federation for World Peace and Unification, *Pyeong Hwa Gyeong*, (Seoul: Sung Hwa Publishing, 2015), 1646 [Eng].
6   True Father, 1999.01.05

Chapter 1   Heavenly Parent's Dream and the Heavenly Tribal Messiah

1   FFWPU, *Pyeong Hwa Gyeong*, 574.
2   True Mother, to a 2015 Global Top Gun Special Gathering, 2015.08.19, Cheon Jeong Gung.
3   True Mother, Culture of Heart Performing Arts Youth Camp Special Gathering, 2017.01.06, Cheon Jeong Gung.
4   FFWPU, *Pyeong Hwa Gyeong*, 574 [Eng].
5   The "cosmos" refers to the earth plus heaven: the physical world and the spiritual world.
6   True Mother, Speech at a special gathering during the 2015 Global Top Gun Workshop, 2015.08.19, Cheon Jeong Gung
7   FFWPU, *Pyeong Hwa Shin Gyeong*, 14.
8   True Father, 1999.09.05, Belvedere Training Center.

9   FFWPU, *Pyeong Hwa Shin Gyeong*, 14.
10 FFWPU, *Pyeong Hwa Gyeong*, 606.
11 Family Federation for World Peace and Unification, ed., *Pyeong Hwa Gyeong*, 859–860 [Eng].
12 FFWPU, *Pyeong Hwa Gyeong*, 298–299 [Eng].
13 *Sermons*, vol. 12, 99, 1962.12.10.
14 FFWPU, *Pyeong Hwa Gyeong*, 816.
15 True Mother, Speech at the 3rd Anniversary of Cheon Il Guk Foundation Day, 2016.02.20, CheongShim Peace World Center.
16 True Mother, Speech at the 49th True Heavenly Parent's Day Commemoration, 2016.02.08, Cheon Jeong Gung.
17 Family Federation for World Peace and Unification, ed., *Cheon Seong Gyeong* (Seoul: Sung Hwa Publishing, 2014), 1646 [Eng].
18 Family Federation for World Peace and Unification, *True Parents' Life Courses*, vol. 10 (Seoul: Sung Hwa Publishing, 2000), 96.
19 *True Parents' Life Courses*, vol. 10, 98.
20 *Sermons*, vol. 20, 342, 1968.7.20.
21 True Father, 2009.06.04, Cheon Jeong Gung.
22 *Sermons*, vol. 248, 99, 1993.08.01.
23 True Mother, "The Mission of Eve," *Tongil Segye*, No. 251, (Seoul: Sung Hwa Publishing, 1991), 85–88
24 Family Federation for World Peace and Unification, *Exposition of the Divine Principle* (Seoul: Sung Hwa Publishing, 1996), 41 [Kor]. cf. in the Divine Principle, the place where God and humanity become one is referred to as the center of the cosmos.
25 True Parents made proclamations on two consecutive days,

November 17 and 18, 2011, at Geomundo,

26   True Mother, Benediction Prayer at the Cheon Il Guk Foundation Registration Blessing Ceremony, 2013.01.13, CheongShim Peace World Center.

27   True Father, Special Speech by the True Parents of Heaven, Earth and Humankind, 2012.04.21, CheongShim Peace World Center.

28   True Mother, Speech at Worldwide Joint Worship for Completing the Heavenly *Tribal Messiah* Mission, 2014.10.26, CheongShim Peace World Center.

29   True Mother, 2014.10.29, Cheonan District Church.

30   FFWPU, *Cheon Seong Gyeong*, 702 [Kor].

31   FFWPU, *Cheon Seong Gyeong*, 1440 [Eng].

32   FFWPU, *Pyeong Hwa Shin Gyeong*, 89–90.

33   FFWPU, *Cheon Seong Gyeong*, 687 [Eng].

34   FFWPU, *Cheon Seong Gyeong*, 688 [Eng].

35   FFWPU, *Cheon Seong Gyeong*, 687 [Eng].

36   FFWPU, *Cheon Seong Gyeong*, 714 [Eng].

37   FFWPU, *Cheon Seong Gyeong*, 713 [Eng].

38   FFWPU, *Cheon Seong Gyeong*, 713–714 [Eng].

39   FFWPU, *Cheon Seong Gyeong*, 715 [Eng].

40   FFWPU, *Cheon Seong Gyeong*, 714 [Eng].

41   True Father, 1999.04.11, Belvedere Training Center.

42   FFWPU, *Pyeong Hwa Gyeong*, 1399 [Kor].

43   FFWPU, *Pyeong Hwa Gyeong*, 1404 [Kor].

44   FFWPU, *Cheon Seong Gyeong*, 1444 [Eng].

45   Oh Taek-yong, *Understanding True Parents' Proclamations and*

God's Providence (Asan: Sun Moon University Publishing, 2015), 115.

46   Oh Taek-yong, Understanding True Parents' Proclamations and God's Providence, 115.
47   Oh Taek-yong, Understanding True Parents' Proclamations and God's Providence, 136.
48   Sermons, vol. 346, 265–68, 2001.07.01; vol. 356, 68, 2002.10.16.
49   True Mother, Speech given at the closing session of a Special HJ CheonWon Workshop under the Guidance of True Parents, 2016.08.21, CheongPyeong Training Center

Chapter 2   What Is a Heavenly Tribal Messiah?

1   True Father, 2011.10.17, Cheon Jeong Gung.
2   *Sermons*, vol. 298, 105, 1999.01.01.
3   Yong, Jin-heon, "Hak Ja Han's Hyojeong Ethics," (Doctoral Dissertation, SunHak Universal Peace Graduate University, 2017), 7.
4   Family Federation for World Peace and Unification, *Pyeong Hwa Shin Gyeong*, (Seoul: Sung Hwa Publishing, 2010), 22.
5   *Sermons*, vol. 419, 112, 2003.10.01.
6   FFWPU, *Pyeong Hwa Shin Gyeong*, 22.
7   *Sermons*, vol. 306, 223–227, 1998.09.23.
8   *Sermons*, vol. 37, 56, 1970.12.22.
9   Family Federation for World Peace and Unification, *The Reality of the Spirit World and Life on Earth*, (Seoul: Sung Hwa Publishing,

1997), 349–352.

10 Family Federation for World Peace and Unification, *Exposition of the Divine Principle*, (Seoul: Sung Hwa Publishing, 1996), 30 [Eng].

11 FFWPU, *Pyeong Hwa Shin Gyeong*, 21.

12 Family Federation for World Peace and Unification, *Pyeong Hwa Gyeong*, (Seoul: Sung Hwa Publishing, 2015), 672 [Kor].

13 True Father, "Cosmic Assemblies for the Settlement of the True Parents of Heaven, Earth and Humankind Who, as God's Embodiment, Proclaim the Word," 7–8, 2011.04.24

14 Oh Taek-yong, *Understanding True Parents' Proclamations and God's Providence*, (Asan: Sun Moon University Publishing, 2015), 193.

15 FFWPU, *Exposition*, 265–268 [Kor].

16 Oh Taek-yong, *Understanding True Parents' Proclamations and God's Providence*, 235–238.

17 *Sermons*, vol. 306, 238, 1998.09.23.

18 The six times True Father was imprisoned were in the Gyeonggi Province Police Station (1944.10–1945.02), Jeongju Gwaksan Police Substation (1945.10, about a week), Pyongyang Daedong Detention Center (1946.08.11–11.21), Heungnam Special Labor Camp (1948.02.22–1950.10.14), Seodaemun Prison (1955.07.04–10.04), Danbury Federal Prison (1984.07.20–1985.08.20), and the seventh incident was the helicopter crash near CheongPyeong (2008.07.19).

19 History Compilation Committee, ed., *True Parents' Life Courses*,

vol. 2, (Seoul: Sung Hwa Publishing, 1999) 139.
20 History Compilation Committee, ed., *True Parents' Life Courses*, vol. 3, (Seoul: Sung Hwa Publishing, 1999) 157.
21 FFWPU, *Pyeong Hwa Shin Gyeong*, 17.
22 FFWPU, *Pyeong Hwa Gyeong*, 1122 [Kor].
23 FFWPU, *Pyeong Hwa Gyeong*, 1124 [Kor].
24 *Sermons*, vol. 371, 276–277, 2002.03.03.
25 *Sermons*, vol. 279, 124, 1996.08.01.
26 Oh Taek-yong, *The Meaning of Absolute Sex as Seen Through True Father's Speeches: The Word and Theology 7*, (Asan: Sun Moon University Publishing, 2001), 97–116.
27 FFWPU, *Pyeong Hwa Shin Gyeong*, 25.
28 FFWPU, *Pyeong Hwa Gyeong*, 1026 [Eng].
29 FFWPU, *Pyeong Hwa Gyeong*, 1124 [Kor].
30 FFWPU, *Pyeong Hwa Gyeong*, 1127 [Kor].
31 FFWPU, *Pyeong Hwa Shin Gyeong*, 227.
32 FFWPU, *Pyeong Hwa Shin Gyeong*, 233.
33 FFWPU, *Pyeong Hwa Shin Gyeong*, 235.
34 Unification Thought Institute, *Summarizing Unification Thought*, (Asan: Sun Moon University Publishing, 2007), 66.
35 FFWPU, *Exposition*, 41 [Kor].
36 FFWPU, *Pyeong Hwa Gyeong*, 1093 [Kor].
37 Family Federation for World Peace and Unification, *God's Homeland and the Peace UN*, (Seoul: Sung Hwa Publications, 2004), 107–113.
38 FFWPU, *Cheon Seong Gyeong*, 1446 [Kor].

39 FFWPU, *Exposition*, 40 [Kor].
40 *Sermons*, vol. 416, 84, 2003.08.20.
41 *Sermons*, vol. 279, 112–113, 1996.08.01.
42 FFWPU, *Exposition*, 27 [Kor].
43 FFWPU, *Cheon Seong Gyeong*, 1443 [Kor].
44 *Sermons*, vol. 481, 23–24, 2005.01.01.
45 True Father, 2001.01.31, East Garden
46 Oh Taek-yong, *Understanding True Parents' Proclamations and God's Providence*, 136.
47 *Sermons*, vol. 170, 267, 1987.11.27.
48 *Sermons*, vol. 102, 230, 1979.01.01.
49 Lee, Jae-seok, "For Victory in Home Church," *Tongil Segye*, No. 135, (Seoul: Sung Hwa Publishing, 1982), 42.
50 *Sermons*, vol. 110, 266, 1981.01.01.
51 *Sermons*, vol. 110, 266, 1981.01.01.
52 *Sermons*, vol. 231, 143, 1992.06.02.
53 *Sermons*, vol. 104, 263, 1979.05.27.
54 *Sermons*, vol. 137, 302, 1986.01.03.
55 Park Jung-hyun, "Home Church Activities in New York, Today's Rome," *Tongil Segye*, No. 124 (Seoul: Sung Hwa Publishing, 1981), 67.
56 Kim Won-jong, "The Fire Has Already Been Lit," *Tongil Segye*, No. 98 (Seoul: Sung Hwa Publishing, 1976), 42.
57 True Mother, "The Mission of Eve," *Tongil Segye*, No. 251 (Seoul, Sung Hwa Publishing, 1991), 84–88.
58 True Mother, "The Mission of Eve," 85–88.

59 *Sermons*, vol. 177, 70, 1988.05.15.
60 *Sermons*, vol. 176, 280, 1988.05.11.
61 *Sermons*, vol. 219, 162, 1991.08.29.
62 *Sermons*, vol. 178, 86, 1988.06.01.
63 *Sermons*, vol. 250, 177, 1993.10.14.
64 *Sermons*, vol. 217, 125, 19910.5.12.
65 *Sermons*, vol. 168, 142, 1987.09.13.
66 *Sermons*, vol. 189, 248, 1989.04.09.
67 *Sermons*, vol. 219, 159, 1991.08.29.
68 *Sermons*, vol. 52, 129, 1971.12.26.
69 *Sermons*, vol. 181, 296, 1988.10.03.
70 *Sermons*, vol. 181, 296, 1988.10.03.
71 *Sermons*, vol. 181, 296, 1988.10.03.
72 *Sermons*, vol. 234, 251, 1992.08.24.
73 *Sermons*, vol. 248, 157, 1993.08.01.
74 *Sermons*, vol. 248, 99, 1993.08.01.
75 *Sermons*, vol. 325, 158, 2000.07.01.; vo. 320, 328, 2000.05.05.
76 *Sermons*, vol. 487, 256, 2005.02.17.
77 True Father, 1997.09.13, East Garden.
78 True Father, 1997.10.13, Victoria Plaza Hotel.
79 *Sermons*, vol. 285, 167, 1997.05.01.
80 *Sermons*, vol. 285, 177, 1997.05.01. cf. Assimilation means achieving complete unity through harmony.
81 *Sermons*, vol. 487, 253, 2005.02.17.
82 *Sermons*, vol. 487, 237, 239, 2005.02.17.
83 True Mother, 2014.10.29, Cheonan District Church.

84   *Sermons*, vol. 142, 292, 1986.03.13.

Chapter 3   Why Should We Fulfill the Heavenly Tribal Messiah Mission?

1   FFWPU, *Pyeong Hwa Gyeong*, 654–655 [Eng].
2   Family Federation for World Peace and Unification, *Pyeong Hwa Shin Gyeong*, (Seoul: Sung Hwa Publishing, 2009), 46.
3   FFWPU, *Pyeong Hwa Shin Gyeong*, 47.
4   Family Federation for World Peace and Unification, *Exposition of the Divine Principle*, (Seoul: Sung Hwa Publishing, 1996), 40 [Kor].
5   FFWPU, *Pyeong Hwa Gyeong*, 659 [Eng].
6   FFWPU, *Pyeong Hwa Gyeong*, 591 [Eng].
7   FFWPU, *Pyeong Hwa Gyeong*, 673 [Eng].
8   FFWPU, *Pyeong Hwa Shin Gyeong*, 43.
9   FFWPU, *Pyeong Hwa Gyeong*, 437–438 [Eng].
10 FFWPU, *Pyeong Hwa Shin Gyeong*, 21.
11 FFWPU, *Pyeong Hwa Gyeong*, 660–661 [Eng].
12 FFWPU, *Pyeong Hwa Gyeong*, 592 [Kor].
13 FFWPU, *Pyeong Hwa Gyeong*, 592 [Kor].
14 FFWPU, *Pyeong Hwa Gyeong*, 1026 [Eng].
15 FFWPU, *Pyeong Hwa Gyeong*, 1026 [Eng].
16 FFWPU, *Pyeong Hwa Gyeong*, 1029 [Eng].
17 FFWPU, *Pyeong Hwa Shin Gyeong*, 17.

18 *Sermons*, vol. 247, 253, 1993.05.09.
19 *Sermons*, vol. 56, 312, 1972.05.18.
20 *Sermons*, vol. 202, 348, 1990.05.27.
21 *Sermons*, vol. 219, 97, 1991.08.25.
22 FFWPU, *Pyeong Hwa Shin Gyeong*, 212.
23 FFWPU, *Chambumo Gyeong*, 172 [Eng].
24 *Sermons*, vol. 287, 140–155, 1997.09.14.
25 *Sermons*, vol. 287, 141, 1997.09.14.
26 *Sermons*, vol. 287, 141, 1997.09.14.
27 True Father, 2009.06.04, Cheon Jeong Gung.
28 True Mother, Speech delivered at special assembly of Cheon Il Guk leaders working under the guidance of the True Parents of Heaven, Earth and Humankind for a Heavenly Korea, 2017.12.15, Cheon Jeong Gung
29 *Sermons*, vol. 210, 210–211, 1999.01.05.
30 FFWPU, *Pyeong Hwa Gyeong*, 1076 [Eng].
31 *Sermons*, vol. 280, 124–149, 1996.11.24.
32 FFWPU, *Pyeong Hwa Gyeong*, 1092 [Kor].
33 True Mother, Speech at Worldwide Joint Worship for Completing the Heavenly *Tribal Messiah* Mission, 2014.10.26, CheongShim Peace World Center.
34 *Sermons*, vol. 279, 116, 1996.08.01.
35 *Sermons*, vol. 2, 40, 1956.02.17.
36 True Father, 2012.04.25, Cheon Jeong Gung.
37 True Mother, Speech delivered at special assembly of Cheon Il Guk leaders working under the guidance of the True Parents of

Heaven, Earth and Humankind for a Heavenly Korea, 2017.12.15, Cheon Jeong Gung

38 FFWPU, *Pyeong Hwa Gyeong*, 1144–1145 [Eng].
39 FFWPU, *Pyeong Hwa Gyeong*, 308 [Eng].
40 FFWPU, *Pyeong Hwa Gyeong*, 311 [Eng].
41 FFWPU, *Pyeong Hwa Gyeong*, 307 [Eng].
42 FFWPU, *Pyeong Hwa Gyeong*, 654–311 [Eng].
43 FFWPU, *Pyeong Hwa Gyeong*, 307 [Eng].
44 FFWPU, *Pyeong Hwa Gyeong*, 307–308 [Eng].
45 FFWPU, *Pyeong Hwa Gyeong*, 180 [Eng].
46 Family Federation for World Peace and Unification, *Cheon Seong Gyeong*, (Seoul: Sung Hwa Publishing, 2014), 1646 [Eng].
47 *Sermons*, vol. 52, 52, 1971.12.14.
48 *Sermons*, vol. 410, 119, 2003.07.02.
49 *Sermons*, vol. 210, 188, 1990.12.19.
50 FFWPU, *Pyeong Hwa Gyeong*, 312, [Eng].
51 True Mother, Speech delivered at special assembly of Cheon Il Guk leaders working under the guidance of the True Parents of Heaven, Earth and Humankind for a Heavenly Korea, 2017.12.15, Cheon Jeong Gung
52 *Sermons*, vol. 410, 119, 2003.07.02.
53 *Sermons*, vol. 416, 84, 2003.08.20.
54 Family Federation for World Peace and Unification, God's Homeland and the Peace UN, (Seoul: Sung Hwa Publications, 2004), 107–113.
55 FFWPU, *Cheon Seong Gyeong*, 1446 [Kor]

56 *Exposition*, 40 [Kor]
57 *Sermons*, vol. 481, 23–24, 2005.01.01.
58 FFWPU, *Cheon Seong Gyeong*, 1443 [Kor].
59 FFWPU, *Cheon Seong Gyeong*, 1443 [Kor].

Chapter 4 How to Fulfill the Heavenly Tribal Messiah Mission

1 Family Federation for World Peace and Unification, *Pyeong Hwa Gyeong*, (Seoul: Sung Hwa Publishing, 2013) 1211–1212 [Kor]
2 FFWPU, *Pyeong Hwa Gyeong*, 1193 [Eng].
3 *Sermons*, vol. 407, 142–144, 2003.05.15.
4 *Sermons*, vol. 304, 25, 1999.09.05.
5 *Sermons*, vol. 304, 38–41, 1999.09.05.
6 Family Federation for World Peace and Unification, *Exposition of the Divine Principle*, (Seoul: Sung Hwa Publishing, 1996), 27 [Kor].
7 Family Federation for World Peace and Unification, Sun Myung Moon's Philosophy of Peace, (Seoul: Sung Hwa Publishing, 2002), 94.
8 World Scripture Compilation Committee, World Scriptures II, (Seoul: Universal Peace Federation, 2009), 474.
9 *Exposition*, 308 [Kor]
10 *Sermons*, vol. 466, 293, 2004.09.01.
11 FFWPU, *Pyeong Hwa Gyeong*, 308 [Kor].
12 *Sermons*, vol. 87, 231–232, 1976.06.06.

13 History Compilation Committee, ed., *Important Ceremonies and Proclamations IV*, (Seoul: Sung Hwa Publishing, 2001), 54.

14 Holy Spirit Association for the Unification of World Christianity, *Human Life and the World of the Soul*, (Tokyo: Kogensha, 2001), 246–247, 251, 356.

15 True Father, 1997.12.01, Belvedere Training Center.

16 *Exposition*, 199–215 [Kor]

17 Family Federation for World Peace and Unification, *Cheon Seong Gyeong*, (Seoul: Sung Hwa Publishing, 2014), 1444 [Eng].

18 *Sermons*, vol. 162, 115, 1987.03.30.

19 Family Federation for World Peace and Unification, ed., *Tribal Messiah*, (Seoul: Sung Hwa Publishing), 216.

20 FFWPU, *Tribal Messiah*, 217.

21 FFWPU, *Tribal Messiah*, 218.

22 Family Federation for World Peace and Unification, ed., *Life on Earth and the Spirit World II*, 195.

23 Family Federation for World Peace and Unification, ed., *Life on Earth and the Spirit World I*, 226.

24 FFWPU, *Life on Earth and the Spirit World II*, 207.

25 FFWPU, *Life on Earth and the Spirit World I*, 216.

26 FFWPU, *Life on Earth and the Spirit World I*, 175.

27 True Mother, Speech delivered at special assembly of Cheon Il Guk leaders working under the guidance of the True Parents of Heaven, Earth and Humankind for a Heavenly Korea, 2017.12.15, Cheon Jeong Gung

28 FFWPU, *Tribal Messiah*, 202.

29 FFWPU, *Tribal Messiah*, 202.
30 FFWPU, *Tribal Messiah*, 209.
31 *Sermons*, vol. 298, 145–146, 1999.01.01.
32 *Sermons*, vol. 288, 264, 1997.11.29.
33 FFWPU, *Tribal Messiah*, 213.
34 True Mother, Speech given at the opening session of a Special HJ CheonWon Workshop under the Guidance of True Parents, 2016.08.01, CheongPyeong Training Center
35 True Mother, 2015.05.23, East Garden
36 True Mother, Speech at the "Peace Starts with Me" Hyojeong Cultural Festival, 2017.7.15, Madison Square Garden.
37 *Sermons*, vol. 357, 100, 2001.10.29.
38 True Mother, Speech delivered at special assembly of Cheon Il Guk leaders working under the guidance of the True Parents of Heaven, Earth and Humankind for a Heavenly Korea, 2017.12.15, Cheon Jeong Gung

Chapter 5 What Happens When You Fulfill the Heavenly Tribal Messiah Mission?

1 Family Federation for World Peace and Unification, *Exposition of the Divine Principle*, (Seoul: Sung Hwa Publishing, 1996), 91 [Eng].
2 *Exposition*, 60 [Kor]
3 *Exposition*, 65–68 [Kor]

4   True Father, 2001.01.31, East Garden.
5   True Father, 2011.04.16, Cheon Jeong Gung.
6   *Sermons*, vol. 249, 112, 1993.10.08.
7   Family Federation for World Peace and Unification, *Pyeong Hwa Shin Gyeong*, (Seoul: Sung Hwa Publishing, 2009), 256.
8   *Sermons*, vol. 249, 112, 1993.10.08.
9   *Sermons*, vol. 295, 235, 1998.08.26.
10 *Sermons*, vol. 393, 167, 2002.10.04.
11 *Sermons*, vol. 393, 288, 2002.10.04.
12 True Father, "Cosmic Assemblies for the Settlement of the True Parents of Heaven, Earth and Humankind Who, as God's Embodiment, Proclaim the Word," 58, 2011.04.24
13 *Sermons*, vol. 231, 242, 1992.06.03.

Chapter 6   Life Principles for Those Who Fulfill the Heavenly Tribal Messiah Mission

1   True Father, 1999.03.14, Belvedere Training Center.
2   True Father, 1999.09.05 Belvedere Training Center.
3   True Father, 1999.01.05, Punta del Este, Uruguay.
4   True Father, 2011.07.15, Nigerian Presidential Palace.
5   Family Federation for World Peace and Unification, *Pyeong Hwa Shin Gyeong*, (Seoul: Sung Hwa Publishing, 2009), 89–90.
6   True Mother, Speech at the "Peace Starts with Me" Hyojeong Cultural Festival, 2017.7.15, Madison Square Garden.

7   *Sermons*, vol. 18, 67, 1967.05.21.
8   *Sermons*, vol. 144, 1975.02.02.
9   FFWPU, *Life on Earth and the Spirit World I*, 167.
10 FFWPU, *Life on Earth and the Spirit World I*, 169–170.
11 FFWPU, *Life on Earth and the Spirit World I*, 171–172.
12 FFWPU, *Life on Earth and the Spirit World I*, 172.
13 True Father, 2009.12.22, Cheon Jeong Gung
14 True Father, 2009.10.08, East Garden
15 True Father, 2009.10.08, East Garden
16 True Father, 2009.12.22, Cheon Jeong Gung
17 *Sermons*, vol. 27, 128, 1969.11.30.
18 Family Federation for World Peace and Unification, *Chambumo Gyeong*, (Seoul: Sung Hwa Publishing, 2015), 1477 [Eng].
19 Family Federation for World Peace and Unification, *Pyeong Hwa Gyeong*, (Seoul: Sung Hwa Publishing, 2015), 772 [Eng].
20 *Sermons*, vol. 298, 311, 1999.01.17.
21 FFWPU, *Chambumo Gyeong*, 41 [Kor].
22 True Father, Speech at the Ceremony to mark the 20th Anniversary of the Women's Federation for World Peace, Daejeon Convention Center, Korea, 2012.03.04.
23 Ibid.
24 FFWPU, *Pyeong Hwa Shin Gyeong*, 278.
25 *Sermons*, vol. 289, 284, 1998.02.01.
26 FFWPU, *Pyeong Hwa Shin Gyeong*, 278.
27 FFWPU, *Pyeong Hwa Shin Gyeong*, 88.
28 FFWPU, *Pyeong Hwa Shin Gyeong*, 88.

29 Family Federation for World Peace and Unification, *Exposition of the Divine Principle*, (Seoul: Sung Hwa Publishing, 1996), 106.
30 Family Federation for World Peace and Unification, *Pyeong Hwa Shin Gyeong*, (Seoul: Sung Hwa Publishing, 2009), 283.
31 True Mother, Speech at the 3rd Anniversary of True Father's Seonghwa, 2015.08.30, CheongShim Peace World Center.
32 True Mother, Speech delivered at special assembly of Cheon Il Guk leaders working under the guidance of the True Parents of Heaven, Earth and Humankind for a Heavenly Korea, 2017.12.15, Cheon Jeong Gung

Bibliography

Editorial committee for the Collected Sermons of Sun Myung Moon, Ed. *Collected Sermons of the Rev. Sun Myung Moon*, vol. 2. Seoul: Sung Hwa, 1956.

Editorial committee. *Sermons*, vol. 12. Seoul: Sung Hwa, 1962.
Editorial committee. *Sermons*, vol. 18. Seoul: Sung Hwa, 1967.
Editorial committee. *Sermons*, vol. 20. Seoul: Sung Hwa, 1969.
Editorial committee. *Sermons*, vol. 27. Seoul: Sung Hwa, 1970.
Editorial committee. *Sermons*, vol. 37. Seoul: Sung Hwa, 1970.
Editorial committee. *Sermons*, vol. 52. Seoul: Sung Hwa, 1971.
Editorial committee. *Sermons*, vol. 56. Seoul: Sung Hwa, 1972.
Editorial committee. *Sermons*, vol. 84. Seoul: Sung Hwa, 1976.
Editorial committee. *Sermons*, vol. 87. Seoul: Sung Hwa, 1976.
Editorial committee. *Sermons*, vol. 101. Seoul: Sung Hwa, 1978.
Editorial committee. *Sermons*, vol. 102. Seoul: Sung Hwa, 1979.

Editorial committee. *Sermons*, vol. 104. Seoul: Sung Hwa, 1979.
Editorial committee. *Sermons*, vol. 110. Seoul: Sung Hwa, 1981.
Editorial committee. *Sermons*, vol. 137. Seoul: Sung Hwa, 1986.
Editorial committee. *Sermons*, vol. 142. Seoul: Sung Hwa, 1986.
Editorial committee. *Sermons*, vol. 144. Seoul: Sung Hwa, 1975.
Editorial committee. *Sermons*, vol. 162. Seoul: Sung Hwa, 1987.
Editorial committee. *Sermons*, vol. 168. Seoul: Sung Hwa, 1987.
Editorial committee. *Sermons*, vol. 170. Seoul: Sung Hwa, 1987.
Editorial committee. *Sermons*, vol. 176. Seoul: Sung Hwa, 1988.
Editorial committee. *Sermons*, vol. 177. Seoul: Sung Hwa, 1998.
Editorial committee. *Sermons*, vol. 178. Seoul: Sung Hwa, 1988.
Editorial committee. *Sermons*, vol. 181. Seoul: Sung Hwa, 1988.
Editorial committee. *Sermons*, vol. 189. Seoul: Sung Hwa, 1989.
Editorial committee. *Sermons*, vol. 202. Seoul: Sung Hwa, 1990.
Editorial committee. *Sermons*, vol. 210. Seoul: Sung Hwa, 1999.
Editorial committee. *Sermons*, vol. 217. Seoul: Sung Hwa, 1991.
Editorial committee. *Sermons*, vol. 219. Seoul: Sung Hwa, 1991.
Editorial committee. *Sermons*, vol. 231. Seoul: Sung Hwa, 1992.
Editorial committee. *Sermons*, vol. 234. Seoul: Sung Hwa, 1992.
Editorial committee. *Sermons*, vol. 247. Seoul: Sung Hwa, 1993.
Editorial committee. *Sermons*, vol. 248. Seoul: Sung Hwa, 1993.
Editorial committee. *Sermons*, vol. 249. Seoul: Sung Hwa, 1993.
Editorial committee. *Sermons*, vol. 250. Seoul: Sung Hwa, 1993.
Editorial committee. *Sermons*, vol. 279. Seoul: Sung Hwa, 1996.
Editorial committee. *Sermons*, vol. 280. Seoul: Sung Hwa, 1996.
Editorial committee. *Sermons*, vol. 285. Seoul: Sung Hwa, 1997.

Editorial committee. *Sermons*, vol. 287. Seoul: Sung Hwa, 1997.
Editorial committee. *Sermons*, vol. 288. Seoul: Sung Hwa, 1997.
Editorial committee. *Sermons*, vol. 289. Seoul: Sung Hwa, 1998.
Editorial committee. *Sermons*, vol. 295. Seoul: Sung Hwa, 1998.
Editorial committee. *Sermons*, vol. 298. Seoul: Sung Hwa, 1999.
Editorial committee. *Sermons*, vol. 304. Seoul: Sung Hwa, 1999.
Editorial committee. *Sermons*, vol. 306. Seoul: Sung Hwa, 2003.
Editorial committee. *Sermons*, vol. 320. Seoul: Sung Hwa, 2000.
Editorial committee. *Sermons*, vol. 325. Seoul: Sung Hwa, 2000.
Editorial committee. *Sermons*, vol. 346. Seoul: Sung Hwa, 2001.
Editorial committee. *Sermons*, vol. 356. Seoul: Sung Hwa, 2002.
Editorial committee. *Sermons*, vol. 357. Seoul: Sung Hwa, 2001.
Editorial committee. *Sermons*, vol. 371. Seoul: Sung Hwa, 2002.
Editorial committee. *Sermons*, vol. 393. Seoul: Sung Hwa, 2002.
Editorial committee. *Sermons*, vol. 407. Seoul: Sung Hwa, 2003.
Editorial committee. *Sermons*, vol. 410. Seoul: Sung Hwa, 2003.
Editorial committee. *Sermons*, vol. 416. Seoul: Sung Hwa, 2003.
Editorial committee. *Sermons*, vol. 419. Seoul: Sung Hwa, 2003.
Editorial committee. *Sermons*, vol. 466. Seoul: Sung Hwa, 2004.
Editorial committee. *Sermons*, vol. 481. Seoul: Sung Hwa, 2005.
Editorial committee. *Sermons*, vol. 487. Seoul: Sung Hwa, 2005.
Family Federation for World Peace and Unification. *Exposition of the Divine Principle*. Seoul: Sung Hwa, 1996.
Family Federation for World Peace and Unification *God's Homeland and the Peace UN*. Seoul: Sung Hwa Publications, 2004.
Family Federation for World Peace and Unification, ed. *The Holy Scrip-*

tures of Cheon Il Guk: Cheon Seong Gyeong. Seoul: Sung Hwa, 2013.

Family Federation for World Peace and Unification, ed. *The Holy Scriptures of Cheon Il Guk: Pyeong Hwa Gyeong.* Seoul: Sung Hwa, 2013.

Family Federation for World Peace and Unification, ed. *Life on Earth and the Spirit World I.* Seoul: Sung Hwa, 1997.

Family Federation for World Peace and Unification, ed. *Life on Earth and the Spirit World II.* Seoul: Sung Hwa, 1997.

Family Federation for World Peace and Unification. *Pyeong Hwa Shin Gyeong.* Seoul: Sung Hwa, 2010.

Family Federation for World Peace and Unification. *Sun Myung Moon's Philosophy of Peace.* Seoul: Sung Hwa, 2002.

Family Federation for World Peace and Unification. *Tongil Segye*, No. 251. Seoul, Sung Hwa Publishing, 1991.

Family Federation for World Peace and Unification, ed. *Tribal Messiah.* Seoul: Sung Hwa, 1998.

Family Federation for World Peace and Unification. *True Parents' Life Courses*, vol. 10. Seoul: Sung Hwa, 2001.

History Compilation Committee, ed. *Important Ceremonies and Proclamations IV.* Seoul: Sung Hwa, 2001.

History Compilation Committee, ed. *True Parents' Life Courses*, vol. 2. Seoul: Sung Hwa, 1999.

History Compilation Committee, ed. *True Parents' Life Courses*, vol. 3. Seoul: Sung Hwa, 1999.

Holy Spirit Association for the Unification of World Christianity. *Human*

Life and the World of the Soul. Tokyo: Kogensha, 2001.

Kim Won-jong. "The Fire Has Already Been Lit," *Tongil Segye*, No. 98. Seoul: Sung Hwa, 1976.

Oh Taek-yong. *The Meaning of Absolute Sex as Seen Through True Father's Speeches: The Word and Theology 7.* Asan: Sun Moon University Publishing, 2001.

Oh Taek-yong. *Understanding True Parents' Proclamations and God's Providence.* Asan: Sun Moon University Publishing, 2015.

Park Jung-hyun. "Home Church Activities in New York, Today's Rome," *Tongil Segye*, No. 124. Seoul: Sung Hwa, 1981).

Unification Thought Institute, ed. *Summarizing Unification Thought.* Asan: Sun Moon University Publishing, 2007.

World Scripture Compilation Committee. *World Scriptures II.* Seoul: Universal Peace Federation, 2009.

Yong, Jin-heon. "Hak Ja Han's Hyojeong Ethics," Doctoral Dissertation. Gapyeong: SunHak Universal Peace Graduate University, 2017.

A GLOSSARY OF KEY TERMS

home church :
A style of community ministry that was emphasized in the Unification movement in the 1980s. Each blessed family had the mission to create a model home and family and seek to love and care for 360 families living nearby. Providentially the home church movement had the goal of restoring from Satan the authority of the eldest son.

tribal messiah mission :
The tribal messiah mission was the family ministry that followed home church. Starting in 1991, blessed families were called to return to their home towns and minister to their extended families and others in their home towns. Tribal messiahs worked to bless 160 couples to the Blessing. The tribal messiah age led to the restoration of the authority of parents.

family church / hoondok family church :
The age of hoondok family church was declared in 2005. From this time forward each blessed family was called to establish a hoondok family church, establish

a strong tradition of hoondokhae in their families, and put into practice what they learned through hoondokhae in ministering to their extended families and neighbors. Through hoondok family church the authority of the king was restored.

heavenly tribal messiah mission :
The role of heavenly tribal messiahs was first introduced in March 2012, and True Father emphasized it again in his final prayer. Working in their hometowns or another mission area, heavenly tribal messiahs can shorten the time required for the complete restoration of their lineage from a vertical period of seven generations to as little as one generation, by liberating and blessing 430 vertical generations of their ancestors, and gathering and blessing a horizontal tribe of 430 families, with three generations of their families working together.

home group :
A small group of people, often organized around a few families, who gather regularly as a community of faith, to pray, study, fellowship and minister together. In heavenly tribal messiah activities, a home group sometimes serves as a local pioneer church center.

small group :
see "home group"

midsize group :
A community of faith formed by combining a number of small groups which are in the same vicinity, to work together and support each other, by organizing education programs or community events, for example.

large group :
A larger local church or center which provides opportunities for weekly worship, workshops, and other support services. Parts of the congregation might separate off into small groups and create new pioneer centers.

jeongseong :

An act of devotion, service or care offered to mobilize spiritual support and protection as part of a life of faith. Jeongseong can include prayer, bowing conditions, fasting, taking special care of people, cleaning the church, cooking a special meal, writing letters, and many other types of offering of heart.

"To offer jeongseong means to do your utmost internally and externally. You must offer everything, combining your words, your attitude, your mind and thoughts, all your actions, everything in the internal and external realities of your life." [CSG 11.1.2.1]

hyojeong :

A heart of filial devotion, love given by children in response to the love they have received from their parents, and the exchange of heart between humankind and Heavenly Parent, who also stand in a parent–child relationship. A heart of hyojeong is the starting point of a world that expresses the ideal of creation.

hoondokhae :

Hoondokhae is a meeting where people gather to read, discuss and understand the teachings of True Parents. It is also a time for offering jeongseong of the mind and the body. By engaging in hoondok reading with the whole mind and body, we participate in "hoondok mind-body purification jeongseong."

Cheon Il Guk :

Cheon Il Guk is the shortened name for "Cheonju Pyeonghwa Tongil Guk," which is the "Cosmic Nation of Peace and Unity." Cheon Il Guk is the kingdom of heaven on earth, which we build by practicing what we have learned about love and living for the sake of others.

Seonghwa :

In the Unification movement, the transition from life in the world of air to life in the world of love is call *Seonghwa* (成和: completion and harmony) The end of life in the world of air is nothing to be feared, but is a time of ascending nobly to heaven. When we gather for a Seonghwa Service after somebody has ascended, we celebrate their life up until now, and rejoice for their coming life.

BonHyang Won :
True Father's final resting place above Cheon Jeong Gung is called *BonHyang Won*, which means "garden of the original homeland."

weonjeon / Paju Weonjeon :
Weonjeon is the word used to describe a memorial garden where Unificationists have been laid to rest. The Paju Weonjeon is a special weonjeon in Paju, Korea, for members of the True Family and early church members.

supporters :
Already married couples who received the Blessing through Heavenly Tribal Messiah activities, or other active supporters of FFWPU and/or related providential organizations.

registered members :
Members who attend worship services or donate at least once every six months.

associate members :
Members who donate (tithe if possible) and attend at least two worship services every three months.

regular members :
Members who tithe twice and attend at least six worship services every three months.

Editors
Wonju McDevitt (Head Editor, Chief of Staff, Dr. Hak Ja Han Moon's Secretariat)
Yun Young-ho (Secretary General, FFWPUI HQ)
Yong Jin-hun (Director, FFWPUI HQ Heavenly Tribal Messiah Academy)

Writers
Oh Taek-yong (Publishing Committee Chair, Sun Moon University)
Yong Jin-hun (Director, FFWPUI HQ Heavenly Tribal Messiah Academy)

Heavenly Tribal Messiah Collection 1 Philosophy
What Is a Heavenly Tribal Messiah

Published June 21, 2018

First edition © 2018
Layout by Sung Hwa Publishing Co., Korea
Published by Heavenly Tribal Messiah Academy
Printed by HSA-Books, New York, NY
June, 2019

www.ingramcontent.com/pod-product-compliance
Lightning Source LLC
Chambersburg PA
CBHW050611300426
44112CB00012B/1456